Shakespeare in Modern English
Three Plays

Shakespeare in Modern English

Three Plays

Translated by Hugh Macdonald

As You Like It

Coriolanus

The Tempest

Matador
9 Priory Business Park,
Wistow Road, Kibworth Beauchamp,
Leicestershire. LE8 0RX
Tel: 0116 279 2299
Email: books@troubador.co.uk
Web: www.troubador.co.uk/matador
Twitter: @matadorbooks

ISBN 9781785898402

British Library Cataloguing in Publication Data.
A catalogue record for this book is available from the British Library.

Printed and bound in the UK by TJ International, Padstow, Cornwall

Matador is an imprint of Troubador Publishing Ltd

Contents

Preface: Translating Shakespeare

M Y PURPOSE in rendering Shakespeare into modern English is to enhance the enjoyment and understanding of audiences in the theatre. The translations are emphatically not designed for children or for dummies, but for educated grown-ups for whom Elizabethan English presents a certain barrier to comprehension. When reading Shakespeare, most of us need annotations to explain allusions, mystifying word order, obsolete vocabulary, and deceptive usages of one kind or another which impede understanding, or at least prevent us reading the text at a pace at which we might read Wilde or Shaw plays. The immense accumulation of expert annotation that the plays have attracted over the years is proof that the text itself is rarely self-explanatory. In the theatre, on the other hand, we have no notes to help us, so many of those baffling utterances pass us by. We still get the drift of the words, we sense the dramatic interplay, especially in a good performance, and we enjoy the poetry, but it is an incomplete enjoyment since much of what is said is not understood. As an example, no one who arrives at the theatre unprepared can be expected to make sense of Prospero when in Act V Scene 1 of *The Tempest* he says the following lines, however well he speaks them:

> As great to me as late, and supportable
> To make the dear loss have I means much weaker
> Than you may call to comfort you:

The meaning is there in the text, but it takes a second or two to disentangle it, by which time (in the theatre) the play has moved on.

The experience of seeing Shakespeare is for most English speakers (and I naturally exclude Shakespeare scholars since they are fluent in his language – or should be) is not unlike seeing a play acted in a foreign language with which we are very familiar though not completely fluent. Much is thus missed. When Shakespeare is translated into other languages, the preferred solution is, in most countries that I am aware of, a translation from the nineteenth century or later, which does not present the listener with the sort of difficulties that English speakers face when hearing Shakespeare in the original. Germans do not perform Shakespeare in sixteenth-century German nor Frenchmen in Renaissance French. They prefer Schlegel's or Guizot's or Laroche's version for the very good reason that these versions bring the text fully to life for a modern audience. They could be said to get more today out of seeing these plays in the theatre than Shakespeare's compatriots do. A recent survey revealed that 65 per cent of non-Britons said they enjoyed Shakespeare plays, compared to just 59 per cent of Britons.

My argument is that a modern version set side by side with Shakespeare's text will often prove to be the more intelligible of the two. Not the most colourful perhaps, not the most poetic perhaps, but providing a clearer message:

> Although this lord of weak remembrance, this,
> Who shall be of as little memory
> When he is earthed, hath here almost persuaded –
> For he's a spirit of persuasion, only
> Professes to persuade – the king his son's alive:
> 'Tis as impossible that he's undrowned
> As he that sleeps here swims.

> Although this lord, whose memory is weak – and he
> Himself won't be remembered when he's gone –
> Although he almost had the king believe –
> And it's his job as courtier to persuade him –
> He almost had the king believe his son
> Is still alive. But it's impossible
> He was not drowned. Or else you might believe
> That man is swimming, not asleep.

Even scholars will admit that Shakespeare is sometimes very hard to understand. Countless passages show editors disagreeing about interpretation, and the jokes are notoriously baffling. In performance directors will normally cut lines or passages of which no one can make sense, or at least of which the audience is unlikely to grasp the meaning. A modern translation has to opt for an interpretation that has at least some likelihood of being correct, although sometimes the words are clear but the meaning is not.

It will be objected, no doubt, that the language is too fine to be meddled with and that the poetry is sacrosanct. The zeal with which the notion of translating Shakespeare has been attacked at times suggests paranoia, as if modern translations threaten to delete a sacred monument for ever. Those who rankle at the language being touched are often the very same people who applaud productions which freely change historical and geographical specifics in the staging, change the sequence of lines and scenes, exchange the gender of leading roles, and insert all kinds of topical and inauthentic detail in the direction.

The situation is not unlike the appearance of the New English Bible in 1961. This was greeted with horror by most people brought up on the King James version, even though the latter was known to be often incomprehensible and often wrong. Over the years the virtues of reading the Bible in the modern language (especially aloud) have been accepted by many churches and readers, without any suggestion that the much-loved old texts should be discarded. Both versions serve their purpose.

Many people have committed to memory familiar lines whose replacement will always jar, even when the lines have been stored in the memory without being understood. A modern version may provoke an astonished "So that's what it means!" as readily as "Don't trample on my Shakespeare!" The world is not yet ready for "To live or not to live, that is the question", but it can have no strong objection to "All the world's a stage, and all the men and women merely actors".

As for Shakespeare's poetry, I believe that blank verse is still a superb vehicle for the modern language; so long as verse is rendered as verse and prose as prose, the gains will outweigh the losses. I am not ashamed of passages such as this, from *Coriolanus* III.1:

> May everything that gods and humans swear by
> Bear witness to my closing truth. Two powers,
> Where one disdains the other for good reason,
> The other hurls unjustifiable insults,
> Where gentry, rank and wisdom cannot rule
> Except depending on the yea or nay
> Of widespread ignorance, they will neglect
> Real necessities, and toil instead
> On pointless trifles. Policy thus thwarted,
> No useful things are done. Therefore I beg you,
> You who would rather not be judged as cowards,
> And love the constitution of the state
> More than you fear the effect of change, and prize
> Nobility above your length of life,
> And wish to risk the surgeon's knife to treat
> A body that would surely die without it,
> Pluck out that multitudinous tongue at once!
> Let them not lick the sweet which is their poison!
> Dishonour done to you will warp your judgment

> And rob the state of its integrity,
> Without the power to do the good it should
> Because of all the evils that control it.

This is not Shakespeare's language, to be sure, but it surely conveys the speaker's strength of feeling to a modern audience with conviction.

My translations respect rhyme when it occurs in blank verse as well as the metre. Songs (including "Blow, blow, thou winter wind" and "Where the bee sucks") I have left untranslated. A difficulty arises in *The Tempest* IV.1, the scene where Prospero summons Iris, Ceres and Juno, all of whom speak in rhymed blank verse and sometimes sing songs. My adaptation of this scene is much closer to the original than elsewhere, which gives the scene a certain stagey feeling that may work well in performance.

At certain points translation permits the absorption in the modern text of what are in essence explanatory notes. An example is found in the opening scene of *The Tempest*, where Gonzalo keeps harping on the fact that the Boatswain will not drown, the allusion being to a long-forgotten proverb that stated that "He that is born to be hanged shall never be drowned". Gonzalo's "I have good comfort from this fellow: methinks he hath no drowning mark upon him: his complexion is perfect gallows" is meaningless without familiarity with the proverb. My version is: "I have great faith in this fellow. He that is born to be hanged shall never drown, says the proverb, and his complexion is set rather for the gallows", which scholars will decry as patronising but which audiences will take in their stride, and also understand later allusions to the proverb.

In *As You Like It* III.5 Phebe says, in the original:

> Dead shepherd, now I find thy saw of might,
> "Whoever loved that loved not at first sight?"

This is a quotation from Marlowe's *Hero and Leander*. Perhaps Shakespeare's audience knew the line, but certainly modern audiences do not. It may be frivolous, but it is no more anachronistic or intrusive when I allow Phebe to say:

> O Marlowe, now I find your saying right:
> "Who ever loved that loved not at first sight?"

In the case of some allusions it would be too clumsy to attempt to explain them. The Irish rat, for example, mentioned by Rosalind in *As You Like It* III.2, alluding to the belief that Irish sorcerers could kill animals by means of spells, remains unelucidated.

In *Coriolanus* II.3 there is much talk of "voices" with its double meaning, no longer current, of "voices" and "votes". My solution is in general to leave "voices" in place, but to render it as "votes" in one or two lines in order to convey the interchangeability of meanings. "Maid" too is a word often treated as a *double entendre*, neither of its two meanings being matched in modern vocabulary.

In *The Tempest* IV.1 the barely articulate, drunken Stephano says:

> Mistress line, is not this my jerkin? Now is the jerkin under the line: now, jerkin, you are like to lose your hair and prove a bald jerkin.

The commentators offer "lime" for "line" as the tree on which Stephano finds the jerkin. But recognising "line" as essential to the text, they read "under the line" as meaning either "below the line on which it hung, i.e. on the ground", "below the waist", or "below the equator", or all three, with the follow-up belief that sailors used to shave the heads of those who crossed the equator for the first time. Into the mix can be added the suggestion of syphilis (below the waist) causing loss of hair. The only hope of making this understood in the modern language is the following, which falls short of the suggestion of syphilis (if it is really there):

> Madame line, this jacket's for me, isn't it? Now the jacket's under the line. So, jacket, you're below the equator and so you'll be shaved by sailors and become a bald jacket!

I have replaced the second person singular (thou and thee) with the plural form, since that is universally adopted in modern speech. There is some loss here, since there are social and personal implications in the alternate use of thee and you. But since those implications cannot be instinctively grasped by a modern audience, the gain is greater than the loss. I have adopted modern word order wherever possible, although occasionally when an archaic word order offers no confusion, I have left it unchanged. The city of Milan, stressed on the first syllable by Shakespeare, I stress on its second syllable in accordance with modern usage.

What exactly is modern English? I believe the best solution for translating Shakespeare is not truly modern English, but the language the Edwardians would have recognised as stylish and good. I avoid slang as far as possible, even when Shakespeare throws in words that were slang to him, and I avoid recent neologisms that sound sharply anachronistic. I believe it is possible to reflect Shakespeare's most elevated language in the modern equivalent, and also to adopt a more colloquial tone when he does something similar.

My choice of plays is not entirely random. The decision to translate Shakespeare, an idea long nascent in my mind, was prompted by seeing a production of *As You Like It* in which neither the director nor the actors appeared to have any understanding of the words they were saying. We were told by the director that the play was a gloss on the French Revolution, so the production opened with the storming of the Bastille. Having started with this play, I then went on to *The Tempest* because it contains so many appealing features without being as familiar as the great tragedies, and from there to *Coriolanus* because it is less well known; the plot is not entirely easy to follow, and there are scarcely any lines well enough known to give offence when replaced.

As an experienced translator of opera for singing and an ardent advocate of opera in the vernacular, I find my motives and aims are the same when translating Shakespeare: to make the work better understood in the theatre. Since the current fashion is to sing opera in the original language to audiences who do not understand that language, the problem of comprehension is acute, only crudely addressed by supertitles and the like. Opera audiences have the music to assist understanding, or sometimes to distract them from understanding, so that the loss of a few lines is not so critical as in the spoken theatre.

I expect the same irrational responses to my attempts to translate Shakespeare as those levelled at opera in English, but although I have no desire whatever to banish Shakespeare in the original from the stage, I persist in thinking that the alternative of performing his plays in a modern translation will bring enlightenment and pleasure to many.

Hugh Macdonald
Norwich, 2016

As You Like It

CHARACTERS

Duke Senior, in banishment
Duke Frederick, his brother and usurper
Amiens, a Lord attending Duke Senior
Jaques, a Lord attending Duke Senior
Oliver, elder son of Sir Rowland de Boys
Jaques, second son of Sir Rowland de Boys
Orlando, younger son of Sir Rowland de Boys
Le Beau, a courtier attending Duke Frederick
Charles, a wrestler at court
Adam, an old servant to Sir Rowland de Boys
Dennis, a servant to Oliver
Touchstone, a clown
Sir Oliver Martext, a country curate
Corin, a shepherd
Silvius, a shepherd
William, a country fellow
Hymen, god of marriage

Rosalind, daughter of Duke Senior
Celia, daughter of Duke Frederick
Phebe, a shepherdess
Audrey, a country wench

Lords, Pages and Attendants

Act I Scene 1

Enter Orlando and Adam

ORLANDO   As I remember, Adam, it turned out that just a thousand crowns were bequeathed to me by will, and, as you were saying, my brother was charged, with the blessing of the will, to take good care of me. That was the beginning of my troubles. He keeps my other brother at school, where he gets golden reports of his progress. As for me, he keeps me at home in the country, or to put it more bluntly, he detains me here at home unkept. Do you call that "keeping" a gentleman of my birth when it's no different from an ox in a stall? His horses are better provided for, and as well as getting properly fed, they are trained in dressage and their riders are employed at great expense. But I, his brother, gain nothing from him but growing, which animals on his dunghills get, just the same as I do. Besides this nothing which he gives me so plentifully, the something that nature gave me seems to be taken away by his attitude. He makes me eat with his farmhands, shuts me out of a brother's proper place, and does his utmost to counteract the advantages of my good birth by the education he gives me. That's what troubles me, Adam, and my father's spirit, which I believe I have in me, is beginning to rebel against this servitude. I will not put up with it any more, though as yet I can think of no clever way of escaping it.

Enter Oliver.

ADAM   Here comes my master, your brother.

ORLANDO   Move away a little, Adam, so you'll hear how he'll needle me.

OLIVER   Well, sir, what are you up to here?

ORLANDO   Nothing. I am not taught to get up to anything.

OLIVER   What are you down on then?

ORLANDO   Well, sir, I'm helping you to put down one of God's creatures, a poor unworthy brother of yours, with idleness.

OLIVER   Heavens! You could be better employed than that. To hell with you.

ORLANDO   Shall I take care of the pigs and eat slops with them? Am I the prodigal son that wasted everything and am now reduced to such penury?

OLIVER   Do you know where you are?

ORLANDO   I know very well. Here in your orchard.

OLIVER   Do you know who you're talking to?

ORLANDO   Yes I do, better than he that I'm talking to knows me. I know you are my eldest brother and being of good family you should acknowledge me in the same way. The customs of the world acknowledge you the superior since you were born first, but the same tradition would not deprive me of my good blood even if there were twenty brothers between us. I have as much of my father in me as you, although your precedence in age commands respect more like what is owed to him.

OLIVER   That's enough, boy! [*Strikes him.*]

ORLANDO   Come now, elder brother. You don't have the right experience for this. [*Seizes him.*]

OLIVER   Let go of me, you rat!

ORLANDO   I am no rat. I am the youngest son of Sir Rowland de Boys; he was my father, and whoever says such a father had rats for children is thrice a rat himself. If you weren't my brother I'd not let go of your throat with this hand until the other hand had pulled out your tongue for saying so. You've insulted yourself.

ADAM   Dear masters, calm down! For your father's sake, settle it.

OLIVER   Let me go, I say.

ORLANDO   I won't let go until I want to. You'll hear what I have to say. My father charged you in his will to give me a good education. You have trained me like a peasant, keeping me from a gentleman's accomplishments and concealing them from me. The spirit of my father is strong in me, and I will endure it no longer. So allow me such activities as becomes a gentleman, or give me the modest share of money my father left me in his will, and I'll go and seek my fortune with it. [*Releases him.*]

OLIVER   And what will you do? Go begging when you've spent it? Go on inside. I'll not be bothered with you for long. You'll get some part of what you want. Please leave.

ORLANDO   I'll not offend you any longer than I need for my own advantage.

OLIVER   You go too, you old dog.

ADAM   Is "old dog" my reward? It's true I've lost my teeth in your service. God rest my former master; he would never have spoken to me like that.

Exeunt Orlando, Adam.

OLIVER   Is that it then? Are you beginning to encroach on my position? I'll cure your excessive exuberance, but I'll not give you any thousand crowns. Hey there, Dennis!

Enter Dennis.

DENNIS   Did you call, sir?

OLIVER   Did Charles, the Duke's wrestler, want to speak to me?

DENNIS   Yes, sir, he is there outside, and he'd like to see you.

OLIVER   Call him in. [*Exit Dennis.*] This is a good idea. There's to be wrestling tomorrow.

Enter Charles.

CHARLES   Good day, sir.

OLIVER   Dear Monsieur Charles, what's the new news at the new court?

CHARLES   There's no news at court, sir, only the old news, which is that the old duke has been banished by his younger brother the new duke, and three or four devoted lords have gone into voluntary exile with him. Their land and revenues enrich the new duke, so he's happy to allow them to depart.

OLIVER   Do you know if Rosalind, the duke's daughter, was banished with her father?

CHARLES   Oh no. Her cousin, the duke's daughter, is so fond of her, having been brought up together from the cradle, that she would have gone into exile with her, or died if she'd been left behind. She's at court and is as loved by her uncle as his own daughter. Two ladies never loved each other as they do.

OLIVER   Where will the old duke live?

CHARLES   They say he's already in the Forest of Arden, and many merry men are with him. They live there like old Robin Hood. They say that many young gentlemen are flocking to him every day, and they spend time in the same carefree manner as if they were living in a golden age.

OLIVER   So are you wrestling tomorrow to entertain the new duke?

CHARLES   I am indeed. I came here to tell you about it. I have been informed in confidence, sir, that your younger brother Orlando is planning to come in disguise to try a bout with me. Tomorrow I'll be wrestling for my reputation, and anyone who gets away with no broken limbs will be doing well. Your brother is young and inexperienced, and out of attachment to you I'd be loath to throw him down, which I'd have to do for my own honour if he makes the challenge. So I came to let you know, out of respect, that you should either prevent him from doing as he intends, or be prepared for the disgrace he will bring on himself, it being his own choice and against my own inclination.

OLIVER   Thankyou, Charles, for your devotion to me, for which you will be fully rewarded, as you'll find out. I had been informed of my brother's plan and have surreptitiously tried to dissuade him from it. But he has made up his mind. I tell you, Charles, he is the most stubborn young man in France, full of ambition, envious of other peoples' talents, and secretly, maliciously working against me, his brother. So use your discretion. I'd be just as happy for you to break his neck as his finger. But be careful: because if you humiliate him even a little, or if he fails to gain credit at your expense, he will hatch poisonous plots against you and ensnare you with some malicious trick. He won't let up until he's taken your life by some indirect means or other. I assure you, and it upsets me deeply to say so, there is no person living today who is so young and so villainous. I speak of him just as a brother, but if I had to describe him as he is, I'd blush and weep, and you would turn pale with astonishment.

CHARLES   I'm extremely glad I came to see you. If he comes tomorrow, I'll give him his due. If ever he walks again unaided, I'll give up professional wrestling. God be with you, sir.

OLIVER   Goodbye, Charles. [*Exit Charles*]. I must now stir up that trickster for the match. I hope I'll see the end of him, for my soul, for some reason, hates him more than anything. Yet he's polite, uneducated but learned, full of good intentions, liked by all manner of people he has bewitched. In fact he has been so warmly taken to heart by everyone, especially my own people, who know him best, that I am totally unappreciated. This will not be so for long. That wrestler will solve the problem. All I have to do is fire the boy up for the fight, and that's what I'll do next.   *Exit.*

Act I Scene 2

Enter Rosalind and Celia

CELIA   Please, Rosalind, dear cousin, cheer up.

ROSALIND   Dear Celia, I seem more cheerful than I really am, and yet you want me to cheer up more? Unless you can teach me to forget a banished father, you should not teach me how to recall any particular pleasure.

CELIA   This is how I know you don't love me with the same intensity that I love you. If my uncle, your banished father, had banished your uncle, my father the duke, so that you would still be with me, I could have taught myself to love your father as much as my own. So could you, if your love for me were as perfectly balanced as mine is for you.

ROSALIND   Well then, I'll forget my situation and take pleasure in yours.

CELIA   You know my father has no other child but me, and is not likely to have any. When he dies, you will really be his heir, since what he has taken from your father by force I will give back to you in affection. On my honour, I will, and if I break that promise, let me turn into a monster. So my sweet Rose, my dear Rose, cheer up!

ROSALIND   From now on I will, dear cousin, and I'll find something to distract me. Let me see, what do you think about falling in love?

CELIA   Well certainly, yes, for the fun of it. Don't love someone in earnest, and don't go any further for the fun of it than you can safely get away in honour with an innocent blush.

ROSALIND   How shall we amuse ourselves then?

CELIA   Let's sit and mock the good housewife Fortune spinning her wheel, so that her gifts are bestowed fairly.

ROSALIND   I wish we could, because her favours are extremely unfair in their distribution, and the generous blind goddess makes most of her mistakes in her gifts to women.

CELIA   That's true. Whoever she gives good looks to is usually dishonest, and the honest ones are nothing to look at.

ROSALIND   Be careful: you are confusing Fortune's province with Nature's. Fortune controls worldly advantages, not physical properties, which are Nature's.

Enter Touchstone the Clown.

CELIA   No. When Nature makes a beautiful person, might she not, by misfortune, fall into a fire? Although Nature has given us the intelligence to defy Fortune, wasn't it Fortune that sent this fool here to close the argument?

ROSALIND   Yes indeed. Fortune is being too hard on Nature when Fortune makes Nature's half-wit the one to close off Nature's wit.

CELIA   Perhaps this isn't Fortune's work either, but Nature's. Seeing our natural wits too feeble to talk of such goddesses, she sent us this half-wit as the whetstone with which to sharpen our wits. The fool's bluntness is what can make our wits sharp. Well hello, brainbox! Where are you off to?

TOUCHSTONE   Mistress, you must come back to your father.

CELIA   Were you sent as messenger?

TOUCHSTONE   No, on my honour! But I was told to come for you.

ROSALIND   Where did you learn that oath, fool?

TOUCHSTONE   From a certain knight who swore on his honour they were good pancakes and swore on his honour the mustard was bad. Now I promise you: the pancakes were bad and the mustard was good, yet the knight did not perjure himself.

CELIA   How can you prove that from your immense store of knowledge?

ROSALIND   Yes, go on, unmuzzle that wisdom of yours.

TOUCHSTONE   Both of you, stand here. Stroke your chins and swear by your beards that I am a knave.

CELIA   By our beards, if we had them, you are.

TOUCHSTONE   By my knavery, then, if I had any, I would be. But if you swear by something that doesn't exist you are not perjuring yourself. Nor was the knight when he swore on his honour, since he never had any. Or if he had, he'd sworn it away before he ever saw those pancakes or that mustard.

CELIA   Tell me, who are you talking about?

TOUCHSTONE   Someone dear to old Frederick, your father.

CELIA   My father's love is enough to honour him enough. Don't say any more against him or you'll be whipped for slander one of these days.

TOUCHSTONE   More's the pity that fools may not speak wisely what wise men do foolishly.

CELIA   You're quite right, I assure you, for since the little wit that fools have was silenced, the little folly that wise men have is all the more obvious. Here comes Monsieur Le Beau.

Enter Le Beau.

ROSALIND   With his mouth full of good news.

CELIA   Which he'll stuff into us like pigeons feeding their young.

ROSALIND   Then we'll be news-crammed.

CELIA   All the better. We'll then be plumper and more marketable. Bonjour, Monsieur Le Beau, what's the news?

LE BEAU   Fair princess, you have been missing some good sport.

CELIA   Sport? Of what kind?

LE BEAU   Of what kind, Madame? How am I to answer you?

ROSALIND   As wit and fortune decide.

TOUCHSTONE   Or as the destinies decree.

CELIA   Well said; that was laid on with a trowel.

TOUCHSTONE   What if I lose my rank?

ROSALIND   You'd lose your old smell.

LE BEAU   You confuse me, ladies. I was going to tell you about some good wrestling, which you have lost sight of.

ROSALIND   So tell us about the wrestling.

LE BEAU   I'll tell you the beginning, and if it please your ladyships, you may see the end, for the best is yet to come, and here, where you are now, is where they are coming to perform it.

CELIA   Well, tell us the beginning, the part that's dead and buried.

LE BEAU   There was once an old man and his three sons.

CELIA   I could come up with the beginning of an old tale as good as that.

LE BEAU   Three handsome young men of excellent bearing and presence.

ROSALIND   With notices round their necks: "Be it known to all men by these presents!"

LE BEAU   The eldest of the three wrestled with Charles, the duke's wrestler. Charles quickly threw him down and broke three of his ribs, so there's little hope of life left in him. He treated the second the same way, and the third. They are lying there, with their father, the poor old man, mourning them so pitifully that onlookers start weeping with him.

ROSALIND   Alas!

TOUCHSTONE   But what's the sport, Monsieur, that the ladies have lost?

LE BEAU   This very thing.

TOUCHSTONE   You learn something new every day. This is the first time I've heard of breaking ribs as sport for ladies.

CELIA   First time for me too, I promise.

ROSALIND   But does anyone else long to see his sides broken, like music, in four parts? Does anyone else adore rib-breaking? Shall we go and see this wrestling, cousin?

LE BEAU   You'll certainly see it if you stay here, for this is where the wrestling is to take place, and they're ready to start.

CELIA   There they are, on their way. Let's stay and watch!

> *Flourish. Enter Duke Frederick, Lords,*
> *Orlando, Charles, and Attendants.*

DUKE FREDERICK   Come on now. Since the young man will not be dissuaded, he comes forward at his own peril.

ROSALIND   Is that the man?

LE BEAU   It is, madam.

CELIA   Oh dear! He's too young! But he looks as if he could bring it off.

DUKE FREDERICK   Well now, daughter and niece, have you crept in here to see the wrestling?

ROSALIND   Yes, my lord, if you will kindly give us leave to.

DUKE FREDERICK   You'll get little pleasure from it, I assure you, the odds are so unfairly set. In pity for the challenger's youth I would gladly have dissuaded him, but he would not listen. Speak to him yourselves, ladies; see if you can move him.

CELIA   Call him over, please, Monsieur Le Beau.

DUKE FREDERICK   Do so. I'll step aside.

LE BEAU   Monsieur, challenger, the princess is calling for you.

ORLANDO   I will attend them will all respect and duty.

ROSALIND   Young man, have you challenged Charles the wrestler?

ORLANDO   No, fair princess. He is the general challenger; I take part in this as others do: to try the strength of my youth with him.

CELIA   Young gentleman, your spirit is too brave at your age. You have seen cruel proof of this man's strength. If you saw that with your own eyes or knew your own strength with good judgment, the fear of this adventure would advise you to take on someone your own equal. We beg you for your own sake, think of your own safety and give up the attempt.

ROSALIND   Yes do, young sir. Your reputation will not be damaged. We'll make a case to the duke why the wrestling should not go forward.

ORLANDO   Please don't punish me with your severe thoughts, I beg you, wrong though it would be to refuse such fair and excellent ladies anything. But let your fair eyes and kind wishes support me in the contest. If I'm defeated, there'll be only one person to feel shame and he was never fortunate; if I'm killed, there'll be one dead person who was willing to be so. I'll do my friends no wrong, since I have none who would mourn me. I'll do the world no injury, since I possess nothing. All I do in the world is fill up space which might be better filled when I've made it empty.

ROSALIND   The little strength I have, I wish I could give it to you.

CELIA   And mine too, to eke out hers.

ROSALIND   Good luck! Pray heaven I'm wrong about you!

CELIA   Your heart's desires be with you!

CHARLES   Come on now, where's the young man who's so keen to lie with his mother earth?

ORLANDO   He's ready, sir. But his ambitions are more modest than that.

DUKE FREDERICK   You will play for one fall.

CHARLES   I guarantee, your grace, that you will not beg him to undergo a second contest when you worked so hard to dissuade him from the first.

ORLANDO   You plan to mock me afterwards? You should not have
  mocked me before. Come on, now.

ROSALIND   May Hercules give you strength, young man!

CELIA   I wish I was invisible, then I'd grab the strong fellow by the
  leg!

They wrestle.

ROSALIND   O excellent young man!

CELIA   If I could hurl thunderbolts with my eyes, I know who I'd
  strike down.

Charles is thrown. Shout.

DUKE FREDERICK   Stop, stop!

ORLANDO   I beg your grace. I'm not yet warmed up.

DUKE FREDERICK   How about you, Charles?

LE BEAU   He can't speak, my lord.

DUKE FREDERICK   Take him away. [*Charles is carried out.*] What is
  your name, young man?

ORLANDO   Orlando, my lord, the youngest son of Sir Rowland de
  Boys.

DUKE FREDERICK   I wish you were the son of someone else.
              The world esteemed your father very highly,
              But I have always seen him as my enemy.
              You would have pleased me better with this win
              If you belonged to any other house.
              But all good luck to you. Enjoy your youth.
              I wish you'd told me of a different father.

Exit Duke.

CELIA   Would I do this if, cousin, I were him?

ORLANDO   I'm very proud to be Sir Rowland's son,
              His youngest son, and would not change that boast
              To be adopted heir to Frederick.

ROSALIND   My father loved Sir Rowland very deeply,
              And all the world was of a similar mind.
              If I had known before this was his son,
              I would have pleaded with my tears as well
              As begged him not to fight.

CELIA   Rosalind dear,
              We ought to thank him and encourage him.
              My father's rough and envious attitude
              Appals me greatly. Sir, you've earned your prize.
              If this performance is anything to go by,

And you can win in love as well as strength,
You'll make some woman happy.

ROSALIND   Gentleman, [*Gives chain.*]
Wear this for me, and think of my misfortune;
I'd give you more if I had more to give.
Shall we go, Celia?

CELIA   Yes. Goodbye for now, good sir.

ORLANDO   Am I allowed to thank you? What you see
Is all that's left of any qualities I claim;
I stand here like a solitary post.

ROSALIND   He's calling us. I'm not too proud to ask him
What he wants of us. Sir, did you call us?
Your wrestling was quite splendid. You have conquered
More than your enemies.

CELIA   Are you coming?

ROSALIND   Yes, yes, I'll come. Goodbye!   *Exit with Celia.*

ORLANDO   How could I let my feelings tie my tongue!
She wanted a reply, but I said nothing.

                              Enter Le Beau.

O poor Orlando, you poor loser, you!
You're mastered by a weaker force than Charles!

LE BEAU   Good sir, I've come to tell you as a friend,
Although you have deserved high praise, applause
And commendation here, you should come back.
The duke is giving unambiguous signals
That he misrepresents what you have done.
The duke is moody. No doubt you can imagine
Just what that means more clearly than my words.

ORLANDO   I'm grateful to you. Tell me, those two girls …
Which of the two's the daughter of the duke
Who oversaw the wrestling?

LE BEAU   His manners would suggest that neither can be.
But yet the tall one is indeed his daughter,
The other's daughter of the banished duke,
Detained here by her unforgiving uncle
To keep his daughter company; the pair
Are closer to each other than two sisters.
But I should tell you that of late the duke
Has not been quite so generous to his niece,
The basis of his change of heart is this:
Too many people praise her for her virtue

And pity her for her good father's sake.
Some expression of ill-will against the lady
Can break out any time. I wish you well, sir,
And if things improve in days to come
Perhaps we'll get to know each other better.

ORLANDO   I'm much indebted to you. All God speed.

[Exit Le Beau.]

Next I must pass from one hell to another:
From tyrant duke here to a tyrant brother.
O heavenly Rosalind!

Exit.

Act I Scene 3

Enter Celia and Rosalind

CELIA   Come now, cousin Rosalind, for Cupid's sake, don't you have a single word to tell me?

ROSALIND   Not one I'd even throw at a dog.

CELIA   Your words are too precious to be cast at curs; throw some of them my way. Come on, pelt me with talk.

ROSALIND   Then both cousins would be out of action, one pelted with talk and the other going mad without any.

CELIA   But is this all about your father?

ROSALIND   No, some of it is about my child's father. Oh how full of brambles this workaday world is!

CELIA   They're only burrs, Rosalind, that might be thrown at you in fun. If we stray from the well trodden path our petticoats will catch them.

ROSALIND   I could shake those off my coat; these burrs are in my heart.

CELIA   Cough them up!

ROSALIND   I'd try, if I could say "ahem" and get a-him!

CELIA   Come, come; wrestle with your feelings.

ROSALIND   Oh they turn out to be a better wrestler than I am.

CELIA   Well, good luck to you! You'll manage it some time, even if it takes some wrestling. But joking aside, let's talk seriously. Is it possible to fall so suddenly for old Sir Rowland's youngest son?

ROSALIND   The duke, my father, was very fond of his father.

CELIA   Does it follow that you should be very fond of his son? On that logic I would hate him, since my father hated his father. Yet I don't hate Orlando.

ROSALIND   No, please, for my sake, don't hate him!

CELIA   Why not? Doesn't he deserve it?

Enter Duke Frederick, with Lords.

ROSALIND   Let me love him as he deserves, and you please love him because I do. Look, here comes the Duke.

CELIA   His eyes full of anger.

DUKE FREDERICK   Young lady, with all reasonable speed
        You have to leave our court.

ROSALIND   Me, uncle?

DUKE FREDERICK   Yes.
        If you still linger here within ten days
        As near our public court as twenty miles,
        You'll die for it.

ROSALIND   I do beseech your grace,
        Give me some notion of what wrong I've done.
        However much I search my inmost thoughts,
        Or guess my weaker inclinations,
        Or check I am not dreaming or insane
        (Which surely I am not), believe me, uncle,
        Never so much as in my farthest thoughts
        Did I offend your highness.

DUKE FREDERICK   Those are the words
        All traitors use in their exoneration.
        They sound as innocent as grace itself.
        Let it suffice to say I do not trust you.

ROSALIND   Yet your mistrust cannot make me a traitor.
        Please tell me why suspicion falls on me.

DUKE FREDERICK   You are your father's daughter, that's enough.

ROSALIND   As I was when your highness took his dukedom,
        As I was when your highness banished him.
        Treason is not inherited, my lord.
        Or if we did derive it from our friends,
        What's that to me? My father was no traitor.
        Do not misunderstand me then, your grace,
        Don't think my poverty is treacherous.

CELIA   Dear father, let me speak.

DUKE FREDERICK   She's here for you, remember, Celia,
        For otherwise she would be with her father.

CELIA   I did not ask to let her stay with us;
        It was your pleasure and your own compassion.
        I was too young to value her as friend,

But now I know her well. If she's a traitor,
Then so am I. We've always shared a bedroom,
We've woken up, played, studied, fed together;
Wherever either went, the other too
Was by her side, always inseparable,
Like swans attached to Juno's chariot.

DUKE FREDERICK   She is too crafty for you. And her smoothness,
Her subtle silences, her patience,
Tell people she deserves their sympathy.
You're just a fool. She uses you, you see?
Your virtues will be all the clearer to us
When she has gone. So don't defend her case;
Firm and irrevocable is my decision;
Her sentence is not altered: she is banished.

CELIA   Pronounce that sentence then on me, my lord;
I cannot live without her company.

DUKE FREDERICK   You are a fool. You, niece, take careful note:
If you outstay your time, I guarantee,
My honour is my word: you die.

Exit Duke Frederick, with Lords.

CELIA   O my poor Rosalind, where will you go?
Would you change fathers? I would give you mine.
You could not be more grieved by this than I am.

ROSALIND   I think I should.

CELIA   You have no reason to be.
At least be cheerful. Don't you see the duke
Has banished me, his daughter?

ROSALIND   No, he hasn't.

CELIA   Has not, you say? If only you could see
That love unites us so that we are one.
Shall we be separated, shall we part?
No! Let my father find another heir.
So make a plan with me to get away,
Where we could go, and what to take with us;
Don't try to bear the burden of your grief alone,
We'll share misfortune; never leave me out!
I swear by heaven at this lowest point
Of fortune, we will go along together.

ROSALIND   Where shall we go?

CELIA   To find my uncle in the Forest of Arden.

ROSALIND   But think of all the danger we would face!

The roads are rough for girls who go alone!
A pretty face is more at risk than gold.

CELIA I'll dress in shabby, unattractive clothes
And smear a kind of umber on my face;
You do the same! So as we go our way
We won't attract attention.

ROSALIND   Better yet,
Because I'm taller than the average girl,
Why don't I dress completely as a man?
A gallant cutlass at my belt, and in my hand
A spear for killing boar; if any trace
Of girlish fearfulness remains within,
Externally I'll show a blustering, martial front,
Like all those manly-looking cowards who
Conceal their feebleness with bluff and bluster.

CELIA What shall I call you when you are a man?

ROSALIND The best name I could have is Ganymede,
The name of Jupiter's own servant-boy.
But what will you be called?

CELIA Something that makes a reference to my state:
No longer Celia, but Aliena.

ROSALIND But, cousin dear, suppose we try to lure
That clownish fool away from your father's court!

CELIA He'll go just anywhere on earth with me;
Leave me to win him over. Let's go now
And get our jewels and our money packed.
We have to plan the best and safest way
To hide from the pursuit that will be made
After I leave. So let's away to happiness,
To liberty, and not to banishment!

Exeunt.

Act II Scene 1

*Enter Duke Senior, Amiens, and two or
three Lords, [dressed as] Foresters.*

DUKE SENIOR   Now, my companions, brothers in exile,
Is not this life by ancient custom better
Than all the pomp of court? Are not these woods
Quite free of peril when compared to that?
The punishment that Adam had to bear

Cannot affect us; take the seasons' changes:
The icy bite of winter's churlish wind
Can mercilessly nibble at my body
Until I shrink with cold. I smile and say
"This is no flattery"; these are counsellors
That tell my senses just what man I am.
Sweet are the uses of adversity,
Which, like a toad, ugly and venomous,
Conceals a precious jewel in its head.
This life of ours, far from the public eye,
Finds speech in trees, books in the running brooks,
Sermons in stones, and good in everything.

AMIENS   I wouldn't change it for the world; your grace
Is fortunate to turn such rough misfortune
Into so quiet and so sweet a style.

DUKE SENIOR   Well, shall we go and kill some venison?
It pains me, though, that those poor dappled beasts,
Belonging as they do to this wild wood,
Should suffer in their own domain the fate
Of being gored by arrows.

FIRST LORD   That is, my lord,
What most upsets the melancholy Jaques.
He is convinced you are a worse offender
Than he who stole your land and banished you.
An hour ago Lord Amiens and myself
We crept up close as he was lying there
Beneath an oak whose ancient roots reach out
Into the brook that babbles through the wood.
In that same spot a wretched hunted stag,
Just wounded by a hunter's deadly aim,
Fell to the ground. The animal's dreadful groans
Were so appalling and so keen, my lord,
Each cry seemed it would stretch its leather hide
Almost to bursting, and the big round tears
Flowed one upon another down his innocent nose
In pitiful streams; the creature simply stood,
Watched closely by the melancholy Jaques,
Stood on the very edge of the swift brook
Augmenting it with tears.

DUKE SENIOR   Did Jaques have
Some moral comment on the spectacle?

FIRST LORD   O yes; he had a thousand epigrams.

First, on the tears that filled the flooding stream:
"Poor stag," he said, "you're making a bequest
As humans do, so those who have too much
Get even more." Then, being there alone,
Abandoned by his velvet-coated friend:
"It's right," he said, "that misery should end
A friendship just like that." A herd of cows
Came jostling from the pasture past the place
And paid him no attention. "So," said Jaques,
"Sweep on, you fat and greasy citizens,
Follow the fashion; take a fleeting glance
At that poor broken, lifeless creature there!"
With more invective such as that he pierced
The heart of our society, city, court,
And even human life, swearing that we
Are mere usurpers, tyrants, worse than that,
For chasing animals and killing them
In their assigned and natural dwelling-place.

DUKE SENIOR   And did you go and leave him to his thoughts?

SECOND LORD   We did, my lord, weeping and mumbling on
About the sobbing deer.

DUKE SENIOR   Show me the place.
I love to challenge him when he's like that,
That's when he's full of fight.

FIRST LORD   I'll take you there at once.

Exeunt.

Act II Scene 2

Enter Duke Frederick, with Lords.

DUKE FREDERICK   Can it be possible that no one saw them?
It cannot be; some troublemakers here
Must surely have connived at their escape.

FIRST LORD   I haven't heard from anyone who saw her.
The ladies who attend her in her chamber
Saw her to bed, but in the morning early
They found the bed abandoned by their mistress.

SECOND LORD   My lord, the stupid clown at whose dry wit
Your grace has often laughed is also missing.
Hisperia, the lady's gentlewoman,
Confesses that she slyly overheard

> Your daughter and her cousin speaking warmly
> About the qualities of that young man
> Who recently threw down the brawny Charles,
> And she believes, wherever they have gone,
> That he is surely in their company.

DUKE FREDERICK   Go to his brother, bring that young man here.
If he's not there, then let the brother come.
I'll make him find him. Be off at once,
And spare no effort in the search until
You bring these foolish runaways back here.

Exeunt.

Act II Scene 3

Enter Orlando and Adam.

ORLANDO   Who's there?

ADAM   What, my young master, O my gentle master,
O my good master, you remind me so
Of old Sir Rowland. Why, what brings you here?
Why are you gifted? Why do people love you?
How is it you are gentle, strong and valiant?
How could you be so foolish as to throw
The angry duke's prize wrestler as you did?
The word of your success has got round quickly.
Perhaps you know, sir, that for certain men
Their qualities can do more harm than good.
This may be so for you. Your virtues, sir,
Are like a sacred gift that can betray you.
Oh what a world this is, when loveliness
Can turn to poison and destroy itself.

ORLANDO   Why, what's the matter?

ADAM   O unhappy child!
Do not set foot in here. Beneath this roof
Resides the enemy of everything you stand for.
Your brother – no, no brother! – well, the son
(But not the son, I cannot call him son)
Of him I was about to call his father,
Has heard your praises sung, and so tonight
He plans to burn the lodgings where you live
With you inside. And if this fails, he has
Another way to make an end of you.

I overheard him and his wicked plot.
This is no place, this house is just a slaughterhouse.
Avoid it, shun it, do not enter it!

ORLANDO   Then tell me, Adam, where I ought to go.

ADAM   No matter where, so long as it's not here.

ORLANDO   So would you let me go and beg for food,
Or rob and steal my way by force,
A murderous sword and dagger in my hand?
If this won't do, I don't know what to do.
Whatever else I do, I'll not do that.
I'd rather suffer the malicious will
Of a depraved and blood-besotted brother.

ADAM   But don't do that! I have five hundred crowns,
Saved from the wages which your father paid me.
I thought I'd need it one day to assist me
When my old limbs begin to fail the call
Of service, putting old men out to grass.
Take this, and may our Lord who feeds the ravens
And generously caters for the sparrow,
Be comfort for my age. Here is the gold,
All this I give you. Let me be your servant;
Though I look old, I'm still quite strong and vigorous,
For in my youth I never would allow
A drop of raging liquor pass my lips.
Nor ever did I shamelessly pursue
Depraved debilitating sport.
Therefore my age is like a lusty winter,
Frosty, but kindly. Let me go with you;
I'll serve you with devotion like a younger man
In all your business and necessities.

ORLANDO   O good old man, how well you represent
The faithful standards of an earlier age,
When duty, not reward, led men to serve!
The fashion of our day is not for you,
With people sweating solely for promotion,
Who having gained it feel no obligation
To serve a moment more. You're not like that.
But, poor old man, you prune a rotten tree
On which no trace of blossom ever grows,
For all your careful work and husbandry.
But let that be; we'll go along together.
Before those well-earned wages are all spent

ADAM

We'll find a simple way to be content.
Master, go on, and I will follow you;
To the last gasp you'll find me good and true.
From seventeen till now almost fourscore
Have I lived here, but now that is no more.
At seventeen some boys their fortune seek,
But at fourscore an old man is too weak;
Yet fortune cannot recompense me better
Than to die well, and not my master's debtor.

Exeunt.

Act II Scene 4

Enter Rosalind dressed as Ganymede,
Celia dressed as Aliena, and Touchstone.

ROSALIND   O Jupiter, how weary are my spirits!

TOUCHSTONE   I'd worry about spirits if my legs weren't weary.

ROSALIND   I'm inclined to disgrace my man's clothes and cry like a woman, but I must comfort the weaker sex, since doublet and hose should show courage before a petticoat. So take courage, good Aliena!

CELIA   Please bear with me; I can go no further.

TOUCHSTONE   For my part, I'd rather bear with you than bear you. Yet I'd bear no cross if I did bear you, since you don't have any of those coins with crosses in your purse.

ROSALIND   Well, this is the Forest of Arden.

TOUCHSTONE   Ay, now I am in Arden, the more fool I. When I was at home, I was in a better place, but travellers must be content.

Enter Corin and Silvius.

ROSALIND   Yes, you should be, good Touchstone. Look who's coming!

A young man and an old man deep in talk.

CORIN   But that's the way to make her scorn you more!

SILVIUS   If only, Corin, you knew how much I love her!

CORIN   Well I can guess; I've been in love myself.

SILVIUS   No, Corin, really. You're too old to guess,
Though in your youth you were as keen a lover
As ever sighed into his midnight pillow.
But if your love was ever strong as mine
(And I'm convinced no one has ever matched it),
How many mad exploits did you get up to

	Possessed by passion and a crazy dream?
CORIN	At least a thousand, which I've now forgotten.
SILVIUS	Well then you never loved wholeheartedly.
	You can't remember anything you did,
	However foolish, in response to love.
	You've never loved!
	Or if you've never sat as I do now
	Wearying your hearer singing some girl's praise,
	You've never loved!
	Or if you've never walked hotheadedly away
	From someone's company as I do now,
	You've never loved!
	O Phebe, Phebe, Phebe! *Exit.*
ROSALIND	Alas, poor shepherd! Hearing your distress
	I find myself more troubled by my own.

TOUCHSTONE   And I by mine. I remember, when I was in love I smashed my sword on a stone, saying "Take that!" for visiting Jane Smile at night. And I remember kissing her kitchen spoon and the cow's udders her pretty chapped hands had milked. And I remember wooing a peapod instead of her; I took two codpieces from her and gave them back, and said, in tears: "Wear these for my sake." We that are true lovers get up to some strange games; but as everything in nature is mortal, so all nature in love is mortal in folly.

ROSALIND   You speak more wisely than you know.

TOUCHSTONE   No, I'll never know my own wit until I break my shins on it.

ROSALIND   By Jove! This shepherd's passion is very like my own.

TOUCHSTONE   Mine too, except my passion's somewhat stale.

CELIA	I beg you, please would someone ask that man
	If he can give us any food for money.
	I'm almost dying.

TOUCHSTONE   Hey there, you old bumpkin!

ROSALIND   Steady there! He's not one of your relations!

CORIN   Who's calling?

TOUCHSTONE   Your betters, sir.

CORIN   If they're not, they're very wretched.

ROSALIND   Steady, I said! Good evening to you, my friend.

CORIN   And to you, sir, and to the others there.

ROSALIND	Please tell us, shepherd, if in this wild place
	Refreshment may be had for love or money?
	Please take us somewhere where there's food and rest.

This young girl here is very tired from travelling,
She's quite exhausted.

CORIN   Sir, I truly pity her,
And wish, for her sake rather than my own,
I had more ample means to offer her relief;
But I am shepherd for another man
And do not shear the fleeces that I graze.
My master is of churlish disposition
And never reckons he will get to heaven
By doing deeds of hospitality.
Besides, his house, his flocks, and all his fields
Are now for sale, and at our farmhouse now,
By reason of his absence, there is nothing
For you to feed on. But come, see what's there;
By me at least most welcome you will be.

ROSALIND   And do you know who'll buy the flock and pasture?

CORIN   You saw him here just now: that keen young man
Who has no interest in buying things.

ROSALIND   May I propose that, if this be allowed,
You buy the cottage, pasture and the flock,
And you will get the money back from us.

CELIA   And we will raise your wage. I like this place
And willingly could waste my time in it.

CORIN   Assuredly the thing is to be sold.
Come with me; if you find the soil, the forest,
And the life in these rough woods appealing,
I will be glad to serve you from today,
And buy it with your money straight away.

Exeunt.

Act II Scene 5

Enter Amiens, Jaques, and others.

AMIENS   *Song*

Under the greenwood tree
    Who loves to lie with me,
And turn his merry note
    Unto the sweet bird's throat,
Come hither, come hither, come hither.
    Here shall he see no enemy
But winter and rough weather.

JAQUES   More, more, please more!

AMIENS   It will make you melancholy, Monsieur Jaques.

JAQUES   All the better! More, please, more! I can suck melancholy out of a song as a weasel sucks eggs. More please, more!

AMIENS   My voice is rough. I know I can't please you.

JAQUES   I don't need you to please me; I need you to sing. Come, more! Another stanza! Do you call them stanzas?

AMIENS   Whatever you like, Monsieur Jaques.

JAQUES   No, I don't care about their names, they don't owe me any money. Will you sing?

AMIENS   More at your request than to please myself.

JAQUES   Well then, if I ever thank anyone I'll thank you. But what they call politeness is like the encounter of two baboons; when a man thanks me heartily, I think I've given him a penny for which he offers effusive thanks. Come on, sing! And those of you who don't, keep quiet.

AMIENS   Well, I'll conclude the song. You there, prepare our meal meanwhile. The duke will drink under this tree. He has been looking for you all day.

JAQUES   And I have been avoiding him all day. He's too argumentative for me. I think about as many subjects as he does, but I thank heavens I don't boast about them. Come on, warble!

Song
All together here.

> Who doth ambition shun
> > And loves to live i' th' sun,
> Seeking the food he eats,
> > And pleased with what he gets,
> Come hither, come hither, come hither.
> > Here shall he see no enemy
> But winter and rough weather.

JAQUES   I'll give you a verse to this tune which I wrote yesterday despite my lack of imagination.

AMIENS   And I'll sing it.

JAQUES   Here it is.

> If it do come to pass
> > That any man turn ass,
> Leaving his wealth and ease
> > A stubborn will to please,
> Duc-da-me, duc-da-me, duc-da-me,

Here shall he see gross fools as he
An if he will come to me.

AMIENS   What's this "duc-da-me"?

JAQUES   It's a Greek invocation for summoning fools into a circle. I'll go and sleep, if I can. If I can't, I'll rail against all the first-born of Egypt.

AMIENS   And I'll go and find the duke. His banquet is ready.

Exeunt.

Act II Scene 6

Enter Orlando and Adam.

ADAM   Dear master, I can go no further. I'm dying of hunger. I'll lie down here and measure out my grave. Goodbye, dear master.

ORLANDO   What's all this, Adam? No more strength left? Live a little longer, cheer up a bit! If this untidy forest produces any wild beast, I'll either be food for it or I'll bring it as food for you. Your imagination is nearer death than your actual strength. For my sake, cheer up. Keep death at arm's length a little while longer. I'll be back shortly and if I don't have something for you to eat, you have my permission to die. But if you die before I get back, you'll be wasting my efforts. Well done, you're looking more cheerful, and I'll get back quickly. But you're lying in a draughty spot; come on, I'll move you to some shelter, and you'll not die for lack of a dinner if there's anything living in this wild place. Cheerio, good Adam.

Exeunt.

Act II Scene 7

Enter Duke Senior, and Lords, dressed as outlaws.

DUKE SENIOR   I think he's now become an animal,
I see no trace of him here as a man.

FIRST LORD   My lord, he left this spot not long ago.
He listened to a song here, having fun.

DUKE SENIOR   He is so full of discord that his singing
Will jar with the sweet music of the spheres.
Go find him; I would like a word with him.

Enter Jaques.

FIRST LORD   He saves me trouble; he's already here.

DUKE SENIOR   Well now, Monsieur, what sort of life is this
                That your poor friends must seek your company?
                Well, you look cheerful.
JAQUES   A fool, a fool! I met a fool in the forest,
                A motley fool! A miserable world!
                As I do live on food, I met a fool
                Who lay down in the sun and basked awhile
                And railed at Lady Fortune in strong terms,
                In well-practised terms, and yet a motley fool.
                "Good morning, fool," I said. "No, sir," said he,
                "Don't call me fool till heaven sends me luck."
                And then he took a sundial from his pocket,
                And looking at it with lacklustre eye,
                Says very wisely: "It is ten o'clock.
                Thus we may see," said he, "how the world wags.
                'Tis but an hour since it was nine o'clock,
                And after one more hour it will be eleven;
                And so from hour to hour we grow mature,
                And then from hour to hour we turn to rot.
                And thereby hangs a tale." On hearing him,
                That motley fool, discoursing thus on time,
                My lungs sang like a cock-a-doodle-doo
                That fools should be so thoughtful and profound;
                I started laughing and kept on at least
                An hour by his dial. O noble fool,
                A worthy fool! The motley suits you well.
DUKE SENIOR   Which fool was this?
JAQUES   O worthy fool! He used to be a courtier,
                And says if ladies are still young and fair
                They have the gift to know it. And in his brain,
                Which is as dry as a leftover ship's biscuit
                After a voyage, he's crammed each nook and cranny
                With observations which he then brings out
                In mangled form. Oh that I were a fool!
                I truly yearn to wear a motley coat.
DUKE SENIOR   You shall have one.
JAQUES   It is my only wish,
                Provided that you clear your better judgments
                Of all opinions festering in your head
                That I am wise. I must have liberty
                Along with it, unfettered as the wind,
                To blow on anyone I please, as fools do.

And those who are offended by my fooling
Must laugh the most. And why, sir, must they so?
It's plain as any road that leads to church.
He whom a fool attacks with all his wisdom
Is very foolish, even if it hurts,
Not to ignore the insult. For if not,
The wise man's folly is laid bare to all,
Even to the random glances of the fool.
Invest me in my motley, give me leave
To speak my mind, and I will through and through
Cleanse the foul body of the infected world,
If it will patiently receive my medicine.

DUKE SENIOR For shame! I can tell what you would do.

JAQUES What? Just to argue, would I do some good?

DUKE SENIOR Hypocrisy most foul in chiding sin!
For you have a been a libertine yourself,
With lusts as sensual as an animal;
And all the boils and scabs you gave yourself
From going freely all about the world
You'd pass to others with no further thought.

JAQUES Why now, who's fulminating against pride
And censuring a person's private thoughts?
Does pride not flow in torrents like the sea
Until the means to feed it fade and ebb?
What woman in the city do I name
If I should say the city woman bears
The cost of princes on unworthy shoulders?
Who could accuse me of intending her
When she has neighbours much the same?
Or what about the man of low degree
Who says I do not pay for what he wears,
Thinking that I mean him – but suits his words,
As wild as ever, to the spirit of my speech.
There then, how then, what then? Let me see just how
My words have wronged him. If I got him right,
Then he has wronged himself. If he is blameless,
My charge is like the goose that flies away,
Unclaimed by anyone. But who is this?

Enter Orlando.

ORLANDO Stop that! No more eating!

JAQUES I've not eaten anything yet.

ORLANDO   And you won't, until necessity is served.

JAQUES   What kind of troublemaker is this?

DUKE SENIOR   Are you so fraught, young man, by your distress,
              Or else perhaps so scornful of good manners
              That you show no awareness of civility?

ORLANDO   You've put your finger on it. Yes, the sting
              Of dire distress has taken all my sense
              Of due civility; yet I was well brought up
              And know my manners. But still stop, I say!
              If anyone should touch that fruit set there
              Before my urgent case is heard, he dies.

JAQUES   If reason will not meet your case, I'll die.

DUKE SENIOR   What do you need? Your breeding as a gentleman
              Will carry force before your force moves us to gentleness.

ORLANDO   I'm almost dead from lack of food. Let me have some!

DUKE SENIOR   Sit down and eat, and welcome to our table.

ORLANDO   You speak politely! Pardon me, I beg you.
              Expecting only savage manners here,
              I thought a threatening, violent tone was right
              To get my way. Whoever you may be,
              You who let endless hours of time creep by
              In this remote and wild, uncharted wood,
              Beneath the shade of melancholy boughs,
              If ever you have looked on better days,
              If ever you've been called by bells to church,
              If ever you've partaken of a feast,
              If ever you've had cause to wipe a tear,
              And know what it is to pity and be pitied,
              Let gentleness show how to force my way;
              I blush to say it, and I hide my sword.

DUKE SENIOR   It's true that we have looked on better days,
              And have been called by holy bells to church,
              And sat as guests at feasts, and wiped our eyes
              To mop the tears that pity draws from us;
              So sit and share our hospitality
              And take whatever food and drink you need;
              Our help in any form is here to serve you.

ORLANDO   Then just hold back from starting on your meal
              While like a doe I go and find my fawn
              And give it food. There is a poor old man
              Who limped and crawled behind me every step
              Out of pure love. Until he's had his fill,

                    Oppressed by two weak evils, age and hunger,
                    I will not touch a thing.
DUKE SENIOR   Go, find him then;
                    We'll leave it all untouched till you return.
ORLANDO   I thank you; bless you all for your good comfort.   *Exit.*
DUKE SENIOR   You see then we are not the only ones to suffer.
                    The universal theatre of this world
                    Presents more tragic pageants than the stage
                    On which you see us.
JAQUES   All the world's a stage,
                    And all the men and women merely actors;
                    They have their exits and their entrances,
                    And one man in his time plays many parts,
                    His acts being seven ages. At first, the infant,
                    Mewling and puking in his nurse's arms.
                    Then the whining schoolboy with his satchel,
                    His face all freshly scrubbed, creeping like a snail
                    Unwillingly to school. And then the lover,
                    With sighs and tears and sentimental ballads
                    Praising his lady's eyebrows. Then a soldier,
                    Full of strange oaths and fashionably bearded,
                    Jealous of honour, quick to pick a quarrel,
                    And desperate to puff his reputation
                    Even in the face of cannonfire. Then comes
                    The magistrate, his belly full and round,
                    His look severe, his beard neat and well trimmed,
                    A man of wisdom and experience.
                    And so he plays his part. The sixth age shifts
                    To wearing slippers, looking thin and foolish,
                    With spectacles on nose and purse on side,
                    His stocking, saved for years, too large by far
                    For his spare frame, and his big manly voice,
                    Turning again toward a childish treble,
                    Just squeaks and whistles. The last scene of all,
                    Which ends this strange eventful history,
                    Is second chidhood, leading to oblivion,
                    No teeth, no sight, no taste, no anything.

                    Enter Orlando, with Adam.

DUKE SENIOR   Welcome. Set down your venerable burden
                    And let him feed.
ORLANDO   Thankyou on his behalf.

ADAM   A useful deed,
          Since I can scarcely speak my thanks myself.
DUKE SENIOR   Welcome, help yourselves. I'll wait awhile
          Before I trouble you to tell your story.
          Let's have some music. Please, dear cousin, sing!

AMIENS   *Song*

          Blow, blow, thou winter wind,
          Thou art not so unkind
              As man's ingratitude:
          Thy tooth is not so keen,
          Because thou art not seen,
              Although thy breath be rude.
          Heigh-ho, sing heigh-ho, unto the green holly.
          Most friendship is faining, most loving mere folly:
              Then heigh-ho, the holly.
              This life is most jolly.

          Freeze, freeze, thou bitter sky
          That does not bite so nigh
              As benefits forgot:
          Though thou the waters warp,
          Thy sting is not so sharp
              As friend remembered not.
          Heigh-ho, sing heigh-ho, unto the green holly.
          Most friendship is faining, most loving mere folly:
              Then heigh-ho, the holly.
              This life is most jolly.

DUKE SENIOR   If you are really good Sir Rowland's son,
          As you have hinted that that's who you are,
          And since I see his likeness there outlined
          In clearest features in your face,
          Be truly welcome here. I am the duke
          That loved your father. Later in my cave
          You'll tell me all your story. Good old man,
          You are most welcome, as your master is.
          Support him by the arm. Give me your hand,
          I know there's plenty more to understand.
                        Exeunt.

Act III Scene 1

Enter Duke Frederick, Lords, and Oliver.

DUKE FREDERICK   Not seen him since? Sir, sir, that cannot be.
If I were not myself inclined to mercy,
I would not seek revenge on him, not here,
With you here present. Look for him, I say;
Go find your brother, wherever he may be,
Leave not a stone unturned, and bring him in
Dead or alive, within the year, or else
You should not seek a living in our lands.
Your properties and anything that's yours
Worth seizing we will seize without remorse
Until you can acquit yourself by having
Your brother speak on your behalf.

OLIVER   I wish your highness knew my heart in this!
I never loved my brother in my life.

DUKE FREDERICK   The worse for you. Well, push him out the door,
And let my officers whose job it is
Take stock of his domains and lands.
Do this immediately and throw him out.

Exeunt.

Act III Scene 2

Enter Orlando.

ORLANDO   Hang there, my verse in witness of my love;
And thou, thrice-crownèd Queen of Night, survey
With thy chaste eye, from thy pale sphere above,
Thy huntress' name that my full life doth sway.
O Rosalind! these trees shall be my books,
And in their barks my thoughts I'll character,
That every eye which in this forest looks
Shall see thy virtue witnessed everywhere.
Run, run, Orlando, carve on every tree
The fair, the chaste, and unexpressive she.   *Exit.*

Enter Corin and Touchstone the Clown.

CORIN   So how do you like this shepherd's life, Master Touchstone?

TOUCHSTONE   To tell the truth, shepherd, in itself it's a good life; but
as a shepherd's life it's nothing. As a solitary life, I like it a lot. As a
private life, it's vile. Being in the fields, it pleases me much. But not

being at court, it's tedious. As it's a meagre life, mind you, it suits me well. But since there's not much abundance in it, it goes much against my stomach. Are you a philosopher, shepherd?

CORIN   All I know is that the sicker you get the worse you feel; he who has no money, income or property is without three good friends; that the property of rain is to wet and of fire to burn; that good pasture makes fat sheep, and that a main cause of the night is lack of the sun; and that he that is born with no intelligence or skill may lament the lack of good breeding, or he comes from a very ungifted family.

TOUCHSTONE   That makes a natural philosopher. Were you ever at court, shepherd?

CORIN   Certainly not.

TOUCHSTONE   Then you are damned.

CORIN   I hope not!

TOUCHSTONE   You are definitely damned, like a badly cooked egg, all on one side.

CORIN   For not being at court? Your reason?

TOUCHSTONE   Because if you were never at court you never saw good manners; if you never saw good manners, then your manners must be wicked; and wickedness is a sin, and sin leads to damnation. You are in a parlous state, shepherd.

CORIN   Not at all, Touchstone. What's seen as good manners at court are as ridiculous in the country as country behaviour seems ridiculous at court. You told me you don't salute at court but kiss hands. That courtesy would be unclean if courtiers were shepherds.

TOUCHSTONE   Give me an example, briefly. Come on, an example.

CORIN   Well, we are always handling our ewes, and their fleeces, as you know, are greasy.

TOUCHSTONE   Well, don't courtiers' hands sweat? Isn't mutton grease as wholesome as the sweat of a man? That's a shallow argument, shallow. A better example, please. Come on.

CORIN   In addition, our hands are hard.

TOUCHSTONE   Your lips will feel them sooner. That's shallow too. A sounder argument, please.

CORIN   And they're often covered in tar from the surgery of our sheep, and would you want us to kiss tar? The courtier's hands are perfumed with civet.

TOUCHSTONE   Extremely shallow! Food for worms compared to a good piece of flesh! Really! Take note of this wisdom and consider: Civet is of a lower order than tar, being the unclean discharge of a cat. Improve on that example, shepherd.

CORIN   You have too courtly a wit for me. I'll take a rest.

TOUCHSTONE   You'll rest damned? God help you, you shallow man. May God do some surgery on you! You're sick.

CORIN   Sir, I am a true labourer. I earn what I eat, buy what I wear, owe no man hate, envy no one's happiness, I am glad about other men's success, uncomplaining about my troubles. And my greatest source of pride is to see my ewes graze and my lambs suck.

TOUCHSTONE   That's another simple sin in you. You bring the rams and ewes together and claim to make a living from the copulation of cattle, you're a pimp to the sheep and serve a twelve-month-old female lamb up to an old cuckold of a ram with crooked horns in a match deprived of all reason. If you are not damned for this, the devil himself will have no shepherds. I can't see how you can escape it.

CORIN   Here comes young master Ganymede, my new mistress's brother.

Enter Rosalind.

ROSALIND   "From the east to western Ind,
                      No jewel is like Rosalind.
                    Her worth, being mounted on the wind,
                    Through all the world bears Rosalind.
                    All the pictures fairest lined
                      Are but black to Rosalind.
                    Let no face be kept in mind
                      But the fair of Rosalind."

TOUCHSTONE   I could write rhymes like that for eight years on end, dinners and suppers and sleeping hours excepted. They're like the rhymes of butterwomen riding to market.

ROSALIND   Go away, fool!

TOUCHSTONE   Try this:

                    If a hart do lack a hind,
                      Let him seek out Rosalind.
                    If the cat will after kind,
                      So be sure will Rosalind.
                    Wintered garments must be lined,
                      So must slender Rosalind.
                    They that reap must sheaf and bind,
                      Then to cart with Rosalind.
                    Sweetest nut hath sourest rind,
                      Such a nut is Rosalind.

> He that sweetest rose will find,
> Must find love's prick, and Rosalind.

This is a very poor piece of verse. Why do you infect yourself with this kind of thing?

ROSALIND   None of that, you stupid fool. I found it on a tree.

TOUCHSTONE   Then it'a tree that bears bad fruit.

ROSALIND   I'll graft it with you and then I'll graft it with a medlar tree. Then it'll be the earliest fruit in the country, since you'll be rotten before you're half ripe and that's the characteristic of the medlar.

TOUCHSTONE   If you say so. But whether wise or not, let the forest judge.

Enter Celia with a paper.

ROSALIND   Quiet! Here comes my sister, reading. Move away.

CELIA   "Why should this a desert be?
                 For it is unpeopled? No.
               Tongues I'll hang on every tree
                 That shall civil sayings show:
               Some, how brief the life of man
                 Runs his erring pilgrimage,
               That the stretching of a span
                 Buckles in his sum of age;
               Some, of violated vows
                 'Twixt the souls of friend and friend;
               But upon the fairest boughs,
                 Or at every sentence end,
               Will I "Rosalinda" write,
                 Teaching all that read to know
               The quintessence of every sprite
                 Heaven would in little show.
               Therefore heaven Nature charged
                 That one body should be filled
               With all graces wide-enlarged.
                 Nature presently distilled
               Helen's cheek, but not her heart,
                 Cleopatra's majesty,
               Atalanta's better part,
                 Sad Lucretia's modesty.
               Thus Rosalind of many parts
                 By heavenly synod was devised,

> Of many faces, eyes, and heart,
>> To have the touches dearest prized.
> Heaven would that she these gifts should have,
>> And I to live and die her slave."

ROSALIND   O gentle preacher, what a tedious sermon of love you've wearied your parishioners with, and never cried out "Have patience, good people!"

CELIA   You want to know? Go away, my friends. Shepherd, give us a little time. You go with him, sir.

TOUCHSTONE   Come on, shepherd, let's make an honourable retreat. Not with bag and baggage, but with scrip and scrippage. *Exit with Corin.*

CELIA   Did you hear that verse?

ROSALIND   Oh yes, I heard it all, and more too, for some of the lines had more feet in them than the verse would bear.

CELIA   That doesn't matter. The feet might bear the verses.

ROSALIND   Yes, but the feet were lame and could not bear themselves without the verse, and so stood lamely in the verse.

CELIA   But didn't you wonder how your name came to be hung and carved on those trees?

ROSALIND   I had gone seven of the nine days' wondering before you came; look at what I found on a palm tree. I have never been set to so many rhymes since the time of Pythagoras, when I was an Irish rat, which I can hardly remember.

CELIA   Do you know who did this?

ROSALIND   Was it a man?

CELIA   And a chain you once wore, round his neck? Are you blushing?

ROSALIND   Who, tell me!

CELIA   Oh Lord, Lord, it's hard for friends to meet, but mountains may be moved by earthquakes and come together.

ROSALIND   But who is it?

CELIA   Is it possible?

ROSALIND   Please, now, I beg you in all earnestness, tell me who it is!

CELIA   Oh wonderful, wonderful, and even more wonderful, wonderful, and once more wonderful and after that far out of range.

ROSALIND   Look at me! Just because I'm dressed as a man, do you think I have a doublet and hose in my temperament? Another moment's delay will be like a voyage of discovery to the South Seas. Please quickly tell me who it is, go on. I wish you had a stammer, then you could pour this concealed man out of your mouth like wine out of a narrow-mouthed bottle: either too much at once or nothing at all. Please take the cork out of your mouth, so I can drink your news.

CELIA   So you can put a man in your belly.

ROSALIND   Is he a human being? What kind of man? Does his head deserve a hat? Does his chin deserve a beard?

CELIA   No, but he has hardly any beard.

ROSALIND   God will give him more if the man is grateful. Let me wait for his beard to grow, unless you hold back my acquaintance with his chin.

CELIA   It's young Orlando, who tripped up the wrestler's heels and your heart both at the same time.

ROSALIND   You're surely mocking me. Speak sad and speak true, girl.

CELIA   Really, cousin, it's him.

ROSALIND   Orlando?

CELIA   Orlando.

ROSALIND   Oh alas! What shall I do with my doublet and hose? What was he doing when you saw him? What did he say? How did he look? What was he wearing? What is he doing here? Did he ask for me? Where is he now? How did he leave you? When will you see him again? Answer me in one word.

CELIA   You'll have to lend me Gargantua's mouth first. It's a word too large for any mouth around today. To say yes and no to those questions is more than you have to answer in the catechism.

ROSALIND   But does he know that I am in this forest, and dressed as a man? Does he look as fresh as he did the day he wrestled?

CELIA   It's easier to count atoms than answer the questions of a lover. But here's a hint of how I found him, and relish it with due respect: I found him under a tree, like a fallen acorn.

ROSALIND   It may well be called Jupiter's tree if it drops such fruit.

CELIA   Listen to me, woman.

ROSALIND   Go on then.

CELIA   He lay there stretched out like a wounded knight.

ROSALIND   It might be pitiful to look at, but it would do honour to the ground.

CELIA   Hold your tongue, please! It leaps out at the wrong time. He was dressed as a hunter.

ROSALIND   Significant! He comes to hunt the heart!

CELIA   I'd prefer to sing my song without the refrain. You're making me sing out of tune.

ROSALIND   Don't you know I'm a woman? When I think, I have to speak. Go on, dear.

Enter Orlando and Jaques.

CELIA   You get me going. Quiet! Isn't that him?

ROSALIND   It is! Take cover and listen.

JAQUES   Thankyou for your company. But truth to tell, I would have been just as happy to be alone.

ORLANDO   And so would I. Yet out of courtesy I thank you too for your company.

JAQUES   God be with you. Let's meet as little as we can.

ORLANDO   I hope we can be better strangers.

JAQUES   Please don't spoil any more trees by writing love songs in the bark.

ORLANDO   Please don't spoil my verse by reading them unsympathetically.

JAQUES   Rosalind is your love's name?

ORLANDO   Yes, exactly.

JAQUES   I don't like her name.

ORLANDO   There was no thought of pleasing you when she was christened.

JAQUES   How tall is she?

ORLANDO   As tall as my heart.

JAQUES   You're full of clever answers. Aren't you acquainted with goldsmiths' wives and have learnt them from their rings?

ORLANDO   Not true. But I give you answers from painted wall hangings, where you got your questions from.

JAQUES   You have a sharp wit, as nimble as Atalanta's pair of heels. Why don't you sit down with me and we will rail together against our mistress the world and all our misery.

ORLANDO   I'll chide no human being but myself, most of whose faults I know.

JAQUES   The worst fault you have is being in love.

ORLANDO   It is a fault that I would not exchange for your best virtue. I'm tired of you.

JAQUES   I swear I was looking for a fool when I found you.

ORLANDO   He drowned in the brook. Just look and you'll see him.

JAQUES   I'll see my own face there.

ORLANDO   Which I take to be either a fool or nothing.

JAQUES   I'll spend no more time with you. Goodbye, Signor Love.

ORLANDO   I'm glad you're going. Adieu, good Monsieur Melancholy.

Exit Jaques.

ROSALIND I'll speak to him like a saucy servant and in that role play a trick on him. Do you hear me, forester?

ORLANDO I hear you very well. What is it?

ROSALIND What's the time, please?

ORLANDO You should ask me what time of day it is. There's no clock in the forest.

ROSALIND Then there's no true lover in the forest, otherwise sighing every minute and groaning every hour would indicate the lazy foot of Time as well as a clock can.

ORLANDO And why not the swift foot of Time? Wouldn't that be just as suitable?

ROSALIND Not at all, sir. Time travels at different speeds with different people. I'll tell you whom Time ambles with, whom Time trots with, whom Time gallops with, and whom he stands still with.

ORLANDO Tell me whom he trots with?

ROSALIND Certainly. He trots meanly with a young girl between her engagement and the day of her marriage. If the interval is just a week, Time's pace is so mean it seems the length of seven years.

ORLANDO Whom does Time amble with?

ROSALIND With a priest that knows no Latin and a rich man without gout; one sleeps easily because he cannot study, the other lives happily because he feels no pain; one lacks the burden of wasteful learning, the other has no knowledge of severe penury. Time ambles with these.

ORLANDO Whom does he gallop with?

ROSALIND With a thief to the gallows. Even if he goes as slowly as a foot can fall, he thinks he's there too soon.

ORLANDO Whom does he stand still with?

ROSALIND With lawyers in vacation. They sleep between one term and the next and so they don't notice Time moving.

ORLANDO Where do you live, you handsome young man?

ROSALIND With this shepherdess, my sister, here on the edge of the forest, like the fringe on a petticoat.

ORLANDO Are you a native of this place?

ROSALIND As native as the rabbit you see living just where she was born.

ORLANDO Your accent is more refined than what you could acquire in so remote a home.

ROSALIND Many people have told me so. An old religious uncle of mine who lived in the city in his youth taught me to speak. He knew courtship too well, for he fell in love there. I've heard him

give many speeches against it. Thank God I am not a woman
tainted with all those giddy failings he accuses the entire sex of.

ORLANDO   Can you remember any of the principal evils he laid to
the charge of women?

ROSALIND   There are no principal ones. They were all as alike as any
penny, each fault seeming quite monstrous until the next one was
said to match it.

ORLANDO   Do tell me some of them.

ROSALIND   No, I won't apply treatment to anyone but the sick.
There's a man who haunts the forest and abuses young saplings by
carving "Rosalind" on the bark, hanging poems on hawthorns and
elegies on brambles, all deifying the name of "Rosalind". If I could
meet that dealer in dreams I'd give him a bit of sound advice, since
he seems to be totally consumed by love.

ORLANDO   I am he that is so love-sick. Please tell me your remedy.

ROSALIND   There are none of my uncle's signs of love on you. He
taught me how to tell a man in love, in which flimsy cage I'm sure
you're not a prisoner.

ORLANDO   What were his marks?

ROSALIND   Thin cheeks, which you don't have; blue, sunken eyes,
which you don't have; an unresponsive manner, which you don't
have; an unruly beard, which you don't have; but I forgive you for
that because just having a skimpy beard is a sign of youth. Then
your stockings should be ungartered, your bonnet unbanded, your
sleeves unbuttoned, your shoes untied, and everything about you
showing a careless laxity. But you are not such a man. You are
rather fastidious in your dress, as if you loved yourself rather than
seeming the lover of someone else.

ORLANDO   Young man, I wish I could make you believe I am in love.

ROSALIND   Me believe it? You might as easily make her whom you
love believe it, which I'm sure she is more likely to do than to
confess she does. That's one of the points in which women always
give the lie to their consciences. But truly now, are you the one
who hangs on trees the poems in which Rosalind is so admired?

ORLANDO   I swear to you, young man, by Rosalind's white hand, that
I am that man, that unfortunate man.

ROSALIND   But are you as much in love as your rhymes declare?

ORLANDO   Neither rhyme nor reason can express how much.

ROSALIND   Love is merely a form of madness. I tell you it deserves
darkened rooms and whipping, just as madmen do. The reason
why lovers are not punished and cured in that way is that lunacy is

so common that the whippers are in love too. Yet I claim to cure it by counselling.

ORLANDO   Have you ever cured anyone in that way?

ROSALIND   Yes, one, like this: he had to imagine me to be his love, his mistress, and I set him every day to woo me. When he did this, I, being a playful young man, would grieve, or act like a woman, changeable, longing and liking, proud, dreamy, apish, shallow, inconstant, full of tears, full of smiles, given to adoring everything a little and adoring nothing truly, as boys and women do, being mostly cattle of that colour. Now I'd like him, now I'd loathe him, then entertain him, then reject him, now weep for him, then spit at him. And so I converted my suitor from his mad fever of love to a real state of madness in which he had to forswear the world and live in a monastic cell. In that way I cured him, and I'll take it upon myself to wash your liver as clean as the heart of a healthy sheep, without a spot of love left in it.

ORLANDO   I do not wish to be cured, young man.

ROSALIND   I would cure you if you just call me Rosalind and come every day to my cottage and woo me.

ORLANDO   Well, confident in my love, I will. Tell me where it is.

ROSALIND   Come with me, and I'll show you where it is, and as we go you can tell me where in the forest you live. Will you come?

ORLANDO   With all my heart, good youth.

ROSALIND   No, call me Rosalind. Will you come too, sister?

Exeunt.

Act III Scene 3

Enter Touchstone the Clown, Audrey; and Jaques.

TOUCHSTONE   Come along, Audrey! I'll fetch your goats, Audrey. And am I yet a man, Audrey? Do my plain features please you?

AUDREY   Your features, Lord protect us! What features?

TOUCHSTONE   I'm here with you and your goats, as that most capricious poet, honest Ovid, was exiled among the Goths.

JAQUES   [*Aside*] Oh misplaced knowledge! Worse than Jupiter visiting a thatched cottage.

TOUCHSTONE   When a man's verse cannot be understood, and a man's good wit cannot be acknowledged by the bright child who understands it, it strikes a man more dead than a great discharge in the smallest room. Truly, I wish the gods had made you poetical.

AUDREY   I don't know what poetical is. Is it honest in deed and word? Is it about truth?

TOUCHSTONE   No, truly. For the truest poetry is the most deceptive and lovers are given to writing poetry. And what they swear in poetry as lovers, it may be said, they pretend.

AUDREY   So do you wish the gods had made me poetical?

TOUCHSTONE   I do truly. You swear to me you are honest. Now, if you were a poet I might have some hope you were pretending.

AUDREY   Wouldn't you want me to be honest?

TOUCHSTONE   No, truly, not unless you were ugly. For honesty coupled with beauty is like adding honey to sugar.

JAQUES   [*Aside*] A fool that makes sense!

AUDREY   Well, I'm not pretty, so therefore I pray the gods make me honest.

TOUCHSTONE   Truly. Casting honesty upon an ugly slut would be like putting good meat on an unclean dish.

AUDREY   I'm not a slut, though I thank the gods I'm ugly.

TOUCHSTONE   Well, the gods be praised for your ugliness! Sluttishness can come later. Be that as it may, I will marry you. And with that in mind I visited Sir Oliver Martext, the vicar of the next village, who has promised to meet me in this part of the forest and to unite us.

JAQUES   [*Aside*] I'd like to see this meeting!

AUDREY   Well, the gods give us joy!

TOUCHSTONE   Amen. If a man was of a nervous disposition, he might falter in this plan. For here there's no church, only the wood. No congregation but animals with horns. But so what. Have courage! Horns may be odious, but they are necessary. It is said that "many a man knows no ends of his goods". Right! Many a man has good horns and knows no end of them. Well, that's his wife's dowry, not something of his own getting. Horns? Even so, just poor men? No, no. The noblest deer has them as huge as the humble deer. Is the single man therefore blest? No. Just as a walled town is better than a village, so the forehead of a married man is more honourable than the bare brow of a bachelor. And just as some defence is better than no skill at all, a horn is more precious than none.

Enter Sir Oliver Martext.

Here comes Sir Oliver. Sir Oliver Martext, you are most welcome. Will you dispatch us here under this tree, or shall we go with you to your chapel?

OLIVER MARTEXT   Is there no one here to give the woman away?

TOUCHSTONE   I won't take her as the gift of any man.

OLIVER MARTEXT   Truly she has to be given away, or the marriage is not lawful.

JAQUES   Proceed, proceed. I'll give her away.

TOUCHSTONE   Good evening, good Master What-ye-call't. How are you, sir? You are very welcome. May God reward you for your recent arrival. I'm very glad to see you. Even for a trivial thing like this. No, please keep your hat on.

JAQUES   Are you to be married, clown?

TOUCHSTONE   As the ox has his yoke, the horse has his bit, and the falcon her bells, so a man has his desires. And as pigeons bill and coo, so marriage would be nibbling.

JAQUES   And will you, being a man of breeding, be married under a bush like a beggar? Go to church and have a good priest tell you what marriage is. This fellow will just join you together the way they join up panelling. Then one of you will prove to be a shrunken panel and like unseasoned timber warp, warp.

TOUCHSTONE   [*Aside*] I'm not sure I wouldn't be better married by him than by someone else. For he's not likely to marry me well, and not being well married, it will be a good excuse later for me to leave my wife.

JAQUES   Come with me and let me give you some advice.

TOUCHSTONE   Come, sweet Audrey. We must be married, or we must live in sin. Farewell, good Sir Oliver. Not

> O sweet Oliver,
> O brave Oliver,
> Leave me not behind thee;

but

> Wind away,
> Be gone, I say;
> I will not to wedding with thee.

Exeunt Jaques, Touchstone and Audrey.

OLIVER MARTEXT   Never mind. No ridiculous knave like that is going to turn me away from my calling.

Exit.

Act III Scene 4

Enter Rosalind and Celia.

ROSALIND Don't talk to me, I might cry.

CELIA Please go ahead. But have the grace to consider that tears do not become a man.

ROSALIND But don't I have good reason to cry?

CELIA As good as you could desire. So cry.

ROSALIND Even his hair is a deceptive colour.

CELIA Rather browner than Judas's. His kisses are as treacherous as Judas's own children.

ROSALIND His hair is really a good colour.

CELIA An excellent colour. Your chestnut was always the only colour.

ROSALIND And his kissing is as full of sanctity as the touch of holy bread.

CELIA He has bought a pair of Diana's unwanted lips. A nun sworn to coldness kisses no more religiously than he. They contain the very ice of chastity.

ROSALIND But why did he swear he would come this morning, but doesn't come?

CELIA Certainly there's no truth in him.

ROSALIND Do you think so?

CELIA Yes. I don't think he's a pickpocket or a horse thief, but for his reliability in love I think he's as hollow as a covered goblet or a worm-eaten nut.

ROSALIND Not true in love?

CELIA Yes, when he's in, but I don't think he's in.

ROSALIND You heard him swear blind that he was.

CELIA "Was" is not "is". Besides, a lover's oath is no better than a barman's. They are both inclined to add up wrong. He's here in the forest in attendance on the duke, your father.

ROSALIND I met the duke yesterday who asked me many questions. He asked me who my parents were. I told him I was of as good parentage as he is. So he laughed and let me go. But why do we talk about fathers when there's such a man as Orlando?

CELIA Oh, he's a fine man. He writes excellent poetry, speaks exceedingly well, swears brave oaths, and breaks them bravely, always coming at you from the side, like a feeble tilter, attacks his lover's heart from the flank, spurs his horse just on one side, and breaks his staff like a perfect idiot. But whatever youth takes on and folly guides is just perfect. Who is this now?

Enter Corin.

CORIN
Mistress and master, you have often asked
About the shepherd that complained of love,
Who you saw sitting by me on the turf,
Praising the proud disdainful shepherdess
That was his mistress.

CELIA
                                        Well, what of him?

CORIN
If you would like to see a scene played out
Between the pale complexion of true love
And the red glow of scorn and proud disdain,
Come with me now and I will take you there
For you to see it.

ROSALIND
                              Yes, let's go with him.
The sight of lovers teaches those in love.
Bring us to this scene and you will say
I'll prove a busy actor in their play.

Exeunt.

Act III Scene 5

Enter Silvius and Phebe.

SILVIUS
Sweet Phebe, do not scorn me; do not, Phebe!
Tell me you do not love me, but don't say it
In bitterness. The public executioner
Whose heart is hardened by the sight of death
Lets fall the axe upon the proffered neck,
But first begs pardon. Will you treat me worse
Than one who lives and dies by spilling blood?

Enter Rosalind, Celia, and Corin.

PHEBE
Don't think I'd be your executioner!
I avoid you so as not to injure you.
You tell me there is murder in my eye.
It's no surprise and even very probable
That eyes, that are the frailest, softest things,
That close their timid lids at any speck,
Should be called tyrants, butchers, murderers.
I mean it when I frown at you like this,
And if my eyes could wound you, then they'd kill you.
Pretend at least to faint and fall down on the ground,
And if you can't, then you should be ashamed
Of lying when you said my eyes are murderers.

           Just show me any injury they caused!
If you should scratch your finger with a pin,
It leaves a scar; and if you grasp a reed
Too firmly there's a mark it clearly leaves
Upon your hand. But yet, although my eyes
Are aimed at you, they don't leave any trace,
In fact I don't believe our eyes can do
The slightest harm.

SILVIUS   O dear Phebe,
If it should ever happen soon or later
You meet in some fresh cheek the power of love,
You'll recognise the wounds you cannot see
That love's keen arrows make.

PHEBE   But till that time
Leave me alone; and when that future time comes
Feel free to mock me pitilessly, knowing
That till that time I will not pity you.

ROSALIND   Why not, I ask you? Whoever brought you up
To be so heartless to him and to triumph
Over his wretchedness? I see no beauty
In you, at least no more than can be seen
Without a candle fumbling in the dark.
Can you afford to be so proud and pitiless?
Now tell me, why do you look at me like this?
I see no more in you than in the commonplace
Of nature's children. Heaven help me now!
I think she means to win me with her eyes!
No, please, dear girl, don't nourish any hope;
Your inky eyebrows and your dark black hair,
Your glaring eyes, your creamy-coloured cheeks,
Cannot ensnare me into loving you.
You, foolish shepherd, why do you persist
In chasing her like chilly wind and rain?
You are a thousand times a finer man
Than she a woman. It is such fools as you
That fill the world with unbecoming children.
She's flattered not by looking in the mirror,
But by you. You make her see herself more handsome
Than any of her features justify.
Young lady, know the truth. Down on your knees,
And thank heaven humbly for a good man's love;
For I must say in friendship in your ear,

> Sell when you can, the market's never stable,
> Beg for his mercy, love him, take his offer;
> An ugly maid should never be a scoffer.
> So take her promptly, shepherd, and farewell.

PHEBE   Please chide me, sweet young man, a whole year long;
> I'd rather hear you chide than this man woo.

ROSALIND   [*Aside*] He's fallen in love with your ugliness, and she'll
fall in love with my anger. If that's so, as fast as she answers you
with frowns I'll annoy her with mean words. [*To Phebe*] Why do
you look at me like that?

PHEBE   I cannot bear you any ill will.

ROSALIND   I beg you, do not fall in love with me.
> I am more false than drunken promises.
> Besides, I do not like you. Over there
> Beside the olive trees is where I live.
> Shall we go, sister? Shepherd, don't give up.
> Come, sister. Shepherdess, be kinder to him
> And don't be proud. If all the world could see,
> They'd know there's no one so abused as he.
> Come on, back to our flock.

> *Exit with Celia and Corin.*

PHEBE   O Marlowe, now I find your saying right:
> "Who ever loved that loved not at first sight?"

SILVIUS   Dear Phebe …

PHEBE   What, Silvius? What did you say?

SILVIUS   Dear Phebe, pity me.

PHEBE   I'm sorry for you truly, gentle Silvius.

SILVIUS   If you are sorry, that's a slight relief.
> If misery in love can make you sorry
> Your sorriness and my downheartedness
> Are both removed by love.

PHEBE   You have my love as if you were my neighbour.

SILVIUS   It's you I'd rather have.

PHEBE   That's covetousness.
> Silvius, there was a time I hated you;
> But that does not mean that I love you now.
> You talk of love so freely and so well,
> I will endure your company, which once
> Was irksome to me. I'll employ you too.
> But do not look for further recompense
> Beyond the satisfaction of employment.

SILVIUS   So holy and so perfect is my love,
And yet so disappointed are my hopes,
That I will think I reap a generous harvest
If I just glean some scattered ears of corn
That others leave behind. Let slip a smile
Toward me now and then; that will sustain me.

PHEBE   Do you know the youth that spoke to me just now?

SILVIUS   Not very well, but I have met him often.
He bought the cottage and some land with it
That once belonged to him they call Carlot.

PHEBE   Don't think I love him, though I ask about him;
He's just a peevish boy. But he speaks well.
What do I care about speech? Yet words do well
When he that speaks them pleases those that hear.
Good-looking, yes, not desperately so;
And yes, he's proud, with pride that suits him well.
He'll make a proper man. The best thing in him
Is his complexion; no sooner does his tongue
Cause some offence his looks can make it up.
He is not very tall, yet for his years he's tall.
His legs are so-so, but they serve him well.
There is a pretty redness in his lips,
A little riper and a richer red
Than colour in his cheeks, just such a difference
As you get between true red and softer pinks.
There are some women, Silvius, if they saw him
As close as I did, surely run the risk
Of falling for him. As for me, I swear,
I neither love nor hate him, and yet
I have more cause to hate him than to love him;
Why did he have to speak so meanly to me?
He said my eyes are black, my hair is black,
And, now I am reminded, scoffed at me.
I don't know why I did not answer back.
But that's all over; silence is not pardon.
I'll write a letter that will taunt and tease him,
And you'll deliver it. Will you, Silvius?

SILVIUS   Phebe, with all my heart.

PHEBE   I'll write it now;
The content's in my head and in my heart;
I will be bitter with him and extremely brief.
Come with me, Silvius.

Exeunt.

Act IV Scene 1

Enter Rosalind, Celia, and Jaques.

JAQUES   Let me get to know you better, you good-looking young man.

ROSALIND   They say you are a melancholy fellow.

JAQUES   I am indeed; I prefer that to laughing.

ROSALIND   Those who are extremely given to one or the other are abominable fellows who lay themselves open to common criticism worse than drunkards.

JAQUES   Well, to be sad and say nothing is good.

ROSALIND   In that case it's good to be a post.

JAQUES   I am not melancholy like a scholar, which would be from rivalry, nor like a musician, which would be from over-elaboration, nor like a courtier, which would be from pride, nor like a soldier, which would be from ambition, nor like a lawyer, which would be from scheming, nor like a lady, which would be from refinement, nor like a lover, which would be from all of these. I am melancholy in my own way, made up of many elements, drawn from many objects, and also from various reflections on my travels which, being often dwelt upon, wrap me in a deep moody sadness.

ROSALIND   A traveller! I'll say you have good reason to be sad. I fear you have sold your own lands in order to see other men's. To have seen much and to have nothing is to have rich eyes and poor hands.

JAQUES   Yes, I have gained much experience.

Enter Orlando.

ROSALIND   And your experience makes you sad. I would rather have a clown make me laugh than experience to make me sad, especially having to travel for it.

ORLANDO   Good day, and happiness, dear Rosalind.

JAQUES   Well then, God be with you, if you are going to speak in blank verse.

ROSALIND   Farewell, Monsieur Traveller. Make sure you adopt an accent and wear strange clothes, disparage all the features of your own country, show no love of your native land, and almost berate God for giving you the physique you have. Otherwise I won't believe you've ever ridden in a gondola.

Exit Jaques.

Well then, Orlando, where have you been all this while? Are you really a lover? If you pretend anything like that again, don't come near my sight.

ORLANDO   My fair Rosalind, I am here within an hour of making my promise.

ROSALIND   Break an hour's promise in love? If someone were to divide a minute into a thousand parts and break part of a thousandth part of a minute in the cause of love, that would be someone that Cupid had tapped on the shoulder. But I guarantee his heart is not broken.

ORLANDO   Forgive me, dear Rosalind.

ROSALIND   No; if you are so late, don't come near my sight. I'd rather be wooed by a snail.

ORLANDO   By a snail?

ROSALIND   Yes, by a snail. Because although he moves slowly, he carries his house on his head, a better marriage settlement, I think, than you offer a woman. Besides, he brings his destiny with him.

ORLANDO   What's that?

ROSALIND   It's his horns. Which men such as you are obliged to credit to your wives. But he comes armed in his fortune and forestalls the slander of his wife.

ORLANDO   Virtue is no maker of horns, and my Rosalind is virtuous.

ROSALIND   And I am your Rosalind.

CELIA   It amuses him to call you that, but he has a better-looking Rosalind than you.

ROSALIND   Come on, woo me, woo me. I'm in a sunny mood and all ready to say yes. What would you say to me now if I was your actual Rosalind?

ORLANDO   I would kiss you before I spoke.

ROSALIND   No, you should speak first, and when you are stuck for lack of something to say, you might have occasion to kiss. Very good orators, when they are out of anything to say, will spit. For lovers who lack something to say – God save us! – the cleverest move is to kiss.

ORLANDO   What if the kiss is refused?

ROSALIND   Then she forces you to plead, and that begins a new stage.

ORLANDO   Who could be silent in the company of his beloved?

ROSALIND   You would be, if I were your girlfriend, or I'd think my honour less pure than my wit.

ORLANDO   What about my suit?

ROSALIND   You're not stuck for lack of clothing, just for lack of words. Am I not your Rosalind?

ORLANDO   I enjoy saying you are because I would be talking of her.

ROSALIND   Well, pretending to be her, I say I will not have you.

ORLANDO   Then, being myself, I die.

ROSALIND   No, not that. Die by proxy. The poor world is almost six thousand years old, and in all this time there has never been anyone who died being himself, by which I mean from being in love. Troilus had his brains dashed out with a Greek club, yet he did his best to die before that, and he illustrates one of the patterns of love. Leander, he would have lived many a long year even if Hero had become a nun if it had not been for a hot midsummer night. The good young man went out to bathe in the Hellespont and was drowned from getting a cramp. The foolish chroniclers of that age said it was because of "Hero of Sestos". Those are all lies. Men have died from time to time and worms have eaten them, but not from love.

ORLANDO   I would not have my real Rosalind think like that, for I am sure her frown might kill me.

ROSALIND   I would not kill a fly with my own hand. But come now, I'll be your Rosalind in a more cooperative frame of mind. Ask me what you like, and I will grant it.

ORLANDO   Then love me, Rosalind.

ROSALIND   Certainly, on Fridays and Saturdays and the rest.

ORLANDO   And will you have me?

ROSALIND   Yes, and twenty more like you.

ORLANDO   What do you mean?

ROSALIND   Are you not good?

ORLANDO   I hope so.

ROSALIND   Well then, can one have too much of a good thing? Come on, sister, you be the priest and marry us. Give me your hand, Orlando. What do you say, sister.

ORLANDO   Please marry us!

CELIA   I don't know the words.

ROSALIND   You should begin, "Will you, Orlando ..."

CELIA   Right. Will you, Orlando, have to wife this Rosalind?

ORLANDO   I will.

ROSALIND   Yes, but when?

ORLANDO   Why, now, as soon as she can marry us.

ROSALIND   Then you must say, "I take thee, Rosalind, for wife."

ORLANDO   I take thee, Rosalind, for wife.

ROSALIND   I might ask you for your authority. But I do take thee, Orlando, for my husband. There's a girl who speaks ahead of the priest. A woman's thoughts run ahead of her actions.

ORLANDO   So do all thoughts; they have wings.

ROSALIND   Now tell me, how long would you have her after you have possessed her.

ORLANDO   For ever and a day.

ROSALIND   Say "a day" without the "ever". No, no, Orlando. Men are April when they woo, December when they wed. Maidens are May when they are maidens, but the sky changes when they are wives. I will be more jealous of you than an African cock pigeon of his hen, more squawking than a parrot in the rain, more fashion-conscious than an ape, more clamorous in my desires than a monkey. I'll weep for no reason, like statues of Diana in fountains, and I'll do the same when you are in a merry mood; I'll laugh like a hyena just when you feel like going to sleep.

ORLANDO   But will my wife Rosalind be like that?

ROSALIND   Assuredly she will do what I would do.

ORLANDO   Oh, but she is wise.

ROSALIND   Otherwise she wouldn't have the wit to do all that. The wiser the waywarder. Open the door on a woman's wit and it'll fly out of the window; shut the window and it will escape through the keyhole. Stop that up and it'll fly up the chimney with the smoke.

ORLANDO   A man who had a wife with such a wit might say "Wit, where, whither?"

ROSALIND   No, you should keep that retort for when you meet your wife's wit going to your neighbour's bed.

ORLANDO   And what wit could wit have to excuse that?

ROSALIND   She'd say she went to find you there. You'll never catch her without an answer unless you catch her without her tongue. Oh, if there were a woman who could not blame her husband for her own faults, she should never nurse her child herself, for she'd be raising a fool.

ORLANDO   For the next two hours, Rosalind, I will leave you.

ROSALIND   Alas, my love, I cannot be without you for two hours!

ORLANDO   I must attend the duke at dinner. By two o'clock I will be with you again.

ROSALIND   Yes, go your way, go your way. I knew what you'd prove to be. My friends told me, and I thought so too. That flattering tongue of yours won me over. It's just one more abandoned woman, and so, come, death! Two o'clock is your time off?

ORLANDO   Yes, sweet Rosalind.

ROSALIND   I swear in earnest, God be my witness, with all those appealing oaths I can muster that if you break one jot of your promise or come back one minute late, I will think you the most pitiful breaker of promises, the most hollow lover, and the most unworthy of her you call Rosalind out of all that enormous band of unfaithful men. So take heed of my warning and keep your promise.

ORLANDO   As religiously as if you were indeed my Rosalind. So
goodbye.

ROSALIND   Well, Time is the old judge that tries all such offenders,
and so let Time sit in judgment. Goodbye.

Exit Orlando.

CELIA   You simply slandered our sex in your lecture about love. We
should strip you of your doublet and hose and show the world
what the bird has done to her own nest.

ROSALIND   O cousin, cousin, dear little cousin, if only you knew
how many fathoms deep I am in love! Too deep to be sounded. My
affection has no known bottom, like the Bay of Portugal.

CELIA   Bottomless, in fact. As fast as you pour affection in, it runs
out.

ROSALIND   No, that same bastard child of Venus, Cupid, begotten of
thought and conceived of spleen, and born of madness; that blind
rascal of a boy that abuses everyone's eyes because he has none
himself, let him be judge of how deeply I am in love. I tell you,
Aliena, I cannot be out of sight of Orlando. I'll go find some shade
and moan until he comes.

CELIA   And I'll sleep.

Exeunt.

Act IV Scene 2

Enter Jaques; and Lords dressed as Foresters.

JAQUES   Who is it that killed the deer?

FIRST LORD   Sir, it was I.

JAQUES   Let's present him to the duke like a Roman conqueror; and
it would be a good idea to set the deer's horns on his head as a
symbol of victory. Do you have a song for this purpose, forester?

SECOND LORD   Yes, sir.

JAQUES   Then sing it. It doesn't matter whether it's in tune so long as
it's loud enough.

Music.

SECOND LORD   What shall he have that killed the deer?
His leather skin and horns to wear:
Then sing him home; the rest shall bear this burden.
Take thou no scorn to wear the horn,
It was a crest ere thou wast born,

Thy father's father wore it,
And thy father bore it.
The horn, the horn, the lusty horn,
Is not a thing to laugh to scorn.

Exeunt.

Act IV Scene 3

Enter Rosalind and Celia.

ROSALIND   What do you think? Isn't it past two o'clock? And no Orlando.

CELIA   I'm certain he's taken his bow and arrows and with pure love and troubled brain has gone off to sleep.

Enter Silvius.

Look who's here.

SILVIUS   My message is for you, young man.
My gentle Phebe sent me here with this.
I don't know what it says, but at a guess
From the stern looks and waspish comments
That came from her as she was writing it,
It's in an angry tone. Forgive me;
I am just the blameless messenger.

ROSALIND   Patience herself would find this letter poor,
Dismissing it severely. Take this, take that!
She says I am not fair, that I lack manners;
She calls me proud, and that she could not love me,
Not even if a man was rare as phoenix.
Her love is not the hare I care to hunt.
Why does she write like this? Well, shepherd, well,
This is a letter of your own devising.

SILVIUS   No, I protest, I do not know its contents.
Phebe did write it.

ROSALIND   Come, come, you are a fool
Who's driven by intense and thoughtless love.
I've seen her hands. She has quite leathery hands,
All tanned like stone. In fact I thought at first
Her gloves were on, but no it was her hands.
She has a housewife's hands, but never mind.
I say it wasn't her that wrote this letter.
The contents are a man's, and so's the hand.

SILVIUS   I say she wrote it.
ROSALIND   But no; the style's unruly, unrefined,
               A fighting person's style. It is a challenge,
               Like Turks against the Christians. Women's brains
               Could not come up with rudeness such as this,
               Such barbarous words, blacker in their effect
               Than in an Ethiopian's face. I'll read …
SILVIUS   Please do, because I haven't heard it yet,
               Just heard too much of Phebe's cruelty.
ROSALIND   She Phebes me. Hear what the tyrant says:

                   "Are you god to shepherd turned
                   That a maiden's heart has burned?"

               Can a woman scoff like that?
SILVIUS   You call it scoffing?
ROSALIND   "Why put your disguise apart
                   Then quarrel with a woman's heart?"

               Did you ever hear such scoffing?

                   "While another man did woo me
                   Who could do no mischief to me."

               Meaning me, a beast.

                   "If the scorn of your bright eyes
                   Can win my love as lover's prize,
                   Alas, in me what strange effect
                   Would they have in mild aspect?
                   When you chide me I do love;
                   How then might your prayers move!
                   He that brings these lines to you
                   Little knows I suffer too;
                   Send a letter under seal
                   Which your answer will reveal
                   Whether you this offer take
                   Of me and all that I can make,
                   Or else, through him, my love deny,
                   And then I'll study how to die."

SILVIUS   You call this chiding?
CELIA   Alas, poor shepherd.
ROSALIND   Do you pity him? No, he deserves no pity. Would you
    love such a woman? So that she can treat you like an instrument
    and play out of tune on you? Not to be endured! Well, go off to
    her, since I see love has made you into a tame snake, and say this

to her: if she loves me, I tell her to love you. If she doesn't love me,
I will never have her unless you ask me on her behalf. If you are a
real lover, be off, and not a word, there are people coming.

Exit Silvius.
Enter Oliver.

OLIVER   Good day, young people. Tell me, do you know
    Where in this forest I might chance to find
    A cottage fenced around with olive trees?

CELIA   West of this place, down in the nearby hollow
    Keep on your right hand by the murmuring stream
    A row of willows, then you'll find the place.
    But at this time the house is all alone,
    There's no one there.

OLIVER   If what I see can learn from what I hear
    Then I should know you by description,
    Those garments and your age: "The boy is fair,
    With feminine features, and he acts as though
    He was an older sister. She is short,
    And darker than her brother." Are you not
    The owner of the house I did enquire of?

CELIA   It is no boast, when asked, to say we are.

OLIVER   Orlando sends his greetings to you both,
    And to the youth he calls his Rosalind
    He sends this bloodstained handkerchief. That's you?

ROSALIND   It is. What must we understand by this?

OLIVER   Something I am ashamed of. Do you wonder
    Who I might be and how and why and where
    The handkerchief was stained?

CELIA   Please tell us how.

OLIVER   When young Orlando left you just a while ago,
    He made a promise to return again
    Within an hour. Then pacing through the forest,
    Chewing the sweet and bitter tastes of love,
    Imagine this: he glanced down at the side
    And there an object did present itself
    Under an oak whose boughs were mossed with age,
    Its topmost branches stripped from years exposed:
    A wretched, ragged man, his hair unkempt,
    Lay sleeping on his back; around his neck
    A green and yellow snake had wreathed itself,
    And with its head thrust to and fro approached

The opening of his mouth. But suddenly
Seeing Orlando, it unlinked itself
And with a gliding movement slipped away
Into a bush, beneath whose murky shade
A lioness, her udders all drawn dry,
Lay crouching, head down low, and like a cat
Watched for the sleeping man to stir. It is
A mark of royal quality in lions
To seek their prey in nothing that seems dead.
Orlando saw this, and approached the man
And found it was his brother, his elder brother.

CELIA   Oh, I have heard him speak of that same brother,
And he described him as the most uncivil
That ever lived.

OLIVER   And well he might do so,
For certainly I know he was unnatural.

ROSALIND   But say: Orlando: did he leave him there,
As food for that dry, hungry lioness?

OLIVER   Twice did he turn his back with that intent,
But kindness, always nobler than revenge
(Although he had a justifiable cause),
And brotherhood drove him to fight the lion,
Which quickly lost the fight, and in the tumult
I suddenly awoke from my unhappy sleep.

CELIA   Are you his brother?

ROSALIND   Did he rescue you?

CELIA   And was it you that made those plans to kill him?

OLIVER   It was, but that was not me. I am proud
To tell you who I was, since my conversion
To who I am feels more than ever right.

ROSALIND   The bloodstained napkin, what is that?

OLIVER   You'll see.
When we had told our stories, his and mine,
We wept to hear what each of us had done,
I told him how I'd wandered in that forest.
In brief, he led me to the friendly duke
Who gave me food and drink and found me clothes,
Entrusting me to his fraternal care.
My brother took me then to his own cave,
And stripped, to show the wound along his arm,
The lioness had torn some flesh away.
The arm was bleeding still, and then he fainted,

Calling out loud the name of Rosalind.
I soon revived him and bound up his wound.
And after a short while his strength came back.
He sent me here, although I do not know you,
To tell this story. Now you'll understand
His broken promise. And he wants this napkin,
Stained with his blood, to be presented to
The shepherd he in fun calls Rosalind.

CELIA   Oh no! Oh steady now, dear Ganymede!

OLIVER   The sight of blood can often make you faint.

CELIA   It's not just that. Come on, now, Ganymede!

OLIVER   Look, he's recovering.

ROSALIND   I wish I were at home.

CELIA   We'll take you there.
I beg you, will you take him by the arm?

OLIVER   Cheer up, young man. Are you a man? That's not a man's
heart.

ROSALIND   Yes, I know that's true. Yes, sir, anyone would think the
pretence was good. Please tell your brother how well I pretended.
Heigh-ho!

OLIVER   That was no pretence. There are too many signs in your face
that it was a serious passion.

ROSALIND   Pretence, I assure you.

OLIVER   Well then, be bold and pretend to be a man.

ROSALIND   I do. But by rights I should have been a woman.

CELIA   Come now, you look paler and paler. Let's go home. Sir, come
with us.

OLIVER   I will, because I have to have the answer
How you excuse my brother, Rosalind.

ROSALIND   I'll think of something. But please put in a good word to
him about my acting. Are you coming?

Exeunt.

Act V Scene 1

Enter Touchstone the Clown and Audrey.

TOUCHSTONE   We'll find a time, Audrey. Be patient, good Audrey.

AUDREY   Well, the priest was good enough, for all the old
gentleman's saying.

TOUCHSTONE   The wicked Sir Oliver, Audrey, that vile Martext. But,
Audrey, there's a young man here in the forest who lays claim to
you.

AUDREY   Yes, I know who it is. He has no claim on me whatsoever. Here comes the man you mean.

Enter William.

TOUCHSTONE   It's meat and drink to me to see a clown; we who have sharp wits have much to answer for, I say. We'll be making fun of him, there's no holding back.

WILLIAM   Good ev'n, Audrey.

AUDREY   Good ev'n, William.

WILLIAM   And good ev'n to you, sir.

TOUCHSTONE   Good ev'n, my respectable friend. Keep your hat on, keep your hat on. No, go on, put it back on. How old are you, my friend?

WILLIAM   Twenty-five, sir.

TOUCHSTONE   A ripe old age. Is your name William?

WILLIAM   William, sir.

TOUCHSTONE   A nice name. Were you born in the forest here?

WILLIAM   Ay, sir, the Lord be thanked.

TOUCHSTONE   "The Lord be thanked." A good answer. Are you rich?

WILLIAM   So-so, sir.

TOUCHSTONE   "So-so" is good, very good, really very good. And yet it's not, it's just so-so. Are you clever?

WILLIAM   Ay, sir, I've a sharp wit.

TOUCHSTONE   Well, you give good answers. I remember a saying: "The fool doth think he is wise, but the wise man knows himself to be a fool." A pagan philosopher, when he wanted to eat a grape, would open his lips when he put it in his mouth, meaning thereby that grapes were made to eat and lips to open. Do you love this girl?

WILLIAM   I do, sir.

TOUCHSTONE   Give me your hand. Are you learned?

WILLIAM   No, sir.

TOUCHSTONE   Then learn this from me: to have is to have; it is a figure in rhetoric that drink, being poured out of a cup into a glass, by filling up one empties the other; all your writers agree that *ipse* is he. Now, you're not *ipse*, for I am he.

WILLIAM   Which he, sir?

TOUCHSTONE   He, sir, that will marry this woman. Therefore, you clown, abandon (in plain language, leave) the society (in rough language, company) of this female (in common language, woman); put together that is: abandon the society of this female, or, clown, you'll perish. Or, put simply, die. Or, to be precise, I'll kill you, make away with you, translate your life into death, your liberty into bondage. I'll serve you up poison, or beat you up, or stab you. I'll debate with you; I'll plot against you; I'll kill you in a hundred and fifty ways. So tremble and go.

AUDREY   Do go, William.

WILLIAM   God rest you, merry sir.   *Exit.*

Enter Corin.

CORIN   Our master and mistress need you. Come back!

TOUCHSTONE   Run away, Audrey, run away! I'm coming, I'm coming.

Exeunt.

Act V Scene 2

Enter Orlando and Oliver

ORLANDO   Is it possible you should like her on so little acquaintance? That you should love her just from seeing her? That because you love her, you should court her, and because you court her she should accept you? And will you persevere until you possess her?

OLIVER   Do not question the impulsiveness of it, or her poverty, our short acquaintance, my sudden wooing, nor her sudden consenting; but say with me, I love Aliena; say with her that she loves me; consent with both that we may enjoy each other. It will be to your advantage, for I will hand over to you my father's house and all old Sir Rowland's revenue, and I'll live and die here a shepherd.

Enter Rosalind.

ORLANDO   You have my consent. Let your wedding be tomorrow; I will invite the duke and all his happy followers. Go and get Aliena ready. Look, here comes my Rosalind.

ROSALIND   Good day, brother.

OLIVER   And to you, dear sister.   *Exit.*

ROSALIND   O my dear Orlando, how it grieves me to see you wearing your heart in a sling!

ORLANDO   It is my arm.

ROSALIND   I thought your heart had been wounded by a lion's claws.

ORLANDO   Wounded yes, but by a lady's eyes.

ROSALIND   Did your brother tell you how I pretended to faint when he showed me your handkerchief?

ORLANDO   Yes, and greater wonders than that.

ROSALIND   Oh, I know what you mean! No, it's true. There has never been anything so sudden except two rams fighting or Caesar's bragging "I came, I saw, I conquered"; for your brother and my sister no sooner met than they looked; no sooner looked than they loved; no sooner loved than they sighed; no sooner sighed than they asked one another the reason; no sooner knew the reason than they sought the remedy; and by these stages they made a staircase to marriage which they will climb precipitately, or else be precipitate before marriage; they are in a complete whirl of love, and they are inseparable. Cudgels couldn't part them.

ORLANDO   They will be married ·tomorrow, and I will invite the duke to the wedding. But oh how bitter it is to look into happiness through another man's eyes! The heavier my heart is tomorrow, the happier will I know my brother to be for having what he wishes for.

ROSALIND   So can I not help you tomorrow with Rosalind?

ORLANDO   I cannot live any longer in my imagination.

ROSALIND   Then I will weary you no longer with idle talk. You should know, and I mean what I say, that I know you are a gentleman of great intelligence. I don't say this to give you a good opinion of my knowledge, insofar as I say I know you are. Nor do I strive for a higher opinion of myself, only to convince you to do good for yourself, not to do me a favour. Please believe then that I can do strange things. Since I was three years old I have been in touch with a magician, most skilled in his art and yet not satanic. If you do love Rosalind as deeply as your actions proclaim, when your brother marries Aliena, you will marry her. I know how desperate her plight is, and it is not impossible for me, so long as it is not inconvenient to you, to set her before your eyes tomorrow, in her normal condition and without any danger.

ORLANDO   Are you telling the real truth?

ROSALIND   On my life, which I prize greatly even though I say I'm a magician, I am. So get yourself up in your finest clothes and invite your friends. For if you would like to be married tomorrow, you shall be; and to Rosalind, if you wish.

Enter Silvius and Phebe.

Look, here comes a lover of mine and a lover of hers.

PHEBE   Young man, it was an unkind thing to do
            To show the letter that I wrote to you.

ROSALIND   Why should I care? I try as best I can
            To seem disdainful and unkind to you.
            Behind you you will see a faithful shepherd:

	Take note of him, love him; he worships you.
PHEBE	Good shepherd, tell him what it means to love.
SILVIUS	It is to suffer constant sighs and tears;
	That's what I feel for Phebe.
PHEBE	And I for Ganymede.
ORLANDO	And I for Rosalind.
ROSALIND	And I for no woman.
SILVIUS	It is to promise ever faithful service.
	That's what I'll do for Phebe.
PHEBE	And I for Ganymede.
ORLANDO	And I for Rosalind.
ROSALIND	And I for no woman.
SILVIUS	It is to be full of fantasy,
	Full of passion, full of wishes,
	All adoration, duty, and observance,
	All humility, all patience, and impatience,
	All purity, all trial, all obedience;
	That's what I am for Phebe.
PHEBE	And so am I for Ganymede.
ORLANDO	And so am I for Rosalind.
ROSALIND	And so am I for no woman.
PHEBE	[*To Rosalind*] If that be true, why blame me if I love you?
SILVIUS	[*To Phebe*] If that be true, why blame me if I love you?
ORLANDO	If that be true, why blame me if I love you?
ROSALIND	Why do you say it too: "Why blame me if I love you?"
ORLANDO	To her who is not here, and does not hear.

ROSALIND Please, that's enough! It's like Irish wolves howling at the moon. [*To Silvius*] I will help you if I can. [*To Phebe*] I would love you if I could. Meet me, everyone, tomorrow. [*To Phebe*] I will marry you if I ever marry a woman, and I'll be married tomorrow. [*To Orlando*] I will satisfy you if I have ever satisfied a man, and you will be married tomorrow. [*To Silvius*] I will make you happy if what pleases you makes you happy, and you will be married tomorrow. [*To Orlando*] As you love Rosalind, meet. [*To Silvius*] As you love Phebe, meet. And as I love no woman, I'll meet. So goodbye. I have left you all your orders.

SILVIUS I'll not fail, if I live.

PHEBE Nor will I.

ORLANDO Nor will I.

Exeunt.

Act V Scene 3

Enter Touchstone the Clown and Audrey.

TOUCHSTONE   Tomorrow is the joyful day, Audrey; tomorrow we
will be married.

AUDREY   I long for it with all my heart; and I hope it is no dishonest
desire to desire to be a woman of the world. Here come two of the
banished duke's pages.

Enter two pages.

FIRST PAGE   Good day, honest gentleman.

TOUCHSTONE   Good day indeed. Come, sit, and let's have a song.

SECOND PAGE   We are ready for you. You sit in the middle.

FIRST PAGE   Shall we start right off, without clearing our throats or
spitting or saying we're hoarse, which are the only ways to excuse
a bad voice?

SECOND PAGE   Certainly, certainly! And take it in turns, like two
gypsies on a horse.

PAGES   It was a lover and his lass,
            With a hey, and a ho, and a hey nonino,
        That o'er the green cornfield did pass
            In springtime, the only pretty ringtime,
        When birds do sing, hey ding a ding, ding.
        Sweet lovers love the spring.

        Between the acres of the rye,
            With a hey, and a ho, and a hey nonino,
        These pretty country folks would lie
            In springtime, the only pretty ringtime,
        When birds do sing, hey ding a ding, ding.
        Sweet lovers love the spring.

        This carol they began that hour,
            With a hey, and a ho, and a hey nonino,
        How that a life was but a flower
            In springtime, the only pretty ringtime,
        When birds do sing, hey ding a ding, ding.
        Sweet lovers love the spring.

        And therefore take the present time,
            With a hey, and a ho, and a hey nonino,
        For love is crowned with the prime
            In springtime, the only pretty ringtime,
        When birds do sing, hey ding a ding, ding.
        Sweet lovers love the spring.

TOUCHSTONE   Truly, young gentlemen, though there was not much
substance in the ditty, it was very out of tune.

FIRST PAGE   You are mistaken, sir. We kept time, we didn't lose the
time.

TOUCHSTONE   Of course, yes. I regard it as a waste of time to listen
to such a foolish song. God be with you, and God improve your
voices. Come on, Audrey.

Exeunt.

Act V Scene 4

Enter Duke Senior, Amiens, Jaques, Orlando, Oliver, Celia.

DUKE SENIOR   Do you believe, Orlando, that young man
Can do all this that he has promised.

ORLANDO   I sometimes do believe, and sometimes do not,
Like those that fear to hope, and know they fear.

Enter Rosalind, Silvius, and Phebe.

ROSALIND   Hold on until we see what we agreed:
You say, if I bring in your Rosalind,
You will bestow her on Orlando here?

DUKE SENIOR   I would, yes, even if it cost me kingdoms.

ROSALIND   And you say you will have her when I bring her?

ORLANDO   I would, yes, even if I were a king.

ROSALIND   You say you'll marry me, if I am willing?

PHEBE   I will, yes, even if I die an hour later.

ROSALIND   And if you do refuse to marry me,
You'll give yourself to this most faithful shepherd?

PHEBE   That is the bargain.

ROSALIND   You say you will have Phebe, if she will?

SILVIUS   Yes, even if she dies I still will have her.

ROSALIND   I've promised to make all these matters clear.
You keep your promise, Duke, to give your daughter;
You yours, Orlando, to accept his daughter;
Keep your word too, Phebe, that you'll marry me,
Or else, refusing me, to wed this shepherd;
Keep your word, Silvius, that you'll marry her
If she refuses me; and so I'll go
And make these mysteries clear.

Exeunt Rosalind and Celia.

DUKE SENIOR   I do remember in this shepherd boy

Some vivid features that my daughter shares.

ORLANDO   My lord, the first time that I ever saw him
I thought he was a brother of your daughter.
But, my good lord, this boy is from the forest,
He has been taught the basic rudiments
Of many country talents by his uncle,
Who is, he says, a wonderful magician
At large somewhere within this very forest.

Enter Touchstone the Clown and Audrey.

JAQUES   There is clearly another Flood on its way, and these couples
are coming into the ark. Here comes a pair of very strange beasts,
known in every language as fools.

TOUCHSTONE   Salutation and greetings to you all.

JAQUES   Sir, my lord, please welcome him. This is the many-sided
gentleman I have often met in the forest. He has been a courtier,
he swears.

TOUCHSTONE   If anyone doubts that, let him put me to the test. I
have learnt to dance; I have courted a lady; I have been tactful with
my friends, smooth with my enemies; I have ruined three tailors; I
have had four quarrels and almost fought one.

JAQUES   And how was it settled?

TOUCHSTONE   Well, we met and found the quarrel was for the
seventh cause.

JAQUES   What do you mean, seventh cause? My lord, like this fellow.

DUKE SENIOR   I like him very much.

TOUCHSTONE   God reward you, sir. I wish you likewise. I put myself
forward here, sir, with these other country couples, to swear
and forswear in accordance with the bonds of marriage and the
commands of passion; a poor virgin, sir, a poor-looking thing, sir,
but mine. A poor impulse of mine, sir, to take someone no one else
will. Rich honesty lives like a miser, sir, in a poor house, like a pearl
in a bad oyster.

DUKE SENIOR   My goodness, he is very quick-witted with his sayings.

TOUCHSTONE   Just like a fool's arrow, and such pleasant diseases.

JAQUES   But back to the seventh cause. How did you resolve the
quarrel on the seventh cause?

TOUCHSTONE   On a lie seven times removed (hold yourself more
modestly, Audrey) as follows: I did object to the cut of a certain
courtier's beard. He sent me word that if I said his beard was not
well cut, he was of the opinion that it was; this is called the Retort
Courteous. If I again sent him word that it was not well cut, he

would send me word he cut it to please himself; this is called the Quip Modest. If again, it was not well cut, he accused me of having no discrimination; this is called the Reply Churlish. If again, it was not well cut, he would answer that I was not telling the truth; this is called the Reproof Valiant. If again, it was not well cut, he would say I lie; this is called the Countercheck Quarrelsome. And so to the Lie Circumstantial and the Lie Direct.

JAQUES   And how often did you say his beard was not well cut?

TOUCHSTONE   I didn't dare go beyound the Lie Circumstantial, and he didn't dare give me the Lie Direct. And so we aligned our swords against one another and parted.

JAQUES   Can you now enumerate in order the degrees of the lie?

TOUCHSTONE   O sir, we quarrel according to the books, according to the rules, as you have books for good manners. I will name the degrees for you. The first the Retort Courteous, the second the Quip Modest, the third the Reply Churlish, the fourth the Reproof Valiant, the fifth the Countercheck Quarrelsome, the sixth the Lie with Circumstance, the seventh the Lie Direct. You can avoid all of these except the Lie Direct, and you may avoid that too with an If. I knew when seven justices could not take up a quarrel, but when the parties themselves met, one of them thought only of an If, as in: "If you said so, then I said so." And they shook hands and swore brotherhood. Your If is the only peacemaker. There's much virtue in If.

JAQUES   Is this not an exceptional fellow, my lord? He's good at everything, but yet he's a fool.

DUKE SENIOR   He uses his folly like a stalking horse, and under the guise of that he aims his wit.

Enter Hymen, Rosalind and Celia. Soft music.

HYMEN   Then there is mirth in heaven
               When earthly things made even
                   Atone together.
               Good duke, receive thy daughter;
               Hymen from heaven brought her,
                   Yes, brought her hither,
               That thou mightst join his hand with his
               Whose heart within his bosom is.

ROSALIND   [*To Duke Senior*] To you I give myself, for I am yours.
             [*To Orlando*] To you I give myself, for I am yours.

DUKE SENIOR   If eyes may be believed, you are my daughter.

ORLANDO   If eyes may be believed, you are my Rosalind.

PHEBE   If sight and shape are true,
                   Why then, my love adieu!
ROSALIND   [*To the Duke*] I'll have no father unless you are he.
                   [*To Orlando*] I'll have no husband unless you are he.
                   [*To Phebe*] Nor ever wed a woman, unless you are she.
HYMEN   Peace ho! I bar confusion:
                   'Tis I must make conclusion
                       Of these most strange events.
                   Here's eight that must take hands
                   To join in Hymen's bands,
                       If truth holds true contents.
                   [*To Orlando and Rosalind*]
                   You and you no cross shall part.
                   [*To Oliver and Celia*] You and you are heart in heart.
                   [*To Phebe*] You to his love must accord,
                   Or have a woman as your lord.
                   [*To Touchstone and Audrey*]
                   You and you are sure together
                   As the winter to foul weather.
                   [*To all*] While a wedlock hymn we sing,
                   Feed yourselves with questioning,
                   That reason wonder may diminish
                   How thus we met, and these things finish.

                          [*All sing*]

                   Wedding is great Juno's crown,
                       O blessed bond of board and bed!
                   'Tis Hymen peoples every town;
                       High wedlock then be honorèd.
                   Honour, high honour and renown
                   To Hymen, god of every town!

DUKE SENIOR   O my dear niece, welcome you are to me,
               Even daughter, welcome in no less degree!
PHEBE   [*To Silvius*] I will not eat my words now you are mine;
               Your faith and my devotion will combine.

                       Enter Jaques de Boys.

JAQUES DE BOYS   Let me have your attention for a moment.
               I am the second son of old Sir Rowland
               With information for this merry company.
               Duke Frederick, when he heard that every day
               Men of great worth were coming to this forest,

Assembled a strong force of foot-soldiers
Which he commanded, with the plan to take
His brother here and put him to the sword;
Arriving at the edge of this wild wood,
He chanced to meet an old religious man.
By argument and talk he was persuaded
To forego his angry vengeance and the world,
And pass his crown on to his banished brother,
Restoring all their lands to those who'd left
In exile with him. That all this is true
I stake my life on it.

DUKE SENIOR   Welcome, young man.
You bring good tiding to your brothers' wedding:
To one his lands given up; and to the other
A broad extensive land, a powerful dukedom.
First, in this forest let us all complete
Those tasks we set ourselves and have begun.
And after, every member of this happy group
That has endured hard days and nights with us
Will share a part of our restored estate
According to their wealth and fair deserts.
Meantime forget this new found dignity
And join in fun and rustic revelry.
Play, music, and you brides and bridegrooms all
In dances, games and merriment leap and fall!

JAQUES   Sir, one thing more. So if I heard you rightly,
The duke has chosen the religious life
And cast aside the pomp of ducal court.

JAQUES DE BOYS   He has.

JAQUES   I'll go and see him. Converts such as these
Can often give abundant food for thought.
[*To the Duke*] I'm glad to see your honour now restored;
Your patience and your virtue well deserve it.
[*To Orlando*] And you a love well earned by your devotion.
[*To Oliver*] And you your land and love and many friends.
[*To Silvius*] And you a loving bed you've well deserved,
[*To Touchstone*] And you a quarrel, since your voyage of love
Has stores for just two months. So, to your pleasure,
I've other things to do than dance the measure.

DUKE SENIOR   Stay, Jaques, stay.

JAQUES   This scene is not for me. Whatever it is,
I'll wait for it in your abandoned cave.   *Exit.*

DUKE SENIOR   Proceed, proceed. Let's now begin these rites
                    As we do trust they'll end: in true delights.

Exeunt.

ROSALIND   It is not the fashion to see a lady as the epilogue, but it is
    no more distressing than to see the lord as the prologue. If it's true
    that a good wine needs no bush, it's true that a good play needs
    no epilogue. Yet for good wine they use good bushes, and good
    plays prove the better from the help of good epilogues. What a
    predicament I'm in, then, being neither a good epilogue nor able
    to ingratiate myself on behalf of a good play! I am not dressed like
    a beggar, so begging is not a good idea. My plan is to win you over,
    and I'll begin with the women. I beg you, women, for the love you
    bear to men, to like as much of this play as you can. And I beg
    you, men, for the love you bear to women (from your simpering
    I observe that none of you hate them) that between you and the
    women the play may give pleasure. If I were a woman, I would kiss
    any of you who had beards that please me, complexions that like
    me and breath that I could stand. And I am sure that those with
    good beards, good faces and sweet breath will do me the favour,
    when I curtsey, of bidding me farewell.

Exit.

Coriolanus

CHARACTERS

Roman Patricians:
Caius Martius, later Caius Martius Coriolanus
Menenius Agrippa, Coriolanus's friend
Titus Lartius, a general
Cominius, consul and commander-in-chief of the army
Volumnia, Coriolanus's mother
Virgilia, his wife
Young Martius, his son
Valeria, Virgilia's friend
Gentlewoman, attendant on Volumnia and Virgilia
Senators
Nobles

Roman Plebeians:
Sicinius Velutus, tribune
Junius Brutus, tribune

Citizens
Soldiers

Volscians:
Tullus Aufidius, a general
Lieutenant to Aufidius
Three servants to Aufidius
Conspirators with Aufidius
Two Senators
Lords
Soldiers
Citizens
Adrian, a spy

Nicanor, a Roman traitor
Roman Aediles
Two officers in the Roman Capitol
Roman herald
Roman lieutenant to Titus Lartius
Messengers
Usher, Drummer, Trumpeter
Scout, Captains, Lictors
Attendants on the Roman women and on Aufidius

ॐ

Act I Scene 1

Enter a group of mutinous citizens with staves, clubs and other weapons

FIRST CITIZEN Before we proceed any further, let me speak.

ALL Speak, speak.

FIRST CITIZEN Are you all resolved to die rather than starve?

ALL Resolved, resolved.

FIRST CITIZEN First, you know Caius Martius is the people's chief enemy?

ALL We know, we know.

FIRST CITIZEN Let's kill him, and we'll have corn at our own price. Is that agreed?

ALL No more talking! Let's do it! Let's go!

SECOND CITIZEN One word, good citizens.

FIRST CITIZEN We're regarded as poor citizens, the patricians are good, at least for credit. What those in authority have too much of would relieve us. If they'd let us have just the excess while it's still fit to eat, we might guess they were relieving us out of compassion. But they think we're not worth it. Our skinniness and the sight of our misery is like a list of what they have in abundance; our suffering is their gain. Let's avenge this with our pikes before we become rakes. The gods know, I say this in hunger for bread, not in thirst for revenge.

SECOND CITIZEN Would you pick on Caius Martius in particular?

ALL On him first. He's a real dog towards the common people.

SECOND CITIZEN Won't you take into account the services he's done for his country?

FIRST CITIZEN Certainly, and we could happily give him a good report for it, but he rewards himself being proud.

SECOND CITIZEN But don't speak maliciously.

FIRST CITIZEN I tell you: what he's famous for doing, he did it for that purpose. Although easy-going people might happily say it was for his country, he did it to please his mother and partly to be proud, which he is to the same degree as he's valiant.

SECOND CITIZEN What he cannot help in his nature you regard as a vice. You must in no way say he is covetous.

FIRST CITIZEN If so, I still don't need to spare the accusations. He has faults, to excess; it would be wearisome to list them. *(Shouts within.)* What's that shouting? The other side of the city's in revolt. Why do we stay here chattering. To the Capitol!

ALL Come on, come!

FIRST CITIZEN   But wait, who's this?

Enter Menenius Agrippa.

SECOND CITIZEN   It's worthy Menenius Agrippa, who has always
loved the people.

FIRST CITIZEN   He's honest enough. Would that all the rest were!

MENENIUS   What plan, my countrymen, is this? Why wield
Those bats and clubs? Please offer me an answer.

SECOND CITIZEN   Our business is not unknown to the Senate. They
have had an inkling of what we intend to do for a fortnight, which
we'll now show them in deeds. They say poor petitioners have
strong lungs; they'll find out we have strong arms too.

MENENIUS   Why, masters, my good friends and honest neighbours,
Will you ruin your case?

SECOND CITIZEN   We cannot, sir; we are ruined already.

MENENIUS   I tell you, friends, the care patricians take
On your behalf is great. As for your wants,
Your suffering in this famine, better would be
To threaten heaven with your sticks than strike
Against the state of Rome, which carries on
Its way, breaking at least ten thousand chains,
Each link much stronger than whatever bar
You plan to throw before them. As for famine,
The gods, not the patricians, are the cause;
Your prayers to them, not arms, must help. Alas,
You are so driven by calamity
That only worse can happen, and you slander
The leaders of the state, whose care for you
Is like a father's, yet like foes you curse them.

SECOND CITIZEN   Care for us? True indeed! They've never cared
for us yet. They allow us to starve while their storehouses are
crammed with grain; they make laws about money-lending to
assist the money-lenders; every day they repeal any wholesome act
enforced against the rich, and every day pass more severe statutes
to chain up and restrain the poor. If wars don't eat us up, they will.
That's all the love they bear us.

MENENIUS   Either you must
Confess you are indeed malicious
Or be accused of folly. I will tell you
A pretty tale. It may be you have heard it,
But since it serves my purpose, I will venture
To bring it out again.

SECOND CITIZEN   Well, I'll hear it, sir; yet you must not think to fob
    off our miseries with a story. But, if you wish, go ahead.
MENENIUS   Well, once upon a time the body's members
    Rebelled against the belly; they all said
    It only acted as a receptacle
    Right in the middle, idle and inactive,
    Hogging the food, and never sharing work
    Equally with the rest, while other organs
    Did see and hear, invent, instruct, walk, feel,
    Participating fairly in the task
    Of serving the affections and the needs
    Of the whole body. The belly answered:
SECOND CITIZEN   Well, sir, what did the belly answer?
MENENIUS   Sir, I'll tell you. With a kind of smile,
    Which wasn't from the lungs, but done like this –
    So watch me: I can make the belly smile
    As well as speak – it tauntingly replied
    To all those grumbling members who were envious
    Of what the belly got; it's just the way
    You speak ill of our senators because
    They're not the same as you.
SECOND CITIZEN   Your belly's answer? What?
    The head with royal crown, the watchful eye,
    The thoughtful heart, the arm our soldier,
    The leg our horse, the tongue our trumpeter,
    With other useful features large and small
    In this our body, if they are all …
MENENIUS   What then?
    Upon my soul, this fellow talks! What then?
SECOND CITIZEN   If they are held in check by greedy belly,
    That sink-hole of the body, …
MENENIUS   Well, what then?
SECOND CITIZEN   If all those active body parts complained,
    What would the belly answer?
MENENIUS   I will tell you,
    If you can spare a little of that little
    Patience you have, you'll hear the belly's answer.
SECOND CITIZEN   You take your time with it.
MENENIUS   Hear this, good friend.
    Your actual belly was deliberate,
    Not rash like his accusers, so he said:
    "It's true, friends of one body," said he,

"That I'm the first to get the general food
Which you all live on; that's a fitting thing
Because I am the storehouse and the shop
Of the whole body. But, if you remember,
I send it through the rivers of your blood
Up to the heart, and even to the brain,
Along the channels and the body's paths;
The strongest nerves and small inferior veins
Receive from me the sustenance they need
To live by. And although each part cannot …
That's you, my friends" – this is the belly speaking –

SECOND CITIZEN   Yes, sir, we get it.

MENENIUS   "Though each part cannot
See what I send out, nor how much or where,
Yet I can keep a record of it all
And know that each part gets the flour,
And leaves the husks behind." So what d'you think?

SECOND CITIZEN   It was an answer. How does it apply?

MENENIUS   The senators of Rome are that good belly,
And you're the mutinous members. If you take
Their counsels and their help, and then digest
Whatever serves the common good, you'll find
No public benefit which you receive
That is not handed down from them to you,
And never from yourselves. What do you think,
You, the big toe of the assembly?

SECOND CITIZEN   Me the big toe? Why the big toe?

MENENIUS   Because you are the lowest, basest, poorest
Of this astute rebellion, and in front.
You ill-bred dog, the lowest of the breed,
You lead the pack when something's to be gained.
So get your clubs and rebel weapons ready;
Rome and her rats are on the verge of battle,
And one side has to lose.

Enter Caius Martius.

                                   Hail, noble Martius!

MARTIUS   Thanks. What's the matter, you rebellious rogues?
By rubbing that sore itch of your opinions
You'll soon get scabs.

SECOND CITIZEN   We have here your good word.

MARTIUS   Whoever offers you good words will flatter you

Intolerably. What is it you want,
You dogs, who hate both peace and war? The first
Alarms you, while the second makes you proud.
Whoever looks for lions in you finds
Just hares; for foxes, geese. No more dependable
Than coal fires lit on frozen water, or
A hailstone in the sun. For you it's virtuous
To honour any man who is convicted
And curse the sentence. Those who earn distinction
Will also earn your hate. And being loved
By you is what a sick man craves; he longs
For more of what will make his sickness worse.
Needing your favours is akin to swimming
With fins of lead, or cutting down an oak
With reeds. Should you be trusted? Never!
At any minute you will change your mind,
And honour any man that you now hate,
Reviling those you earlier praised. How come
You shout, in several areas of the city,
Abuse against the noble senate, who,
Under the gods, take care of you, who otherwise
Would feed on one another? What do they want?

MENENIUS   They ask for corn at their own rates; they say
The city's stocks are ample.

MARTIUS   Hang 'em! "They say"!
They sit at home and then presume to know
What goes on in the Capitol, who's on the rise,
Who thrives and who declines; they set up factions
And shape alignments, making some groups strong
And weakening those who don't appeal to men
In hobnailed boots. They say there's enough grain!
Would that the nobles set aside their scruples
And let me use my sword, I'd make a stack
Of thousands of these slaughtered slaves, as high
As I could throw my lance.

MENENIUS   These men are almost thoroughly convinced,
For though they seem to act without restraint,
They're cowards through and through; but tell me,
What news of other riots?

MARTIUS   They are contained. Hang 'em!
They said they were half starved, and quoted proverbs:
That hunger broke stone walls, that dogs must eat,

That meat was made for mouths, that corn was sent
By heaven not just for rich men. With such lines
They vented their complaints, to which in answer
Leave to petition was granted, a strange step
That dealt the final blow to noble interests
And made authority look weak. They threw
Their caps up high as if to reach the moon,
Out-shouting one another.

MENENIUS   What was granted?

MARTIUS   Five tribunes to defend their vulgar interests,
Of their own choice. One's Junius Brutus,
Sicinius Velutus, and some others.
My God, the rabble would have had to tear
The roofs from every house before I'd give
An inch to them. They will in time obtain
More power still, and make yet further claims
To justify revolt.

MENENIUS   I find it strange.

MARTIUS   Go, get you home, you scraps.

Enter a Messenger in haste.

MESSENGER   Where's Caius Martius?

MARTIUS   Here. What's the matter?

MESSENGER   The news is, sir, the Volscians are in arms.

MARTIUS   I'm glad to hear it. Now we'll have a way
To cast aside superfluous persons.

Enter Sicinius Velutus, Junius Brutus, Cominius,
Titus Lartius, with other Senators.

                                          Look, the best of us.

FIRST SENATOR   Martius, it's true, as you've been warning us.
The Volscians are in arms.

MARTIUS   They have a leader,
Tullus Aufidius, who will test you greatly.
I'm wrong to envy his nobility,
And if I were any other than I am,
I'd wish only to be him.

COMINIUS   You have fought together.

MARTIUS   If half the world took arms against the other half
And he were on my side, I'd switch to fight
Against him, just for that. He is a lion
That I am proud to hunt.

FIRST SENATOR   Then, worthy Martius,

	Give notice to Cominius that you'll fight.
COMINIUS	It's what you promised earlier.
MARTIUS	Yes, it is,
	And you can trust me. Titus Lartius, you
	Will see me strike at Tullus's face once more.
	What, are you hurt? Not fighting?
LARTIUS	No, Caius Martius.
	One crutch I'll use to lean on and the other
	To fight with, I could never stand and watch.
MENENIUS	Oh what breeding!
A SENATOR	Move on now to the Capitol where I know
	Our powerful friends expect us.
LARTIUS	[*To Cominius*] You lead on.
	[*To Martius*] Follow Cominius. We must follow you,
	Priority is yours.
COMINIUS	Noble Martius!
A SENATOR	Back to your homes, be off!
MARTIUS	No, let them follow.
	The Volscians have good stocks of corn; these rats
	Can gnaw their granaries. Esteemed insurgents,
	Your valour promises well. Please follow.

Citizens steal away. Exeunt all but Sicinius and Brutus.

SICINIUS	Was ever anyone so proud as Martius?
BRUTUS	He has no equal.
SICINIUS	When we were named as tribunes for the people, ...
BRUTUS	You saw his lips and eyes?
SICINIUS	I heard his taunts!
BRUTUS	He'll even mock the gods when he is angry.
SICINIUS	He'd mock the modest moon!
BRUTUS	Let's hope this war destroys him. He's too proud
	Of being so courageous.
SICINIUS	Such a nature,
	Encouraged by success, scorns his own shadow
	Even at noon. That makes me wonder how
	His insolence can bear to be commanded
	Under Cominius.
BRUTUS	The goddess Fame,
	In whose good graces he's already high,
	Can better be attained and held secure
	From second-in-command. For what miscarries
	Will be the general's fault, no matter how

SICINIUS

Prodigiously he acts, and heady censure
Will roar from Martius's lips: "If only I
Had run the business!"
               Besides, if things go well,
The honour of success assigned to Martius
Will rob Cominius of his deserts.

BRUTUS

Of all Cominius's honours half will go
To Martius, unearned. And all his errors
Will show up Martius well, a source of honour
Entirely undeserved.

SICINIUS

               Let's go and hear
How things will be decided, and, allowing
For his desire to stand alone, let's see
What action he will take.

BRUTUS

               Let's go.

Exeunt.

Act I Scene 2

Enter Tullus Aufidius with Senators of Corioli.

FIRST SENATOR So, your opinion is, Aufidius,
The Romans are acquainted with our plans
And know what we will do.

AUFIDIUS

               Don't you think so?
Have matters ever been debated here
Or action taken without Rome aware
Of everything we do? I've not heard news
For four days now. These are the words – I think
I have the letter here; yes, here it is.
"An army has been raised, but no one knows
What purpose it is for. Supplies are low,
The people mutinous. And it is rumoured
Cominius, Martius (your old enemy,
Resented more by Romans than by you)
And Titus Lartius, a courageous Roman,
These three command the preparations,
They're aimed, most probably, in your direction.
Take careful note."

FIRST SENATOR   Our army's in the field.
We've never had a doubt that Rome was ready
To confront us.

AUFIDIUS   You did not think it foolish
                        To keep your grand design a secret till
                        The time came to reveal it, learned at once,
                        It seems, by Rome. By that discovery
                        We'll have to aim for less, and not expect
                        To capture many towns before the Romans
                        Know what we're up to.
SECOND SENATOR   Noble Aufidius,
                        Take your commission; go join your troops.
                        Leave it to us to guard Corioli.
                        If they lay siege, then you can bring your army
                        And come to our relief. I think you'll find
                        They're not prepared for us.
AUFIDIUS   Oh, there's no doubt.
                        I speak from certainties. What's more,
                        Some units of their army have set out
                        In this direction. I'll take my leave.
                        If I and Caius Martius chance to meet,
                        We're bound on oath to fight it out until
                        In one of us there's no fight left.
ALL SENATORS   The gods assist you!
AUFIDIUS   And keep you safe!
FIRST SENATOR   Farewell.
SECOND SENATOR   Farewell.
ALL   Farewell.

                        Exeunt.

Act I Scene 3

Enter Volumnia and Virgilia, Martius's mother and wife.
They sit on two low stools and sew.

VOLUMNIA   Please, dear daughter, do sing or express yourself in a
    more cheerful manner. If my son were my husband, I would take
    more pleasure in his absence, away winning honours, than in his
    embraces in his bed, where he'd show most love. When he was just
    a weakling, the only son of my womb, when he was a handsome
    youth attracting gazes all around, when even if kings begged her
    for a whole day, a mother would not let him out of her sight even
    for an hour, knowing how such a one would merit honour and
    that it was no better than hanging a picture on the wall if he were
    not animated by ambition for renown, I was happy to let him seek

danger wherever he might find fame. I sent him to a cruel war, from which he returned with his brow crowned with oak leaves. I tell you, daughter, I rejoiced no more at first learning he was a baby boy than then when I saw he had proved himself a man.

VIRGILIA   But if he had died in that affair, mother, what then?

VOLUMNIA   Then his good record would have been my son. I would have treated his death as my child. Let me tell you in all sincerity: if I had a dozen sons and I loved them all equally, and none less dear to me than our good Martius, I would rather that eleven die nobly for their country than one indulge himself voluptuously away from the action.

Enter a Gentlewoman.

GENTLEWOMAN Madam, the Lady Valeria has come to visit you.

VIRGILIA   Would you kindly allow me to withdraw?

VOLUMNIA   Certainly not.
            I think I hear your husband's drum approaching.
            I see him grab Aufidius by the hair,
            The Volscians fleeing, like children from a bear,
            I see him stamp, like this, and shout, like this:
            "Come on, you cowards, you, conceived in fear
            Though you were born in Rome!" I see him wipe
            His bloodstained brow with mailed glove, then march
            To battle like a labourer hired to mow,
            Who'd lose his wages if it were not done.

VIRGILIA   His bloodstained brow? O Jupiter, no blood!

VOLUMNIA   Come, come, fool! It's more fitting on a man
            Than gilding on a trophy. Hecuba's breasts,
            When she was nursing Hector, looked no lovelier
            Than Hector's forehead when a Grecian sword
            Caused it to spit out blood. Go tell Valeria
            We will receive her now.

Exit Gentlewoman.

VIRGILIA   Heaven save my lord from fierce Aufidius!

VOLUMNIA   He'll beat Aufidius's head below his knees
            And tread upon his neck.

Enter Valeria with an Usher and a Gentlewoman.

VALERIA   My ladies both, good day to you.

VOLUMNIA   Dear Madam.

VIRGILIA   I'm glad to see your ladyship.

VALERIA   How are you both? You are clearly keeping house. What

are you sewing? An excellent pattern, I'm sure. How is your little
son?

VIRGILIA   Thankyou, your ladyship, he is well.

VOLUMNIA   He'd rather watch swords and listen to drums than look
at his schoolmaster.

VALERIA   Definitely his father's son! I'm sure he's a fine-looking boy.
In fact I watched him last Wednesday for a full half hour. He has
such a determined look. I saw him run after a bright-coloured
butterfly, and when he caught it he let it go again, and then ran
after it again, falling head over heels, then he got up and caught
it again. Whether or not it was falling that enraged him, he was
determined to get it. Oh how he tore it to pieces, I tell you.

VOLUMNIA   In one of his father's moods.

VALERIA   Most clearly. He's a noble child.

VIRGILIA   A lively boy, madam.

VALERIA   Come now, put down your sewing. I'd like you to play the
idle housewife with me this afternoon.

VIRGILIA   No, dear madam, I won't be going out.

VALERIA   Not go out?

VOLUMNIA   She will, she will.

VIRGILIA   Indeed, no, if you will permit. I won't go past the threshold
until my lord returns from the war.

VALERIA   Well, you confine yourself most unreasonably. Come, you
should visit the good lady who's expecting.

VIRGILIA   I'll wish her all strength and think of her in my prayers,
but I cannot go there.

VOLUMNIA   Why, tell me?

VIRGILIA   It's not to save the effort, not that I'm in need of friends.

VALERIA   You're like another Penelope. They say all the yarn she
spun in Ulysses's absence just filled Ithaca with moths. Come now,
I wish your embroidery was as sensitive as your finger, then you
might stop pricking it, out of pity. Come on, you'll go with us.

VIRGILIA   No, dear madam, forgive me; I really will not go out.

VALERIA   Really now, you come with me and I'll tell you excellent
news of your husband.

VIRGILIA   O, dear madam, there cannot be any yet.

VALERIA   I'm truly not jesting with you. News came from him last
night.

VIRGILIA   It did?

VALERIA   Yes, it's true. I heard a senator report it. It's this: the
Volscians have fielded an army and against them the general
Cominius is marching with one part of our Roman forces. Your

lord and Titus Lartius are entrenched around their city of Corioli. They are confident of prevailing and keeping the war brief. This is true, on my honour, so please come with us.

VIRGILIA   Please excuse me, dear madam. I will obey you in everything in future.

VOLUMNIA   Leave her alone, lady. As she is now, she'll just poison our happier mood.

VALERIA   You're right, I think she would. Goodbye then. Come, dear lady. I beg you, Virgilia, get out of your solemn mood and come along with us.

VIRGILIA   No, in a word, madam. I really must not. I hope you'll find enjoyment.

VALERIA   Well then, farewell.

Exeunt.

Act I Scene 4

Enter Martius and Titus Lartius, with drum and colours, with captains and soldiers, outside the city of Corioli. A messenger joins them.

MARTIUS   Here comes some news. I wager they have met.

LARTIUS   I bet my horse they've not.

MARTIUS   You're on!

LARTIUS   Agreed.

MARTIUS   Say, has our general met the enemy?

MESSENGER   They face each other but have not yet fought.

LARTIUS   So the good horse is mine!

MARTIUS   I'll buy him from you.

LARTIUS   No, I'll not sell or give him away; I'll lend him to you
For half a hundred years. Summon the town.

MARTIUS   How far off are those armies?

MESSENGER   Within a mile and a half.

MARTIUS   Then we will hear their bugles, and they ours.
O Mars, I pray you make us quick to win,
So we may march from here with smoking swords
To help our fighting friends! Come, blow your blast.

They sound a parley.
Enter two Senators with others on the walls of Corioli.

Tullus Aufidius, is he within your walls?

FIRST SENATOR   No, nor anyone less afraid of you than he;
That's much less than a little.

Drum far off.

　　　　　　　　　　　　Listen, our drums
Are bringing up our youth. We'll make a break-out
And prevent an encirclement. Our gates,
Which still seem shut, are only held with rushes.
They'll open by themselves.

Alarm far off.

　　　　　　　　　　　　Listen, far away!
Aufidius is there. Just see what work he makes
Of your divided army.

MARTIUS　　　　　　　　Oh, they are at it!

LARTIUS That noise will be our signal. Fetch the ladders!

Enter the Volscian army.

MARTIUS They're not afraid; they're coming out towards us.
Put up your shields before your hearts and fight,
Your hearts as tough as shields. Move up, brave Titus.
They scorn us, yet we know our real strength,
Which makes me sweat with rage. Come on, my fellows!
If anyone retreats, I'll take him for a Volscian,
And he will feel my blade.

Alarm. The Romans are beaten back to their trenches.
Enter Martius, cursing.

MARTIUS May all those plagues from southern lands attack you,
You shameful sons of Rome! May boils and sores
Spread through your body so they'll all avoid you
Keeping their distance, and the infection will
Be carried over a mile against the wind!
You geese disguised as men, how can you run
From slaves that even apes could beat? Hell's teeth!
All those back there are wounded, faces pale
From flight and feverish fear! Get up, and charge,
Or by the fires of heaven I'll leave the fight
And turn my war on you! Be careful! Come on!
If you stand fast, we'll drive them back to their wives,
As they would us to our trenches. Follow me!

Another bugle call.
The Volscians flee and Martius follows them to the gates.

So now the gates are open. Show me your support!
Good fortune flings them wide for those who follow,
But not for those who flee. So come where I lead.

He enters the gates.

FIRST SOLDIER   Foolhardiness! Not I!
SECOND SOLDIER   Nor I!

Martius is shut in. Alarm continues.

FIRST SOLDIER   Look! They've shut him in!
ALL   He'll be cut to pieces, for certain.

Enter Titus Lartius.

LARTIUS   What has become of Martius?
ALL SOLDIERS   Killed, sir, for sure.
FIRST SOLDIER   Pursuing close the enemy in retreat,
                        He went inside behind them, then they suddenly
                        Clapped shut the gates. And now he's there alone
                        To face the city himself.
LARTIUS   O noble fellow!
                        More daring than your sword, which bends,
                        But you do not. O Martius, you are lost!
                        A perfect ruby, even as big as you,
                        Would be less precious. You were such a soldier
                        As Cato would have wished, both fierce and terrifying,
                        Not only with the sword, but in your looks and voice;
                        The thunderous percussion of that sound
                        Would make an enemy quake, as if the world
                        Itself were shaking from a fever.

Enter Martius, bleeding, assaulted by the enemy.

FIRST SOLDIER   Look, sir!
LARTIUS   Yes, it's Martius!
                        Let's rescue him or stay to share his fate.

They fight, and all enter the city.

Act I Scene 5

Enter some Romans, with spoils.

FIRST ROMAN   I'll take this back to Rome.
SECOND ROMAN And I'll take this.
THIRD ROMAN   Dammit, I thought this was silver!

Alarm continues far off.
Enter Martius and Titus Lartius with a trumpeter.

MARTIUS   Look at those busybodies who consider
                        Their time so worthless! Cushions, spoons of lead,

Cheap weapons, overgarments that the hangman
Would bury with the wearer! These base slaves
Prepare to leave while battle rages. Down with them!
And listen, that's our general's call. Let's go!
The man my soul most hates is there: Aufidius,
Piercing our Roman troops. So, valiant Titus, take
What men you need to hold the city here,
While I will hasten with whoever dares
To help Cominius.

LARTIUS   Good sir, you're bleeding.
Your exploits here have been too violent
For a second bout of fighting.

MARTIUS   Don't praise me so.
My work has barely warmed me yet. Farewell.
The loss of blood will do nothing but good,
No danger springs from that. Blooded like this
I shall confront Aufidius and fight.

LARTIUS   May Fortune fall in love with you and deftly
Deflect your opponents' swords. Bold gentleman,
May victory attend you!

MARTIUS   You too deserve
That love as much as anyone. So, farewell.

LARTIUS   Great, worthy Martius!

Exit Martius.

Go sound the trumpet in the market-place,
And summon all the officers of the town
To hear what's forming in our mind. Away!

Exeunt.

Act I Scene 6

Enter Cominius, as if in retreat, with soldiers.

COMINIUS   Rest now, my friends. Well fought. We disengaged
Like Romans, neither foolishly persisting
Nor cowardly in retreat. Believe me, sirs,
We'll be attacked again. While we were fighting,
Occasional gusts of wind conveyed the sound
Of action by our friends. We pray the gods
Will lead them to success along with us,
So both divisions may give thankful sacrifice

For something good to smile about.

Enter a messenger.

What news?

MESSENGER   The citizens of Corioli broke out
And challenged Lartius and Martius in battle.
I saw our fellows driven to their trenches,
And then I came away.

COMINIUS   I'm sure that's true,
Though not a welcome truth. How long ago was it?

MESSENGER   Over an hour, my lord.

COMINIUS   It's not a mile away, we heard their drums
Just then. How could it take you a full hour,
The news you bring is late.

MESSENGER   Some Volscian spies
Pursued me, so that I was forced to circle
Three or four miles around. Or otherwise
You would have heard this half an hour ago.

Enter Martius.

COMINIUS   Who's this? Seems he's been flayed! O gods!
That's Martius's figure, and I've seen him thus,
So badly wounded, in the past.

MARTIUS   Am I too late?

COMINIUS   A shepherd can distinguish drum from thunder
As clearly as I know the voice of Martius.
It's not like that of meaner men.

MARTIUS   Am I too late?

COMINIUS   Too late, yes, if the blood that garbs you is
Your own, not that of others.

MARTIUS   Oh, let me grasp you
In arms as sound as when I wooed, with heart
As merry as when our wedding day was done
And candles lit the bedroom.

COMINIUS   O flower of our fighting men! How's Titus Lartius?

MARTIUS   As busy as a man making decrees:
Condemning some to death, and some to exile,
Ransoming some, he'll spare or threaten others,
Holding Corioli in the name of Rome
Just like a fawning greyhound on the leash
To let it loose at will.

COMINIUS   Where is that slave
Who told me they had driven you to your trenches?

Where is he? Call him here.

MARTIUS   Let him alone.
He did tell you the truth. As for our gentlemen,
The rank and file, a plague! Tribunes for them!
No mouse fled faster from a cat than they did
From rascals worse than them.

COMINIUS   How did you win?

MARTIUS Do I have time to tell you? I don't think so.
Where is the enemy? Do you control the field?
If not, why quit the fight before you do?

COMINIUS Martius, we were outnumbered, so
Retreat was better strategy.

MARTIUS What is their field formation? Do you know
Which side their trusted men are on?

COMINIUS   I guess
Their vanguard soldiers are from Antium,
Their sturdiest force, led by Aufidius;
He is their greatest hope.

MARTIUS   I ask a favour,
By all the battles we have fought together,
By the blood we've shed and all the vows that bind us
As friends for life, assign me please, I beg,
Against Aufidius and his Antium troops.
Do not let slip this opportunity,
But fill the air with swords and spears upraised
And prove our valour now.

COMINIUS   Though I might wish
That you be taken to a soothing bath
With balms and bandages applied, I dare not
Refuse you when you ask. Select the men
Who best can aid you in your action.

MARTIUS   They must
Be willing, first and foremost. If there's anyone –
Can there be any doubt? – who loves this painting
With which you see me smeared; if any fear
A bad report more than his personal safety;
If any think brave death outweighs bad life,
And that his country's dearer than himself,
Let him stand up, with others of like mind,
And wave his sword to show his readiness
To follow Martius.

They all shout and wave their swords,
take him up in their arms and throw up their caps.

If this display does not deceive me, each
Of you is worth at least four Volscians. All
Of you can hold a shield as tough as what
The great Aufidius carries. I will select
A certain number, but with thanks to all.
The rest will do their duty in some other fight,
Wherever you are called. March forward now,
And I will shortly pick my special troop
Of men best fitted for it.

COMINIUS   March on, my men,
Make good the loyalty you claim, and you
Will all share in the honour.

Exeunt.

Act I Scene 7

Titus Lartius, having set a guard on Corioli, goes with a drummer
and a trumpeter towards Cominius and Caius Martius, and
enters with a Lieutenant, other soldiers and a scout.

LARTIUS   Make sure the gates are guarded. Keep your duties
As I have set them down. If sent for, see
That extra troops come to our aid. The rest
Will hold the city. If we lose the field,
We cannot keep the town.

LIEUTENANT   This will be done, sir.

LARTIUS   Go back, and close the gates behind us.
Come, guide. Conduct us to the Roman camp.

Exeunt.

Act I Scene 8

Alarm, as in battle.
Enter Martius and Aufidius from different directions.

MARTIUS   I'll fight no one but you, for I detest you
Worse than a man who breaks a promise.

AUFIDIUS   I too
Bear hatred. There's no snake in Africa
I abhor more than your envious fame. Stand to.

MARTIUS	Let him who first gives in die slave to the other,
	And be doomed by the gods thereafter.
AUFIDIUS	If I fly,
	Then hunt me like a hare.
MARTIUS	Within these last three hours
	I fought alone within the walls of Corioli
	And acted as I pleased. It's not my blood
	You see across my face. To be avenged
	You'll need your greatest strength.
AUFIDIUS	Even if
	You were great Hector, scourge of your forebears,
	You'd not escape me here.

Here they fight and certain Volscians come to Aufidius's aid.

Your interference shames me; that's not courage,
It's damnable to assist me.

Martius fights until they are driven in breathless. Exeunt.

Act I Scene 9

*Alarm. A retreat is sounded. Enter from one direction Cominius
with the Romans; from another Martius, with his arm in a sling.*

COMINIUS	If I should tell you everything you did
	Today, you'd not believe it all. But I
	Will give a full report where senators
	May mingle tears with smiles, where great patricians
	Will listen, shrug, and in the end admire.
	I'll tell it where the ladies will be frightened,
	Enjoying their alarm, and beg for more;
	Where those dull tribunes who resent your fame
	As do the smelly plebs, despite themselves
	Will say "We thank the gods that Rome
	Has such a gallant soldier."
	Yet you had just a morsel of this feast,
	Having fully dined before.

Enter Titus Lartius with his troop, from the pursuit.

LARTIUS	O general,
	Here is the horse, we're just its ornament.
	If you had seen …
MARTIUS	Enough, I say. My mother,
	Who has good reason to extol her breeding,

                Upsets me when she praises me. I did
                What you did, namely what I can. Inspired,
                As you have been, to serve my country well.
                Whoever carried out his good intentions
                Achieved as much as me.

COMINIUS   You must not be
                Allowed to hide your merits. Rome must know
                The value of her people. It would be
                Concealment worse than theft, even detraction,
                To hide your doings and to silence what
                Would seem mere modest praise, proclaimed
                From roof to spire. Therefore, I beseech you,
                In recognition of your qualities,
                Not of your deeds, before our army, hear me!

MARTIUS   My body bears some wounds which give me pain
                To hear themselves remembered.

COMINIUS   Otherwise
                They might well fester at ingratitude
                And cure themselves with death. Of all the horses,
                Of which we captured many, and the treasure
                Collected from the battlefield and city,
                We offer you one tenth, to be taken
                Before the general distribution, at
                Your choice alone.

MARTIUS   I thank you, general,
                But cannot make my heart consent to take
                A bribe to pay my sword. I do refuse it,
                And will accept only an equal share
                With those that served in action.

A long flourish. They all cry "Martius! Martius!", throw up their
caps and lances. Cominius and Lartius stand bare-headed.

                May all those instruments which you abuse
                Henceforth be silent! When those drums and trumpets
                Are used for flattery, all courts and cities
                Are nothing but hypocrisy. When steel
                Grows soft as silk, the parasite will take
                The glory won in war. Enough, I say!
                Because I have not washed my bleeding nose
                Or floored some feeble wretch, which many others
                Have done unnoticed, you all shout my praises
                In hyperbolical acclaim, as if

I loved my modest actions to be fattened up
In praises sauced with lies.

COMINIUS   You are too modest.
Rejecting good reports and without gratitude
To us who judge you fairly. By your leave,
If you are furious with yourself, we'll put you,
Like someone bent on injuring himself,
In chains, then reason safely with you. Therefore
Let all the world know what we know: the garland
Of victory is owed to Caius Martius,
In token of which I give my noble steed
Will all its fine accoutrements. Henceforth,
For what he did before Corioli,
With all the army's clamour, let us name him
Martius Caius Coriolanus!
Parade this noble title evermore!

Flourish. Trumpets sound and drums.

ALL   Martius Caius Coriolanus!
CORIOLANUS I will go wash,
And when my face is clean you will observe
Whether I blush or not. At all events
I thank you. I will bestride your horse.
This good addition to my crest and title
I'll honour at all times.

COMINIUS   Back to my tent
I'll go, and there before it's time to rest
I'll write to Rome of our success. You, Lartius,
Go back to Corioli; send to Rome
Their best negotiators for the peace,
For their own good and ours.

LARTIUS   I shall, my lord.
CORIOLANUS No doubt the gods will mock me … Having now
Refused some princely gifts, I wish to beg
A favour of my general.

COMINIUS   By all means. What is it?
CORIOLANUS Once here in Corioli I was a guest
In a poor man's house. He treated me most kindly.
When he was taken prisoner, he cried out.
But then Aufidius was in my view
And rage displaced my pity. I request you
To give my poor host freedom.

COMINIUS   A fine request!
                    If he had been the butcher of my son,
                    He'd be as free as air. Release him, Titus.
LARTIUS   Martius, his name?
CORIOLANUS   Great heavens, I've forgotten!
                    I'm weary; that's why my memory is tired.
                    Have we no wine here?
COMINIUS   We'll go to my tent.
                    The blood has dried up on your face. It's time
                    It was attended to. Come.

                              Exeunt.

                          Act I Scene 10

                         A flourish. Cornets.
           Enter Tullus Aufidius, bleeding, with two or three soldiers.

AUFIDIUS   The town is taken.
A SOLDIER   It'll be restored when conditions are right.
AUFIDIUS   Conditions!
                    I wish I were a Roman, but can only
                    Be what I am, a Volscian. Conditions!
                    What good conditions can a treaty have
                    For the defeated side? Five times, Martius,
                    I've fought with you; you beat me every time,
                    And would do so, I think, if we should meet
                    As often as we eat. In principle,
                    If again we face each other beard to beard,
                    He's mine, or I am his. My rivalry
                    Is less impelled by honour than it was;
                    Whereas I hoped to win on equal terms,
                    True sword to sword, I'll get a stab at him,
                    If rage or guile assist me.
A SOLDIER   He's the devil.
AUFIDIUS   Bolder, though not so subtle. The disgrace
                    I've suffered at his hand poisons my valour,
                    Which will break loose against him. Being naked,
                    Or sick, protected by a temple or the Capitol,
                    By prayers of priests, by sacrificial rites –
                    All mollifiers of fury – none of these
                    Shall claim their rotten privilege against
                    My hate of Martius. Where I find him, whether

At home, under my brother's guard, even there
Against the law of hospitality I will
Bathe my fierce hand in his heart. Go off to the city,
Learn how it's held, and who has been selected
As hostages for Rome.

A SOLDIER   Will you not go?
AUFIDIUS   I am expected at the cypress grove. I'd like you
To bring me word there (south of the city mills)
What news there is, so I can plan my journey
Accordingly.

A SOLDIER   I shall, sir.

Exeunt.

Act II Scene 1

Enter Menenius with the two Tribunes of the people,
Sicinius and Brutus.

MENENIUS   The soothsayer tells me we'll have news tonight.
BRUTUS   Good or bad?
MENENIUS   Not in line with the people's prayers, since they have no
love for Martius.
SICINIUS   Nature teaches animals to know their friends.
MENENIUS   Tell me, who does the wolf love?
SICINIUS   The lamb.
MENENIUS   Yes, to eat him, just like the hungry plebeians would eat
Martius.
BRUTUS   He's a lamb that baas like a bear.
MENENIUS   He's a bear that lives like a lamb. You two are old men.
Let me ask you one thing.
BOTH TRIBUNES   Well, what?
MENENIUS   In what vice can Martius be said to be poor, that you two
don't have in abundance?
BRUTUS   He's poor in no one fault, but well supplied with all.
SICINIUS   Especially pride.
BRUTUS   And worse than everyone in boasting.
MENENIUS   This is strange now. Do you two know how you are
criticised here in the city, I mean by us of the right-leaning party?
Do you?
BOTH TRIBUNES   Why? How are we criticised?
MENENIUS   Since you mentioned pride just now, won't you be angry?
BOTH TRIBUNES   Well, let's see.

MENENIUS   It's not important. The slightest pretext will rob you of your patience. Give vent to your feeling and be as angry as you like, at least if you take pleasure in it. You blame Martius for being proud.

BRUTUS   We're not alone, sir.

MENENIUS   I know you can do very little alone, for you have plenty of help, or else your actions would be remarkably solitary. Your abilities are too infantile to do much alone. You talk of pride. If only you could turn your eyes to face the napes of your neck and make an interior examination of your good selves! If only!

BOTH TRIBUNES   What then, sir?

MENENIUS   Why, then you'd discover a pair of undeserving, proud, violent, testy magistrates, otherwise known as fools, as any in Rome.

SICINIUS   Menenius, you're pretty well known too.

MENENIUS   I'm known to be a capricious patrician who loves a cup of hot wine unadulterated by Tiber water; I'm said to be somewhat at fault in favouring the plaintiff first, and hasty and hot-tempered for the slightest reason; I keep company with the buttocks of the night more than with the forehead of the morning. I say what's in my mind and exhaust my malice in words. Meeting two such statesmen as you – I cannot call you wise Lycurguses – if the drink you give me disagrees with my palate, I'll screw up my face at it. I cannot say your worships have argued the matter well when I find something assinine in almost every syllable you utter. And though I must be content to bear with those that say you are venerable, grave men, yet they tell a terrible lie who say you have good faces. If you can see any of this in my face, which is a map of my microcosm, does it follow that I too am well enough known? What harm can your blind insights glean from this character, if I too am well enough known?

BRUTUS   Come, come, sir. We know you well enough.

MENENIUS   You know neither me, nor yourselves, nor anything. You are ambitious to be saluted by poor knaves. You waste a whole morning hearing a case between an orange-wife and a spigot-seller, and then adjourn a dispute about threepence to a second day's hearing. When you preside over a matter between two parties, if you happen to get an attack of colic, you make faces like mime artists, declare war on any thought of patience, and while calling for a chamber-pot dismiss the controversy unresolved, made more complicated by your hearing. The only fairness you offer is in calling both parties knaves. You are a pair of strange ones.

BRUTUS Come, come, you're better known for being witty at the dinner table than a useful official in the Capitol.

MENENIUS Even our priests would be amused if they encountered such ridiculous citizens as you. When you speak most to the point, it's not worth wagging your beard, and your beards don't deserve as honourable a grave as to stuff a cobbler's cushion or be entombed in an ass's pack-saddle. Yet you have to say Martius is proud, he who, in a cautious estimate, is worth all your predecessors since the Flood, although maybe some of the best of them were hereditary hangmen. Good evening to your worships. Any more of your conversation would affect my brain, you being herdsmen of the beastly plebeians. I will venture to take my leave of you.

Brutus and Sicinius step aside.
Enter Volumnia, Virgilia and Valeria.

Greetings, my ladies, as fair as you are noble, and as fair as the moon, what are you in such a hurry to see?

VOLUMNIA Honourable Menenius, my boy Martius is coming. For the love of Juno, let's go.

MENENIUS Really? Martius coming home?

VOLUMNIA Yes, worthy Menenius, to an enthusiastic reception.

MENENIUS Take my cap, Jupiter, with my thanks. What ho! Martius coming home?

VIRGILIA and VALERIA Yes, it's true.

VOLUMNIA Look, here's a letter from him. The government has another, his wife another, and I think there's one at home for you.

MENENIUS I'll see that there's celebration at my house tonight. A letter for me?

VIRGILIA Yes, definitely, there's a letter for you. I saw it.

MENENIUS A letter for me! It endows me with seven years' good health, during which I will scorn any physician. The most respected prescription in Galen is mere quackery, and compared to this letter no more effective than a dose of horse medicine. Is he not wounded? He has usually come home wounded.

VIRGILIA Oh no, no, no!

VOLUMNIA Oh, he is wounded. I thank the gods for that.

MENENIUS So do I, if it's not serious. Is he bringing back victory in his pocket? The wounds do him honour.

VOLUMNIA On his brow. Menenius, he comes home for the third time with a garland of oak leaves.

MENENIUS Has he taught Aufidius a sound lesson?

VOLUMNIA   Titus Lartius writes that they fought together, but
Aufidius got away.

MENENIUS   It was time for him too, I'll grant him that. If he had
stayed close by, I wouldn't have been so Aufidiussed for all the
treasure chests in Corioli and the gold that's in them. Does the
senate know all this?

VOLUMNIA   Good ladies, let's go. Yes, yes, yes. The senate has letters
from the general in which he gives my son the whole honour of
the war. In this action he has doubly exceeded his earlier deeds.

VALERIA   There are really remarkable things being said of him.

MENENIUS   Remarkable? Yes, I'm sure. And not without genuinely
earning them.

VIRGILIA   May the gods grant they be true!

VOLUMNIA   True? Ha ha!

MENENIUS   True? I'll swear they're true. Where is he wounded?
[*To the Tribunes*] God save your worships! Martius is coming
home. He has yet more to be proud of. [*To Volumnia*] Where is he
wounded?

VOLUMNIA   In the shoulder and in the left arm. There will be some
big scars to show the people when he stands for office. In the
defeat of Tarquinius he received seven wounds to the body.

MENENIUS   One in the neck and two in the thigh, there are nine I
know about.

VOLUMNIA   He had, before this last expedition, twenty-five wounds
all told.

MENENIUS   Now it's twenty-seven. Every gash was an enemy's grave.

A shout and flourish.

Listen: the trumpets!

VOLUMNIA   Those are Marius's escort. Ahead of him he has noise,
and behind him he leaves tears.

   Death, that dark spirit, in his sinewy arm does lie;
   The arm advances and comes down, and then men die.

*A sennet. Trumpets sound. Enter Cominius the general and
Titus Lartius; between them Coriolanus, crowned with an
oak garland; with captains and soldiers and a herald.*

HERALD   Hear, Rome, how Martius fought the fight alone
                Within Corioli's gates, where he has won,
                As well as fame, a name for Martius Caius; he
                Now bears the honorific "Coriolanus".
                Welcome to Rome, victorious Coriolanus!

Flourish.

ALL   Welcome to Rome, victorious Coriolanus!
CORIOLANUS No more of this! It all offends my heart.
                   Please now, no more!
COMINIUS   Look, sir, your mother.
CORIOLANUS   Oh!
                   You have, I know, petitioned all the gods
                   For my success.   *Kneels.*
VOLUMNIA   No, my good soldier, stand up.
                   My Martius, my good Caius, newly named
                   In honour of great deeds you have achieved,
                   What is it? "Coriolanus" must I call you?
                   But, oh, your wife!
CORIOLANUS   My gracious silence, greetings.
                   You weep to see me triumph; does that mean
                   You would have laughed if I was in my coffin?
                   Those are the eyes of Corioli's widows
                   And mothers who've lost sons.
MENENIUS   May the gods crown you!
CORIOLANUS You're still alive? [*To Valeria*] O my dear lady, pardon.
VOLUMNIA   I don't know where to turn. O welcome home!
                   And welcome, general, and welcome to all.
MENENIUS   A hundred thousand welcomes! I could weep
                   And I could laugh; I'm light and heavy. Welcome.
                   May curses spread up into every heart
                   That is not glad to see you! You are three
                   That Rome should dote on; yet it must be said
                   We have some crabby people here that won't
                   Be shifted to your liking. So welcome, warriors!
                   We call a nettle just a nettle, and
                   The faults of fools just folly.
COMINIUS   Quite so.
CORIOLANUS Menenius, well said.
HERALD   Make way there, and proceed.
CORIOLANUS   Your hand; and yours;
                   Before I pass the threshold of our house
                   The good patricians must be visited.
                   From them I have received not only greetings
                   But also new distinctions.
VOLUMNIA   I have lived
                   To see the realisation of my wishes
                   And the consummation of my dreams.
                   There's only one thing lacking, which I'm sure

                Will be conferred by Rome.

CORIOLANUS   I tell you, mother,
                I'd rather be their servant in my way
                Than go along with them in theirs.

COMINIUS   We must proceed now to the Capitol.

Flourish of cornets. Exeunt in state, as before. Enter Brutus and Sicinius.

BRUTUS   All tongues speak of him, and the bleary-eyed
                Put on their spectacles to see him. Nurses
                Just let their babies scream the house down,
                So busy are they prattling. Kitchen maids
                Pin linen scarves around their grimy necks
                And clamber on the walls to view him. Shops
                Are crowded, full of people of all sorts,
                Some riding rooftop ridges like a horse,
                All desperate to see him. Priests emerge
                Into the light and push their way through crowds
                To get a good position. Veiled ladies
                Expose the white and pink of their complexions,
                No longer shaded, to the burning kiss
                Of midday sun. You'd think from the commotion
                That whatsoever god is leading him
                Had slyly crept inside his human frame
                And given him divine impressiveness.

SICINIUS   I have a sudden insight: he'll be consul!

BRUTUS   In which case Tribunes might as well be asleep.

SICINIUS   He cannot exercise restraint in office
                And keep things within proper bounds, but will
                Lose what he's won.

BRUTUS   In that there's comfort.

SICINIUS   Trust
                The commoners, for whom we stand, to let
                Their long resentment overlook his honours,
                Whatever cause he gives them, and I'm certain
                He'll give them cause, just as I know
                He will be proud to do so.

BRUTUS   I heard him swear
                That if he were to stand for consul, never
                Would he appear in public, nor put on
                The threadbare garment of humility.
                Nor would he show his wounds to the people
                To win their stinking votes, as others might.

SICINIUS	You're right.
BRUTUS	Yes, he'd forgo the office rather
	Than hold it only at the service of the gentry
	And the desire of the nobles.
SICINIUS	What I wish
	Is that he'd hold that purpose and put it
	Into effect.
BRUTUS	Most probably he will.
SICINIUS	It will be certain ruin for him then,
	And in our interest too.
BRUTUS	This must be how
	His future looks, or our authority is ended.
	We must persuade the people how he hates them
	And always has, and that he'd like to treat them
	Like mules by silencing their partisans
	And limiting their freedom, regarding them
	In human action and capacity
	Of no more worth or value for the world
	Than camels in the war, which get their fodder
	Only for bearing burdens and get whipped
	For sinking under them.
SICINIUS	This should be done
	Some time when his unbridled arrogance
	Is stirring up the people. Such a time
	Will come quite soon if he's provoked to it,
	And that's as easy as to let a dog chase sheep.
	His fire will kindle their dry stubble, and
	Their blaze will quench his flame for ever.

Enter a Messenger.

BRUTUS	What's the news?
MESSENGER	You are requested at the Capitol. It's thought
	That Martius will be consul. Deaf and dumb
	Press forward just to see him, and the blind
	To hear him speak. Women were flinging gloves
	Towards him as he passed, ladies and maids
	Their scarves and handkerchiefs. The nobles bowed
	As if to Jove's statue, and the people made
	A shower and thunder with their caps and shouts.
	I've never seen anything like it.
BRUTUS	Let's go there
	And watch the present with our eyes and ears

And save our hearts for the future.

SICINIUS   I'm with you!

Exeunt.

Act II Scene 2

Enter two officers, to lay cushions, as it were in the Capitol.

FIRST OFFICER   Come on, they're almost here. How many people are standing for the consulship?

SECOND OFFICER   Three, they say, but everyone thinks Coriolanus will carry it.

FIRST OFFICER   He's a brave fellow, but he's exceedingly proud and has no love for the common people.

SECOND OFFICER   Well, there have been many great men that have flattered the people without loving them, and there are many the people have loved without knowing why. If they can love without knowing why, they can hate for no better reason. Therefore for Coriolanus not to care whether they love or hate him displays the true understanding he has of their attitudes, and out of his patrician indifference he lets them see it plainly.

FIRST OFFICER   If he didn't care whether he had their love or not, he'd waver impartially between doing them neither good nor harm; but he seeks their hate with greater devotion than they can return it, and leaves nothing undone that may reveal him as their opponent. Now to seem to seek out the malice and displeasure of the people is as bad as what he himself dislikes: flattering them for their love.

SECOND OFFICER   He has deserved well of his country, and his ascent has not been by such easy steps as for those who are flexible and courteous to the people and greet them respectfully, without any further accomplishment to win their esteem and good opinion. But he has so thoroughly displayed his honours to their eyes and his actions to their hearts that for their tongues to be silent and not confess so much would be a rather ungrateful insult. To react in any other way would be malicious, and, giving itself the lie, would earn reproof and rebuke from every ear that heard it.

FIRST OFFICER   Let's say no more about him; he's a fine man. Here they are.

A sennet. Enter the Patricians and the Tribunes of the people, with lictors before them; Coriolanus, Menenius, Cominius the Consul. Sicinus and Brutus take their places a little apart. Coriolanus stands.

MENENIUS   Having decided how to treat the Volscians,
             And to send for Titus Lartius, it remains
             As the main point for this assembled gathering
             To show our gratitude to him whose service
             Nobly defended this our country. Therefore,
             Most reverend Roman elders, may it please you
             To ask the consul and last general
             In our recent successes to report
             A little on those worthy deeds performed
             By Martius Caius Coriolanus, whom
             We meet here both to thank and to remember
             With honours well deserved.

FIRST SENATOR   Speak, good Cominius.
             Leave nothing out, and make us think that Rome
             Is more defective in its offers of reward
             Than short on gratitude. Masters of the people,
             We do request your keen attention and
             Your influence within the common people
             To endorse what we do here.

SICINIUS   We are convened
             For admirable purposes, and mean
             To look with favour on whatever theme
             Is put before our assembly.

BRUTUS   We'll be glad
             To do so all the more if he displays
             A kinder estimation of the people
             Than what he's shown before.

MENENIUS   Now now; be careful!
             I'd rather you had held your tongue. Do you wish
             To hear Cominius speak?

BRUTUS   Most willingly;
             But yet my warning was more pertinent
             Than the rebuke you gave it.

MENENIUS   He loves your people,
             But don't expect much intimacy from him.
             Worthy Cominius, speak.

             Coriolanus rises and starts to go away.

A SENATOR   No, keep your place.
             Sit, Coriolanus. No need to feel ashamed
             Of your such noble deeds.

CORIOLANUS Forgive me, sirs.

                    I'd rather suffer all those wounds again
                    Than hear how they were dealt.
BRUTUS   Sir, I hope
                    My words did not cause you to leave?
CORIOLANUS   No, sir.
                    Yet words often offend me more than blows.
                    You did not flatter me, so did not hurt me.
                    I love your people for their virtue.
MENENIUS   Please, sit down.
CORIOLANUS I'd rather have a pat on the head in the sun
                    When battle calls than sit here idly hearing
                    My feeble deeds exaggerated.   *Exit.*
MENENIUS   Tribunes,
                    How can he flatter your fast-breeding crowd –
                    Just one good man in a thousand – when you see
                    He'd rather venture all his limbs for honour
                    Than one of his ears to hear it? Proceed, Cominius.
COMINIUS   My words will not suffice, too feebly uttered
                    To extol the deeds of Coriolanus justly.
                    It's said that valour is the greatest virtue,
                    Reflecting best on him who has it. If so,
                    The man I speak of cannot in this world
                    Be equalled. No more than sixteen years of age
                    When Tarquin made a march on Rome, he fought
                    Outstandingly for us. Our then dictator,
                    Whom I am pleased to point to, saw him fight
                    When with his chin still beardless he drove back
                    The hairy faces ranged against him. Once
                    He stood above a hard-pressed Roman soldier,
                    And killed three of the enemy. Tarquin
                    Himself he wounded in the knee. That day,
                    When he was young enough to play a woman's part,
                    He proved himself the best and was rewarded
                    With wreaths of oak placed on his brow. At manhood
                    He thus arrived still young, and swelled up like the sea.
                    He took the brunt of seventeen battles since
                    And won the garland's honours every time.
                    About this recent action at Corioli
                    I cannot say enough. He stopped deserters,
                    And by his rare example turned their terror
                    Around, as if the fight were sport. Like weeds
                    In front of sailing ships, the men obeyed

And bowed to his command. His sword dealt death
At every mark it struck. From foot to face
He was a thing of blood; his every motion
Was met with dying cries. Alone he entered
Those fateful city gates, whose destiny
He painted blood-red, then returned unaided.
With reinforcements he attacked Corioli
Just like a thunderbolt. The day seemed won,
When soon his lively senses heard the din
Of distant action. Immediately his spirit,
With double force, revived his lagging limbs.
He joined the battle, where his sword soon reeked
With blood from men whose lives he wasted
As if it were perpetual slaughter. Till
We called both field and city ours, not once
Did he allow his breast to pause for breath.

MENENIUS   A worthy man!

A SENATOR   Beyond dispute he measures up to all
The honours we propose.

COMINIUS   He kicked at booty
And looked at precious spoils as if they were
The common muck of the world. His needs are less
Than what a pauper has; the satisfaction
His deeds give is reward enough. He's happy
To spend his time with no particular purpose.

MENENIUS   Truly noble!
Let him be called in.

A SENATOR   Call Coriolanus.

OFFICER   He is present.

Enter Coriolanus.

MENENIUS   The senate, Coriolanus, is well pleased
To make you consul.

CORIOLANUS   I do owe them still
My life and service.

MENENIUS   It then remains
For you to speak to the people.

CORIOLANUS   I beg you,
Let me be spared this custom, for I cannot
Put on the gown, stand there unarmed, and ask them
For my wounds' sake to give their vote. So please,
Allow me not to do so.

SICINIUS   Sir, the people
                    Must have their voices heard; they will
                    Not do without one jot of ceremony.
MENENIUS   Don't ask them that. Accommodate the custom:
                    Observe formalities, as earlier consuls have,
                    Tied to the award of honours.
CORIOLANUS   It is a part
                    I'll blush to play; this license should perhaps
                    Be taken from the people.
BRUTUS   What was that!
CORIOLANUS To boast to them "I did this, I did that"
                    And show my healed scars, which I should hide,
                    As if I had received them just to win
                    The people's vote.
MENENIUS   Do not insist on it.
                    We recommend to you, tribunes of the people,
                    Our purpose; to them and to our noble consul
                    We wish all joy and honour.
SENATORS   To Coriolanus come all joy and honour!

Flourish of cornets. Exeunt all except Sicinius and Brutus.

BRUTUS   You see how he intends to treat the people.
SICINIUS   I hope they'll notice his intentions. Next
                    He will solicit their support as if he was
                    In favour of those very things we know
                    He has condemned.
BRUTUS   Come, we'll inform them
                    Of our proceedings here. I know they are
                    Expecting us in the market place.

Exeunt.

Act II Scene 3

Enter seven or eight citizens.

FIRST CITIZEN   Once and for all, if he requests our votes, we ought
not deny him them.
SECOND CITIZEN   We may, sir, if we wish.
THIRD CITIZEN   We have power in ourselves to do it, but it's a
power we have no power to do. For if he shows us his wounds
and tells us about his deeds, we are to put our tongues into those
wounds and speak for them; so if he tells us about his noble deeds,

we must also tell him our noble acceptance of them. Ingratitude is monstrous, and for the multitude to be ungrateful would make a monster of the multitude, of which we, being members, should bring ourselves to be monstrous members.

FIRST CITIZEN   To make us no better thought of than that, it will not require much effort. Once when we stood up to him about the corn, he didn't hesitate to call us the many-headed multitude.

THIRD CITIZEN   We've been called that many times, not that some of our heads are brown, some black, some fair, some bald, but that our wits are different colours too. I truly think that if all our wits were to issue out of one skull, they would fly east, west, north and south, and their agreement to go in one direction would end up as going to all points of the compass.

SECOND CITIZEN   Do you think so? Which way do you think my wit would fly?

THIRD CITIZEN   Your wit wouldn't be out before someone else's was. It's firmly wedged up in a blockhead. But if it were at liberty, it would defintely fly south.

SECOND CITIZEN   Why that way?

THIRD CITIZEN   To lose itself in a fog where, being three quarters melted away with rotten odours, the fourth would return for conscience's sake to help find you a wife.

SECOND CITIZEN   You're always up to your tricks. That's all right with us.

THIRD CITIZEN   Have you all decided to give your votes? But never mind, the majority vote wins. I say that if he'd listen to the people, there was never a worthier man.

Enter Coriolanus in a gown of humility, with Menenius.

Here he comes, in the gown of humility. Watch his behaviour. We are not to stay all together but to approach him where he stands in ones, twos and threes. He's to make his requests to individuals, which gives each one of us the singular honour of giving him our own vote with our own voice. So follow me and I'll explain how you are to approach him.

ALL CITIZENS   Good plan!

Exeunt Citizens.

MENENIUS   O sir, this isn't right. Did you not know
That all successful men have done it?

CORIOLANUS   Well,
Should I say "Please, sir"? Dammit, nothing will
Persuade my tongue to say that. "Look, my wounds.

I got them in my country's service, when
A number of your brethren screamed and ran
Away from our own drums."

MENENIUS   Oh no, my god,
You mustn't mention that. You must persuade them
To think about you.

CORIOLANUS   Think about me? Hang 'em!
I'd rather they forgot me, like the morals
Our priests quite fail to teach them.

MENENIUS   You'll go wrong.
I'll leave you. But I beg you speak to them
In a wholesome manner.   *Exit*

Enter three of the citizens.

CORIOLANUS   Tell them wash their faces
And clean their teeth? Like that? Here come a couple.
You know the reason I am standing here?

THIRD CITIZEN   We do, sir. Tell us, what persuaded you to come?

CORIOLANUS   My own deserts.

SECOND CITIZEN   Your own deserts?

CORIOLANUS   Yes, but not my own desire.

THIRD CITIZEN   Why not your own desire?

CORIOLANUS   No, sir, it was never my desire to trouble the poor
with begging.

THIRD CITIZEN   You must think we hope to get something from you
if we give you anything.

CORIOLANUS   Well then, tell me your price for the consulship?

FIRST CITIZEN   The price is to ask for it kindly.

CORIOLANUS   Kindly, sir, please let me have it. I have wounds to
show you, which you may see in private. Your opinion, sir, what do
you say?

SECOND CITIZEN   You shall have it, worthy sir.

CORIOLANUS   It's a deal! There are two worthy people I've begged. I
have your support. Goodbye.

THIRD CITIZEN   There's something strange about this.

SECOND CITIZEN   If it were to be repeated … But never mind.

Exeunt citizens. Enter two other citizens.

CORIOLANUS   Look at this: if it's in accord with your opinions that I
should be consul, I have here the traditional gown.

FOURTH CITIZEN   You have deserved well of your country and you
have not deserved well.

CORIOLANUS What do you mean by that?

FOURTH CITIZEN You have been the scourge of Rome's enemies, you have been a rod to her friends. You have not loved the common people.

CORIOLANUS You should consider me more virtuous because I have not been common in my love. I will, sir, flatter my sworn brother, the people, to earn a warmer opinion from them; that's behaviour they consider noble. And since in their wisdom they have chosen rather to have my hat than my heart, I will practise the ingratiating nod and hypocritically doff my hat. In other words, I will imitate the bewitching charms of some popular person and deliver this to those who want it in abundance. So I'm asking to be consul.

FIFTH CITIZEN We hope you'll be our friend, so we give you our vote enthusiastically.

FOURTH CITIZEN You have received many wounds for your country.

CORIOLANUS I will not confirm your statement by showing them. I will take advantage of your votes and so trouble you no further.

BOTH CITIZENS The gods give you joy, sir, in abundance! *Exeunt.*

CORIOLANUS Music to the ear!

> Better it is to die, better to starve,
> Than beg for praise which clearly we deserve.
> Why in this wolf-like gown should I stand here
> To beg any Tom or Dick who may appear
> For their endorsement. Custom calls me to it.
> Whatever custom orders, we should do it.
> The dust on old traditions is unswept;
> So high are hallowed passed-down errors heaped
> That truth cannot be seen. I'll not dissemble so –
> Let highest office and the honour go
> To him that does. But still, I'm half way through;
> One half I've suffered, so the rest I'll do.

Enter three more citizens.

> Here come more voices.
> Your voices! For your voices I have fought,
> Watched for your voices, for your voices took
> Two dozen wounds or more; in eighteen battles,
> Or thereabouts, I've fought; for your voices have
> I done all kinds of this and that; your voices!
> For sure I will be consul!

SIXTH CITIZEN Indeed he has done splendidly, and should have the voice and vote of every honest man.

SEVENTH CITIZEN   So let him be consul! May the gods bring him
   joy and make him a good friend to the people!
ALL CITIZENS   Amen, amen. God save you, noble consul!

Exeunt citizens.

CORIOLANUS   Worthy voices!

Enter Menenius, with Brutus and Sicinius.

MENENIUS   You've filled the time allotted, and the tribunes
   Endow you with the people's vote. Remains
   For you to attend a session of the senate
   With all the insignia of office.
CORIOLANUS   Is that done?
SICINIUS   You have discharged the custom of request.
   The people do admit you; they are due
   To meet quite soon to ratify their vote.
CORIOLANUS Where? At the senate-house?
SICINIUS   There, Coriolanus.
CORIOLANUS May I change these clothese?
SICINIUS   You may, sir.
CORIOLANUS I will do so at once, and in familiar guise
   Go to the senate-house.
MENENIUS   I'll keep you company.
   [*To the Tribunes*]   Will you go too?
BRUTUS   We'll stay here for the people.
SICINIUS   So goodbye.

Exeunt Coriolanus and Menenius.

   He has it now, and from the way he looks
   He's pleased with it.
BRUTUS   He wore those humble clothes
   With pride, we saw. Will you dismiss the people?

Enter the Plebeians.

SICINIUS   Well now, my good men, have you chosen him?
FIRST CITIZEN   He has our votes, sir.
BRUTUS   We pray the gods that he deserves your love.
SECOND CITIZEN   We too, sir. In my very modest judgment,
   When begging for our votes, he was mocking us.
THIRD CITIZEN   Definitely, he downright flouted us.
FIRST CITIZEN   No, that's his way of speaking. It wasn't mockery.
SECOND CITIZEN   Except for you, each one of us agrees
   He treated us most scornfully. He should
   Have shown his wounds to us, earned for his country.

SICINIUS   I'm sure he did.

ALL CITIZENS   No, no. No one saw them.

THIRD CITIZEN   He said he'd wounds he'd show in private.
He took his hat and waved it scornfully,
And said "For sure I will be consul! Custom
Will not permit my claim but with your votes.
So give your vote!" And when we'd granted that,
He said "I thank you for your voices. Thankyou,
Your precious voices. Now you've given your voices,
That's all I need from you." Wasn't that mockery?

SICINIUS   Well, either you were blind and didn't see it,
Or saw it and were moved by childish friendliness
To grant your voices.

BRUTUS   Could you not have told him,
What you had learned: that when he had no power
He was a minor servant to the state.
He was your enemy, and always spoke
Against the liberties and charters that you have
By constitutional right. And now, attaining
A higher place of power in the state,
If he should still remain so ill-disposed
Toward the common people, then your votes
May come to hurt you. What you should have said
Is that his famous deeds themselves sufficed
To claim high honour, so his gracious nature
Should be indebted for your voices, and
Transform his malice towards you into love,
As friendly lord and patron.

SICINIUS   If you said
What you were told to say, you would have put
His spirit to the test. You would have either
Received a gracious promise which, if need be,
You could have held him to, to keep his word.
Or else it would have galled his surly nature
Which cannot easily endure conditions
Restricting him at all. Once in a rage,
He'd give you the advantage and excuse
To see him not elected.

BRUTUS   Did you notice
That he was openly contemptuous
When needing your support, and do you think
That his contempt will not endanger you

When he has power to wield? Were there no hearts
Within those bodies? Did your tongues rebel
Against all reasonable action?

SICINIUS   Have you
Ever in the past denied requests? Yet
To him who did not ask but simply mocked
You gave your voice and tongue.

THIRD CITIZEN   He's not confirmed. We could deny him still.
SECOND CITIZEN   We will deny him.
I'll get five hundred voices for that call.

FIRST CITIZEN   And I'll round up a thousand, and their friends.
BRUTUS   Go off at once and tell those friends of yours
That they have chosen someone who will steal
Their liberties and treat their voices as
No more than those of dogs they beat for barking,
And kept for that same purpose.

SICINIUS   See they assemble
And all revoke that ignorant election
And make a sounder judgment. Stress his pride
And his old hatred of you. Don't forget
How grudgingly he wore the humble gown,
And how he scorned and wooed you both together.
Impressed by his achievements, your affection
Caused you to overlook his haughty bearing
Which he has shaped and fashioned as an insult
Arising from the inveterate hate he bears you.

BRUTUS   The blame you may assign to us, your tribunes,
Because we urged that nothing should prevent you
From voting for him.

SICINIUS   You can say you chose him
More at our urging than from being guided
By your own real feelings, and that your minds,
Preoccupied with what you must do rather
Than what you should, made you give him your voice
Despite your better judgment. It's our fault.

BRUTUS   Quite so, don't spare us, say we lectured you
How young he was when he began to serve
His country, and how long he's served, what stock
He springs from: it's the noble house of Martius,
From Ancus Martius, Numa's daughter's son,
Who was the next king after great Hostilius.
Publius and Quintus both were of that house;

They built great aqueducts to bring us water.
And Censorinus, darling of the people,
So named because he twice served Rome as Censor,
Was his great ancestor.

SICINIUS   It was this man
We recommended to you, conscious of
His personal record and his sterling merit.
But when you weigh his present attitude
Against his earlier bearing, you have found
That he's your real enemy, and revoke
Your hasty approbation.

BRUTUS   Say you'd never
Have done it, had we not persuaded you.
And presently, when you are all assembled,
Repair to the Capitol.

ALL CITIZENS   We will. We all,
Or almost all, regret our choice.

Exeunt Plebeians.

BRUTUS   Let them
Go on. This mutiny is better hazarded
At once, not wait for better opportunity.
If, as he well might, he gets into a rage
When they refuse him, we should take advantage
Of his intemperate anger.

SICINIUS   To the Capitol, come.
We will be there before most of the people;
And this will seem, as partly it is, their own
Revolt, which we have goaded and supported.

Exeunt.

Act III Scene 1

*Cornets. Enter Coriolanus, Menenius, all the gentry,
Cominius, Titus Lartius, and other Senators.*

CORIOLANUS Aufidius then had raised another army?
LARTIUS   He had, my lord, that's why we came to terms
As soon as we were able.
CORIOLANUS So then the Volscian strength is as it was,
Ready at any time to launch a raid
On us.
COMINIUS   My lord, their armies are so weak

We can't expect to see their banners waving
In our time again.

CORIOLANUS   You saw Aufidius?

LARTIUS   His safety guaranteed, he came to me
And cursed the Volscians for the town's surrender.
He's now withdrawn to Antium.

CORIOLANUS   And did he
Remember me?

LARTIUS   He did, my lord.

CORIOLANUS   How? What?

LARTIUS   How often he and you had fought with swords;
That of all things on earth he hates the most
You are the one; that he would pawn his treasure
Beyond a hope of seeing it again,
If he could once defeat you.

CORIOLANUS   He lives at Antium?

LARTIUS   At Antium.

CORIOLANUS I wish I had a cause to go and find him,
To show I hate him equally. Welcome home.

Enter Sicinius and Brutus.

See here, these are the tribunes of the people,
The tongues of the common mouth. I do despise them
Because they dress above their proper station,
Beyond the endurance of the nobles.

SICINIUS   Pass no further.

CORIOLANUS Hey! What's this?

BRUTUS   It will be dangerous to go on. No further!

CORIOLANUS What's the reason for this?

MENENIUS   What's the matter?

COMINIUS   Has he not been approved both by the nobles
And by the common people too?

BRUTUS   Cominius, no.

CORIOLANUS   Have children voted for me?

FIRST SENATOR Tribunes, give way. He's due in the market place.

BRUTUS   The people are incensed against him.

SICINIUS   Stop,
Or tumult will erupt.

CORIOLANUS   Are they your herd?
Should such men vote, when they can vote one way,
Then change their minds at once? What are your duties?
If you're their mouthpiece, can't you rule their teeth?

        Did you not urge them on?

MENENIUS   Keep calm, keep calm.

CORIOLANUS It's a conspiracy whose purpose is
        To curb the power of the nobility.
        Allow it, and you'll have to live with people
        Who cannot rule and never will be ruled.

BRUTUS   Don't call it a conspiracy. The people
        Resent it when you mock them, and of late,
        When corn was given out gratis, you complained.
        You slandered those who stood up for the people,
        And called them enemies of the nobles.

CORIOLANUS But this was known before.

BRUTUS   Not to them all.

CORIOLANUS Have you informed them since?

BRUTUS   How? I inform them?

CORIOLANUS That's business that you do.

BRUTUS   I do it better than you do your own.

CORIOLANUS Why then should I be consul? For heaven's sake,
        If I'm as undeserving as you say,
        Let me be tribune too.

SICINIUS   You show too much that side
        Of you which irks the people. If you plan
        To reach your destination and get lost,
        You have to ask the way much more politely,
        Or never be so noble as a consul,
        And never sink to being tribune.

MENENIUS   Let's keep calm.

COMINIUS   The people have a grievance. Let's move on.
        Equivocation is not helpful, nor has
        Coriolanus merited obstructions
        Put up by his accusers.

CORIOLANUS   What about corn?
        That was my speech, and I will say it again.

MENENIUS   Not now, not now.

FIRST SENATOR   Not in this heat, sir, now.

CORIOLANUS Now, as I live, I will.
        My nobler friends, I crave your pardon. For
        The fickle, smelly multitude, let them
        Take note of what I say. I do not flatter,
        But describe them as they are. I say again,
        By soothing them we nourish insurrection
        Against our senate, discord and sedition

Which we ourselves have ploughed for, sowed and scattered,
By mingling them with us, virtuous patricians,
Whose only loss of power has been occasioned
By passing it to beggars.

MENENIUS   That's enough.
FIRST SENATOR No more speech, we beg you.
CORIOLANUS   What? No more?
I feared no foreign force when for my country
I shed my blood, so why expect my lungs
To mince my words against those measly scabs
From whom we fear infection and yet seek
New ways to catch it?
BRUTUS   You speak of the people
As if you were a god with power to punish,
And not a man of human flesh.
SICINIUS   We should
Inform the people.
MENENIUS   What? Of what? His rage?
CORIOLANUS My rage!
If I were calm, as if asleep at midnight,
By Jove, my thoughts would be the same.
SICINIUS   They're thoughts
That shall remain a poison where they are,
Not poison any further.
CORIOLANUS   "Shall remain"?
D'you hear this captain of the minnows? D'you hear
His insistent "shall"?
                                    That's out of order.
COMINIUS   "Shall"?
CORIOLANUS O good but most unwise patricians, why,
You grave but reckless senators, did you
Allow the many-headed populace
To choose an officer to blast and blare
On their behalf, who with his stubborn "shall"
Has insolence enough to say he'll seize
Authority from you. If he has power,
Accept your impotence. If not, dispel
Your dangerous softness. If you are wise,
You'll not act foolishly; but if you're not,
Let them enjoy the cushioned senate seats.
If they are senators, you are plebeians.
If you and they combine, the strongest taste

Will come from them. They choose as magistrate
A man who sets his "shall", his popular "shall",
Against a more deliberative body
Than ever ruled in Greece. By Jove himself,
It drags the consuls down, and my soul aches
To know, when two authorities share power,
Neither supreme, how soon confusion
Will fill the gap between them and mistake
The one for the other.

COMINIUS   Let's go to the market-place.

CORIOLANUS Whoever argued that it would be wise
To give the people warehouse corn for free,
As once was done in Greece?

MENENIUS   Don't touch on that!

CORIOLANUS Though there the people had more absolute power,
I say they nourished disobedience,
And fed the ruin of the state.

BRUTUS   Why should
The people give their votes to anyone
Who speaks like that?

CORIOLANUS   I'll give my reasons, more
Persuasive than their votes. They know the corn
Was not our payment to them, and they know
They had not earned it. Conscripts in the war –
A time when every body of the state was touched –
They would not charge the gates. This kind of service
Did not deserve corn gratis. Being in the war,
Their mutinous behaviour, which displayed
Much valour, did not help their cause. The charge
Which they have often made against the senate,
Unjustifiably, was not the reason
For our most generous largesse. So, what then?
How will that many-bosomed mob accept
The senate's courtesy? Let deeds express
What they will surely say in words: "We did
Request it. We have numbers on our side;
They gave us our demands in fear." That way
We undervalue our authority,
And make the rabble think we act from fear.
In time they'll break the senate doors wide open
And let the crows peck at the eagles.

MENENIUS   Come, enough!

BRUTUS   Enough, more than enough.
CORIOLANUS   No, no, I've more.
                May everything that gods and humans swear by
                Bear witness to my closing truth. Two powers,
                Where one disdains the other for good reason,
                The other hurls unjustifiable insults,
                Where gentry, rank and wisdom cannot rule
                Except depending on the yea or nay
                Of widespread ignorance, they will neglect
                Real necessities, and toil instead
                On pointless trifles. Policy thus thwarted,
                No useful things are done. Therefore I beg you,
                You who would rather not be judged as cowards,
                And love the constitution of the state
                More than you fear the effect of change, and prize
                Nobility above your length of life,
                And wish to risk the surgeon's knife to treat
                A body that would surely die without it,
                Pluck out that multitudinous tongue at once!
                Let them not lick the sweet which is their poison!
                Dishonour done to you will warp your judgment
                And rob the state of its integrity,
                Without the power to do the good it should
                Because of all the evils that control it.
BRUTUS   He's said enough.
SICINIUS   He's spoken like a traitor and shall answer
                As traitors do.
CORIOLANUS   You wretch, beneath contempt!
                What should the people do with these bald tribunes?
                Their leadership defies obedience to
                The senior body. They were chosen when
                Rebellion was the cause, out of necessity,
                Of acts that were not right. Let us declare
                That at a better time what's right is right,
                And throw their power in the dust.
BRUTUS   Manifest treason!
SICINIUS   Is this a consul? No.
BRUTUS   Aediles, here!

                        Enter an Aedile.

                                Let him be apprehended.
SICINIUS   Go, call the people, in whose name I do

Arrest you as a rebel and a traitor,
An enemy of the state. Proceed at once
To your interrogation.

CORIOLANUS   Hence, old goat!

ALL PATRICIANS We will stand bail for him.

COMINIUS   Hands off, old man!

CORIOLANUS Get off, you stinking wretch, or I will shake
Your bones out of your clothes.

SICINIUS   Help, citizens!

Enter a rabble of Plebeians with the Aediles.

MENENIUS   On both sides, more respect!

SICINIUS   Here is the man who'd take all power from you.

BRUTUS   Seize him, Aediles!

ALL PLEBEIANS Down with him! Down with him!

SECOND SENATOR   Weapons, weapons, weapons!

They all bustle around Coriolanus.

ALL   Tribunes! Patricians! Citizens! What ho! Sicinius! Brutus!
Coriolanus! Citizens! Peace, peace, peace! Hold it! Peace!

MENENIUS   What's going on? I'm breathless with alarm.
Disorder everywhere! You tribunes, calm
The people! Coriolanus, patience!
Sicinius, you speak.

SICINIUS   Now hear me, people!

ALL PLEBEIANS Let's hear our tribune. Quiet! Speak, speak, speak.

SICINIUS   You are about to lose your liberties.
Martius plans to take them all, Martius,
Whom recently you named as consul.

MENENIUS   Careful!
You are inflaming tempers, you should quench them.

FIRST SENATOR This is destructive, you will lay the city flat!

SICINIUS   What is the city if it's not the people?

ALL PLEBEIANS True. The people are the city.

BRUTUS   By the consent of all we were appointed
The people's magistrates.

ALL PLEBEIANS You are that still.

MENENIUS   And probably will continue.

COMINIUS   That, I agree, is bound to lay the city flat,
Reducing roofs to rubble, under which
The city, now laid out in orderly array,
Will end up left in ruins.

SICINIUS   This deserves death.

BRUTUS   We have to stand on our authority
                Or we will lose it. We do here pronounce,
                As spokesmen for the people by whose voice
                We were elected, that Martius deserves
                To die at once.

SICINIUS   Therefore, lay hold of him.
                Take him to the Tarpeian Rock, and throw
                Him from the highest point.

BRUTUS   Go, Aediles, seize him!

ALL PLEBEIANS   Surrender, Martius!

MENENIUS   Let me say one thing.
                I beg you, tribunes, let me say just this:

AEDILES   Quiet! Quiet!

MENENIUS   If you're truly loyal to your country,
                Hold back and exercise restraint
                In this rash action.

BRUTUS   Sir, that cool approach,
                Which seems so prudent, is quite poisonous
                When the disease is rampant. Seize him, guards,
                And take him to the Rock.

                    Coriolanus draws his sword.

CORIOLANUS   No, I'll die here!
                A number of you here have seen me fight.
                Come, see if you yourselves can do the same.

MENENIUS   Put down that sword! Tribunes, withdraw a while.

BRUTUS   Have him tied up!

MENENIUS   Help Martius, help him!
                You nobles, help him, whether young or old!

ALL PLEBEIANS   Down with him! Down with him!

In this uproar the Tribunes, Aediles and the people are driven off.

MENENIUS   Go back home to your house. Be gone! Away!
                Or else disaster looms.

SECOND SENATOR   Be off!

CORIOLANUS   Stand fast!
                We have as many friends as enemies.

MENENIUS   Is that the way to settle it?

FIRST SENATOR   God forbid.
                I pray you, noble friend, go back to your house.
                Leave us to solve this problem.

MENENIUS   It's a sore
                We suffer which you cannot treat yourself.

COMINIUS   Come, sir, along with us.
CORIOLANUS I wish they were barbarians, since they
                    Are certainly not Romans, even if they
                    Were born like pigs in litters here in Rome.
MENENIUS   Be off! Your rage, however justifiable,
                    Should not be spoken. There will come a time
                    To compensate for this.
CORIOLANUS   In fair conditions
                    I could beat forty of them.
MENENIUS   I could myself
                    Take on a brace of their best men, even
                    The tribunes!
COMINIUS   But now the odds are badly tipped against us.
                    Bravado is but folly when it tries
                    To stop a building falling. Get you gone
                    Before the mob returns; their rage can tear
                    Apart whatever stands against them, like
                    A surging river bursting both its banks.
MENENIUS   Be off! I'll see if my old brain is still of use
                    With people who have none. This must be patched
                    With cloth of any colour.
COMINIUS   Come on now.

                    Exeunt Coriolanus and Cominius.

A PATRICIAN That man has wrecked his future.
MENENIUS   His nature is too noble for the world.
                    He would not flatter Neptune for his trident,
                    Or Jove to steal his thunder. His heart's his mouth.
                    What his breast forges, that his tongue must utter,
                    And, when he's angry, he forgets he'd ever
                    Heard the name of death.

                            A noise within.

                    Here's trouble!
A PATRICIAN   I just wish they were in bed!
MENENIUS   I wish they were in the Tiber! Could he not
                    Speak courteously to them?

            Enter Brutus and Sicinius with the rabble again.

SICINIUS   Where is that viper
                    Who'd like the city empty and be every
                    Citizen himself?
MENENIUS   You worthy tribunes …

SICINIUS   He will be thrown from the Tarpeian Rock
               Without delay. He has defied the law,
               And therefore he cannot expect a trial
               Beyond the public's judgment, which he scorns
               And sets at nought.

FIRST CITIZEN   He'll soon see that the tribunes
               Are, as it were, the people's mouths, and we
               Their hands.

ALL PLEBEIANS   He will, he surely will.

MENENIUS   Sir, sir!

SICINIUS   Quiet!

MENENIUS   Your hunt's without a proper licence, therefore
               Hold off the kill!

SICINIUS   How did it come about
               That you attempt a rescue?

MENENIUS   Let me speak.
               Since I am conscious of the consul's worth,
               I also know his faults.

SICINIUS   Consul? What consul?

MENENIUS   The consul Coriolanus.

BRUTUS   He consul!

ALL PLEBEIANS   No, no, no, no, no!

MENENIUS   If, by the tribunes' leave and yours, good people,
               I may be heard, I crave a word or two,
               Which will not inconvenience you, save
               To take a little time.

SICINIUS   Speak briefly, then.
               For we are now determined to dispatch
               This viperous traitor. It was dangerous
               To throw him out, but certain death for us
               To keep him here. Therefore it is decreed,
               He dies tonight.

MENENIUS   Oh may the gods forbid
               That Rome, the city that records in stone
               Her thanks to all her meritorious children,
               Should ever, like some monstrous mother,
               Devour her offspring!

SICINIUS   He's a disease that must be cut away.

MENENIUS   Oh, he's a limb affected by disease.
               Fatal to cut it off, to cure it easy!
               What has he done to Rome that merits death?
               Killing our enemies? The blood he's lost –

	Which I would guess is more than what he has,
	By many an ounce – he shed it for his country.
	To lose what's left him at his country's hands
	Would be for us that do it and suffer it
	A vile dishonour to the end of time.
SICINIUS	That is quite wrong.
BRUTUS	Completely off the point.
	The country honoured him when *he* loved *it*.
SICINIUS	A foot with gangrene is of little use,
	No matter how effective it once was.
BRUTUS	We've heard enough. Go to his house at once
	And bring him out for fear he may infect us
	With contagion.
MENENIUS	One word more, just one!
	When rage takes hold and like a tiger leaps
	Unthinkingly, it will, too late, slow down,
	As if it carried leaden weights. Proceed
	By all due process of the law, lest parties –
	He has his many admirers – set off strife,
	Inciting Romans to destroy great Rome.
BRUTUS	If it were so …
SICINIUS	Why do you carry on?
	Have we not had a taste of his obedience?
	Our aediles beaten? Us resisted? Come.
MENENIUS	Consider this: since he could hold a sword
	He was bred up for war and is unschooled
	In softer language; flour and husks he treats
	As if they were the same. Permit me therefore,
	I'll go to him and undertake to bring him
	Where he shall answer to a lawful writ,
	In peace, but perilous for him.
FIRST SENATOR	Noble tribunes,
	That is the proper way. The other course
	Will prove too bloody, and the end of it
	Quite unforeseeable.
SICINIUS	Noble Menenius,
	Please act then as the people's officer.
	People, lay down your weapons.
BRUTUS	Don't go home.
SICINIUS	Meet at the market-place.
	[*To Menenius*] We'll await you there,
	And if you don't bring Martius, we'll proceed

	As we first said.
MENENIUS	I'll bring him to you.

[To the Senators]
Let me request your company. He must come,
Or something worse will follow.

FIRST SENATOR   Let's go with you.

Exeunt.

Act III Scene 2

Enter Coriolanus with Nobles

CORIOLANUS Let them do what they like to me, let me
Be broken on the wheel, or ripped apart
By wild horses. Let them pile ten hills
On top of the Tarpeian Rock, so high
That top to bottom is quite out of sight.
Yet I will still be what I am to them.

A NOBLE   That is the nobler course.

Enter Volumnia.

CORIOLANUS   I am surprised
My mother does not back me with more fervour.
She used to call them "woolly vassals", things
Created just to trade in worthless goods,
To doff their caps at their superiors,
And yawn when anyone of rank or title
Stood up to mention peace or war. Why, yes,
I speak of you. Why did you wish I were
More tactful? Would you have me false
To my own nature? Rather, say I play   ·
The man I am.

VOLUMNIA   O sir, sir, sir,
I would have wished you'd win the highest power
Before you wore it out.

CORIOLANUS   Never mind.

VOLUMNIA   You might have been a better man if you
Had tried less hard to be one. Your caprice
Would not have been obstructed quite so much
If you had kept your thinking to yourself
Until they were too weak to cross you.

CORIOLANUS   Hang them!

VOLUMNIA   And burn them too!

Enter Menenius with the Senators.

MENENIUS   Come, come; you've been too rough,
A lot too rough.
You must go back and put it right.

A SENATOR   There's no
Alternative, unless you are prepared
To see the city split in two and perish.

VOLUMNIA   Take my advice. I have a heart like yours,
Unbending; yet my brain can channel anger
To positive advantage.

MENENIUS   That's well said.
Until he stoops to face the common herd,
Which is the only medicine the state can take
In these unruly times, I'll have to wear my armour,
Too heavy for my frame.

CORIOLANUS   What must I do?

MENENIUS   Return to the tribunes.

CORIOLANUS   Well, what then, what then?

MENENIUS   Take back those things you said.

CORIOLANUS   For them? I cannot do it for the gods;
Must I do it for them?

VOLUMNIA   You are too rigid,
Though one can never have too firm a view.
Yet circumstances now require ... You say
In war honour and policy, like close friends,
Must grow together. If that's so, then tell me,
In peacetime what is each of them without,
If they are not united?

CORIOLANUS   What a question!

MENENIUS   A good one!

VOLUMNIA   If in war it's honourable
To seem something you're not, which you adopt
As policy, how is it morally worse
That policy and honour should remain
Companions in peacetime, since in war
And peace alike a policy is needed?

CORIOLANUS   Why do you stress this argument?

VOLUMNIA   Because it now behoves you to address
The people, not from any urge of yours,
Nor on the themes that lie close to your heart,

But with a text that's fixed and memorised
Beforehand, even though the words offend you
And are hardly what your bosom feels.
Now this no more dishonours you at all
Than if you use sweet words to capture towns
When otherwise you'd face the risk of spilling
Much soldiers' blood and possibly your own.
I would dissemble in my actions if
My fortunes or my friends were put at risk,
And count it as an honour. With me are
Your wife, your son, these senators, the nobles;
And you would rather show those common louts
That you can frown, than fawn on them to gain
The recognition of their love, and know
What might be lost without it.

MENENIUS   Noble lady!
[*To Coriolanus*]
Come, go with us. Be fair! You may resolve
Not only present dangers but the loss
Of office.

VOLUMNIA   So I urge you now, my son,
Go to them, with that bonnet in your hand,
And pay elaborate respect with it,
Your knees kissing the ground. In such a gesture
Action is eloquence, and the eyes of the ignorant
Take in more of the message than their ears.
And wave your head, despite your stubborn heart.
Then be as soft as ripened mulberries
That crumble when they're handled. Or say to them,
You are their soldier, bred for battle, so
You lack the softer manners which you need
To ask for their approval; all of this
You must confess. Present yourself henceforth
As one of them, so far as you are able,
Within the limits of your power.

MENENIUS   If you
Take this to heart, why, even as she speaks,
They'll be won over, since they can forgive
As readily as talking to the wind.

VOLUMNIA   Please go, and let yourself be ruled, although
I know you'd rather chase an enemy
Into the flames than flatter him politely.

Enter Cominius.

	Here is Cominius.
COMINIUS	I come directly from the market place.
	You'd better go with strong support, prepared
	To face them calmly, or else stay away.
	They are enraged.
MENENIUS	So choose your words with care.
COMINIUS	This calm approach will work, provided he
	Controls his fiery spirit.
VOLUMNIA	He must, he will.
	So say you will, I beg you, then get to it.
CORIOLANUS	Must I, bare-headed, show myself to them?
	Must I allow my tongue to tell a lie
	My noble heart detests? Well, I will do it.
	If it were only me, this body, at issue,
	This frame of Martius, they should simply grind it
	To dust, and throw it to the winds. Let's go,
	To the market-place! You've cast me in a role
	I scarcely can perform convincingly.
COMINIUS	Come, come, we'll prompt you.
VOLUMNIA	As you may recall,
	My praises made you first a soldier, so,
	To get my praise for this, perform a part
	You have not played before.
CORIOLANUS	Well, I must do it.
	Forget my natural instinct, and replace it
	With a harlot's spirit! May my warrior's shout
	Which blended with my drum, become a pipe
	Just like a eunuch's or a virgin's voice,
	A baby's lullaby! The smiles that knaves
	Adopt must fill my cheeks; my eyes must brim
	With tears, just like a schoolboy. Then my knees,
	That never bend except to stir a stirrup,
	Must take the form of mendicants at alms.
	I will not do it, lest I bring dishonour
	On my own sense of truth, and thus implant
	An everlasting baseness in my mind.
VOLUMNIA	Let it be your choice then. To plead with you
	Dishonours me more than if you abase
	Yourself to them. So welcome rack and ruin!
	Your mother will endure your pride if only

She may be spared your dangerous obstinacy.
I mock at death with courage, just as you do.
Do what you choose. Your fortitude is mine,
You sucked it from me, but your pride's your own.
CORIOLANUS Be happy, mother; I'll go to the forum.
Don't chide me any more. I'll win their love
By bluff. I'll trick them with smooth words, then all
The trades in Rome will love me. Look, I'm going.
Commend me to my wife. I'll return consul,
Or never trust a word my tongue may utter
When flattery is the game.
VOLUMNIA   Do as you wish.   *Exit.*
COMINIUS   Come on. The tribunes are expecting you.
Prepare to answer mildly, since they'll have
Their accusations ready, stronger, as I hear,
Than any they have made before.
CORIOLANUS The word is "mildly". So, come on, let's go.
If they dream up some novel accusation,
I'll answer them with honour.
MENENIUS   Yes, but mildly.
CORIOLANUS Well, mildly it will be, "mildly".

Exeunt.

Act III Scene 3

Enter Sicinius and Brutus.

BRUTUS   Your accusation should be this: that he affects
Tyrannical power. If he evades the charge,
Remind him of his malice to the people
And that the booty won at Antium
Was never shared.

Enter an Aedile.

So, is he coming?

AEDILE   He is.
BRUTUS   Who's with him?
AEDILE   Old Menenius and those senators
That always took his side.
SICINIUS   Have you a list
Of all the votes that have been cast?
AEDILE   We have.

SICINIUS   And was each man allowed a vote?
AEDILE   He was.
SICINIUS   Let all the people now assemble here.
                And when they hear me say "It shall be so
                By the people's common rights", and then the sentence
                Of death, or fine, or banishment, then let them
                Cry "Fine!" if I say "Fine", if "Death" cry "Death!",
                Insisting on the old prerogative
                And power due to the justness of our cause.
AEDILE   I shall inform them.
BRUTUS   And when the people start to shout replies,
                Don't let them stop. Their yells and shouting will
                Enforce the verdict and the execution of
                Whatever sentence we propose.
AEDILE   That's clear.
SICINIUS   And strengthen their resolve, so when we give
                The signal of our choice, let them be ready.
BRUTUS   Get on with it. [*Exit Aedile.*] Provoke his anger first.
                He's used to winning and to overcoming
                All contradiction. If aroused to fury,
                He cannot be restrained, and then he says
                Whatever's in his mind, and that's our chance
                To break his neck.

                Enter Coriolanus, Menenius and Cominius,
                     with Senators and Patricians.

SICINIUS   Well, here he comes.
MENENIUS   Calmly, I do beg you.
CORIOLANUS Yes, like a stable-boy who's called a knave
                Repeatedly and gets no pay. The gods
                Preserve great Rome! May justice rule,
                Guided by worthy men! Plant love among us!
                Fill our large temples with the flags of peace
                And not our streets with war!
FIRST SENATOR   Amen, amen.
MENENIUS   A noble wish.

                Enter the Aedile with the Plebeians.

SICINIUS   Come forward, people.
AEDILE   Let the tribunes speak! Silence! Quiet, I say!
CORIOLANUS Let me speak first.
BOTH TRIBUNES   By all means. Quiet there!
CORIOLANUS Beyond this session now, will I be charged?

Is everything decided here?

SICINIUS   I ask you
If you agree to abide by the people's vote,
Acknowledging their officers, and agree
To suffer lawful censure for your faults
As may be proved against you.

CORIOLANUS   I am content.

MENENIUS   There, citizens! He says he is content.
Consider his brave service in the war,
And all those wounds received, as many
As gravestones in a churchyard.

CORIOLANUS   Scratches only!
Scars fit only for laughter!

MENENIUS   Then there's this:
If you should think his speech is not the people's,
Remember he's a soldier. Do not take
His rougher accent for malicious speech
But rather, as I say, a soldier's voice,
Not one who hates you.

COMINIUS   Well, enough of that.

CORIOLANUS How come that having been elected consul
I am so dishonoured that within the hour
You take it from me?

SICINIUS   Answer questions only.

CORIOLANUS You're right. It's true, I ought to.

SICINIUS   We charge that you have conspired to take
Established offices away from Rome
And give yourself tyrannical powers
For which you are a traitor to the people.

CORIOLANUS What! Traitor?

MENENIUS   Keep your temper, and your promise!

CORIOLANUS The flames of hottest hell consume the people!
You call me "traitor", miserable tribune?
If twenty thousand deaths were what you saw;
If many million deaths were in your hands;
Your lying tongue exceeds those numbers, so
I say "You're lying" with a voice as candid
As when I pray to the gods.

SICINIUS   You heard that, people?

ALL PLEBEIANS   To the rock, to the Tarpeian rock!

SICINIUS   Quiet!
We do not need to make more accusations.

What you have seen him do and heard him say –
Beating your officers, cursing yourselves,
Opposing laws by force and here defying
Those whose authority it is to try him.
Alone this criminal and capital offence
Deserves the punishment of death.

BRUTUS   But since
He's served the city well …

CORIOLANUS   What would you know
Of service?

BRUTUS   I speak of what I know.

CORIOLANUS You?

MENENIUS   Is this the promise that you made your mother?

COMINIUS   Please, understand …

CORIOLANUS   That's all I need to know.
Let them pronounce what sentence they may choose:
Death from the Tarpeian rock, life banishment,
Imprisonment with just one grain a day,
I wouldn't buy their mercy if it cost me
A single word, nor check my inclinations
For anything they have, nor say "Good day"
To get it.

SICINIUS   Since he has, from time to time,
Inveighed with all his might against the people,
Seeking to rob them of their power, and even
Belaboured violently those men whose duty
It is to serve the processes of justice,
In the people's name with the authority
Of us, the tribunes, hereby we declare
That he be banished forthwith from the city,
Never to enter Roman gates again,
In peril of the greater punishment
Of being thrown from the Tarpeian Rock.
In the people's name I say it shall be so.

ALL PLEBEIANS   It shall be so! It shall be so! Send him away!
He's banished, and it shall be so!

COMINIUS   Just hear me, senators and people!

SICINIUS   He's sentenced. No more hearing.

COMINIUS   Let me speak.
I have been consul, and can show for Rome
My enemy's marks upon me. I do love
My country's good with a respect more tender

	More holy and profound than my own life,
	My dear wife's honour, and the very lives
	Of all my children. So I wish to say ...
SICINIUS	We know your drift. What do you have to say?
BRUTUS	There's no more to be said, for he is banished
	As enemy of the people and his country.
	It shall be so.
ALL PLEBEIANS	It shall be so! It shall be so!
CORIOLANUS	You common pack of dogs, whose breath I hate
	Like stinking rotten marshes, whose affection
	I prize as much as human carcasses
	Left long unburied to pollute the air.
	I banish you! While you stay here with all
	Your weaknesses, scared by the slightest rumour,
	Your enemies, just nodding with their plumes,
	Will drive you to despair. Retain the power
	To banish those who could defend you, till
	At length your ignorance, which only learns
	From harsh experience, in order to
	Preserve only yourselves – your own worst enemy –
	Until your ignorance delivers you,
	Humiliated captives, to some nation
	That defeats you without fighting. In contempt
	Of you and of the city, thus I turn my back.
	There is a world elsewhere.

Exeunt Coriolanus, Cominius and Senators.
The people shout and throw up their caps.

AEDILE	The people's enemy has gone. He's gone!
ALL PLEBEIANS	Our enemy is banished. He has gone. Hooray!
SICINIUS	Escort him to the gates and follow him
	With all the insults you can find, as once
	He followed you. Give him all the discomfort
	He has deserved. We need an escort to
	Attend us through the city.
ALL PLEBEIANS	Come on, let's see him out of the gates! Come on!
	The gods preserve our noble tribunes! Come!

Exeunt

Act IV Scene 1

Enter Coriolanus, Volumnia, Virgilia, Menenius,
Cominius, with the young nobility of Rome.

CORIOLANUS Come, no more tears. A brief farewell. The beast
With many heads butts me away. Now, mother,
Where is your former courage? You once said
Extreme conditions test our spirits well,
That ordinary suffering is borne
By ordinary people; when the sea
Is calm, all boats alike float easily.
When fortune strikes her hardest blows,
It takes a gentleman's ability
To bear her wounds. You used to load me up
With precepts that would make the heart withstand
Whatever stood before it.

VIRGILIA   O heavens, O heavens!

CORIOLANUS   Please, I pray you, woman ...

VOLUMNIA   May pestilence strike down all occupations
And trades in Rome!

CORIOLANUS   What, what!
I will be loved when I am missed. Now, mother,
Revive that spirit when you used to say,
If you had been the wife of Hercules,
Six of his labours you'd have done and saved
Your husband so much sweat. Cominius,
Don't droop! Goodbye. Farewell, my wife, my mother,
I will do well. You, old and true Menenius,
Your tears are saltier than those you shed
In youth, and harmful to your eyes. And you,
My former general, I have seen your strength,
For you have witnessed many a gruesome sight.
Tell these sad women that there's little sense
In weeping in the face of the inevitable,
One might as well try laughter. You know, mother,
The risks I took were comforting for you.
Do not discount my promise: though I go
Alone, more feared and talked about than seen,
As if I were a dragon in his lair,
Your son will either shine in his achievements
Or fall a victim of deceit and falsehood.

VOLUMNIA   My son, where will you go? Take good Cominius,

                    At least to start with. And pursue some course
                    That's not random exposure to whatever
                    Appears before you in your path.
VIRGILIA   Ye gods!
COMINIUS   I'll come with you a month, and help you choose
                    Places to rest where you'll have news of us
                    And we of you. So if a time should come
                    When you are summoned back, we will not need
                    To search the whole wide world for you, and lose
                    An opportunity for you which might
                    Go cold if you were absent.
CORIOLANUS   No! Goodbye!
                    You've seen the passing of too many years,
                    Too often in the thick of war, to rove with one
                    Still in his prime. Just take me to the gate.
                    Come, my dear wife, my dearest mother, and
                    My friends from the nobility. As I go,
                    Bid me farewell and smile. So please now, come.
                    While I remain above the ground you will
                    Hear from me sometimes, never anything
                    That jars with what I was.
MENENIUS   That's good to hear,
                    And worthy of you. Come now, let's not weep.
                    If I could shake off even seven years
                    From these old arms and legs, great heavens,
                    I'd join you every step.
CORIOLANUS Give me your hand. There.

                            Exeunt.

Act IV Scene 2

Enter the two Tribunes Sicinius and Brutus, with the Aedile.

SICINIUS   Instruct them to go home. He's gone, and we are done.
                    The nobility who sided with him, as we saw,
                    Are deeply vexed.
BRUTUS   Now we have shown our power,
                    Let's be more humble after the event
                    Than when it was all happening.
SICINIUS   Send them home.
                    Say their great enemy is gone; they can
                    Enjoy their former strength.

BRUTUS	And then dismiss them.
	[*Exit Aedile*] Here comes his mother.

Enter Volumnia, Virgilia and Menenius.

SICINIUS	Let's not meet her.
BRUTUS	Why?
SICINIUS	They say she's mad.
BRUTUS	They've seen us. Keep on your way.
VOLUMNIA	Well met indeed! May all the plagues of heaven
	Repay your love!
MENENIUS	Be quiet, please! Less noise!
VOLUMNIA	If I could weep more silently, you'd still
	Hear plenty. You're not going, are you?
VIRGILIA	You must stay too. I wish I had the power
	To say that to my husband.
SICINIUS	Are you human?
VOLUMNIA	Yes, fool. Should I feel shamed? Note this, you fool:
	My father, was he not a man? Were you
	Clever enough to banish him that struck
	More blows for Rome than you have uttered words?
SICINIUS	O blessed heavens!
VOLUMNIA	More noble blows than all your words of wisdom,
	And for Rome's good. I'll tell you – don't go yet.
	And you stay too. I wish my son were now
	In the Arabian desert, facing all your hordes,
	His good sword in his hand.
SICINIUS	What then?
VIRGILIA	What then!
	He'd make an end of your posterity!
VOLUMNIA	Including bastards!
	Good man! The wounds he bears for Rome!
MENENIUS	Come, come, calm down.
SICINIUS	I wish he had continued in the service
	Of Rome as he began, and not untied
	The noble knot he made.
BRUTUS	I wish he had.
VOLUMNIA	"I wish he had"! 'Twas you who roused the rabble,
	You pair of cats can judge his worth as well
	As I can understand the mysteries
	Which heaven does not want the earth to know.
BRUTUS	Please, let's go.
VOLUMNIA	Indeed, sir, you should go.

                    You've done a brave deed. Now before you go,
                    Hear this: by the degree the Capitol
                    Exceeds in height the meanest house in Rome,
                    By so much does my son, this lady's husband here,
                    Whom you have banished, far exceed you all.

BRUTUS   Well, well, we'll leave you.
SICINIUS   Why should we stay here
                    Just to be baited by a crazy woman?

                          Exeunt Tribunes.

VOLUMNIA   You have my prayers.
                    I wish the gods had nothing else to do
                    But act upon my curses. Once a day,
                    If I could meet them, it would clear my heart
                    Of all its woes.

MENENIUS   You spoke directly to them,
                    And you had cause, I say. We dine together?

VOLUMNIA   Anger's my meat. I feed upon myself,
                    And so I'll starve from eating.
                    [*To Virgilia*]   Come, let's go.
                    Stop whining faintly and lament as I do,
                    In anger, as the goddess Juno does. Come, come.

                              Exeunt.

MENENIUS   Fie, fie, fie!

                            Exit.

Act IV Scene 3

Enter a Roman and a Volscian.

ROMAN   I know you well, sir, and you know me. Your name, I think,
    is Adrian.

VOLSCIAN   That is so, sir. In truth I have forgotten you.

ROMAN   I am a Roman, and I am working, like you, against them. Do
    you know who I am now?

VOLSCIAN   Nicanor, is it?

ROMAN   The same, sir.

VOLSCIAN   You had more beard when I last saw you, but your
    speech confirms who you are. What's the news in Rome? I have
    instructions from the Volscian state to look for you there. You've
    saved me a good day's journey.

ROMAN There's been an unusual insurrection in Rome: the people against the senators, patricians and nobles.

VOLSCIAN Has been? Is it over? Our leaders don't think so. They are preparing seriously for war and had hoped to find them in full conflict.

ROMAN The main blaze of it is over, but a small thing would ignite it again, for the nobles have taken the banishment of that worthy Coriolanus so much to heart that they are keenly ready to take power back from the people and get rid of their tribunes for ever. It's simmering, I tell you, ready to break out violently at any moment.

VOLSCIAN Coriolanus banished?

ROMAN Banished, yes.

VOLSCIAN You will be very welcome with this news, Nicanor.

ROMAN The present moment would help the Volscians. I've heard it said that the best time to corrupt a man's wife is when she's fallen out with her husband. Your noble Tullus Aufidius will do well in this war, his great opponent Coriolanus no longer being wanted by his country.

VOLSCIAN He's bound to. I'm most fortunate to have met you by accident. You've answered my questions, and I'll happily accompany you home.

ROMAN Between now and supper I'll tell you some remarkable things about Rome, all tending to the advantage of their adversaries. Did you say you have an army ready?

VOLSCIAN A most splendid one: the centurions and their troops individually enrolled, already on the payroll, and ready to move at an hour's notice.

ROMAN I'm happy to hear about their readiness and am the one, I believe, that will bring about immediate action. So, sir, heartily well met, a pleasure to have your company.

VOLSCIAN That is what I was going to say, sir. I have the most cause to be glad of yours.

ROMAN Well, let's go together.

Exeunt.

Act IV Scene 4

Enter Coriolanus in shabby clothes, disguised and muffled.

CORIOLANUS A pleasing city is this Antium. City,
'Tis I that made your widows. Many an heir
Of these fine buildings in the heat of battle
Have I heard groan and fall. Don't recognise me,
Or widows armed with spikes and boys with stones
May kill me on the spot.

Enter a Citizen.

Good day, sir.
CITIZEN   And to you.
CORIOLANUS   Direct me, if you'd be so kind,
To where the great Aufidius lives. Is he
In Antium?
CITIZEN   He is, and here tonight
He entertains the nobles of the state.
CORIOLANUS Which is his house, please tell me.
CITIZEN   This one here.
CORIOLANUS Thankyou, sir, and goodbye.

Exit Citizen.

O world, what fickle turns! The closest friends,
Who seem to share one heart within two breasts,
Whose hours, whose beds, whose meals and exercise
Are always shared, inseparable as twins,
Can turn within an hour, because some trifle
Becomes a cause of argument, into
The bitterest of enemies. Then too
The fiercest foes, whose passions and whose plots
For doing harm keep them awake at night,
Some little chance, something not worth an egg,
Can make them dearest friends and bring their lives
Together. So with me. I hate my birthplace,
And focus all my love on this, an enemy town.
I'll enter. If he kills me, that's fair justice.
But if he lets me, then I'll serve his country.

Exit.

Act IV Scene 5

Music plays. Enter a servant.

FIRST SERVANT Wine, wine, wine! What's the matter with the service? I think the others are asleep.   *Exit.*

Enter another servant.

SECOND SERVANT Where's Cotus? My master needs him. Cotus!
                                                                      Exit.

Enter Coriolanus.

CORIOLANUS A splendid house. The feast smells good, but I cannot pass as a guest.

Enter the first servant.

FIRST SERVANT What do you want, friend? Where're you from? This isn't your kind of place. Please leave.   *Exit.*

CORIOLANUS I should expect no better entertainment, as conqueror of Corioli.

Enter second servant.

SECOND SERVANT Where are you from, sir? Has the porter got eyes in his head, if he lets in people like you? Please get out.

CORIOLANUS Get off me!

SECOND SERVANT You get off me!

CORIOLANUS You're being troublesome.

SECOND SERVANT You're going to be insolent? I'll have someone talk to you at once.

Enter third servant, the first meets him.

THIRD SERVANT Who's this fellow?

FIRST SERVANT The strangest type I've ever seen. I can't get him out of the house. Would you call the master?

THIRD SERVANT What are you doing here, fellow? Please keep away from this house.

CORIOLANUS Let me stay here. I will cause no trouble.

THIRD SERVANT What's your rank?

CORIOLANUS A gentleman.

THIRD SERVANT An amazingly poor one.

CORIOLANUS True, that's what I am.

THIRD SERVANT Please, poor gentleman, find some other place to put yourself. This is no place for you. Please leave, come on.

CORIOLANUS Attend to your duties, and feed yourself on scraps.
                                                          Pushes him away.

THIRD SERVANT   What, you refuse? Go and tell the master what a
    strange guest he has here.
SECOND SERVANT   I'll go.
THIRD SERVANT   Where do you live?
CORIOLANUS   Beneath the stars.
THIRD SERVANT   Beneath the stars?
CORIOLANUS   Yes.
THIRD SERVANT   Where's that?
CORIOLANUS   In the city of kites and crows.
THIRD SERVANT   In the city of kites and crows? What an idiot! So
    you live with jackdaws too?
CORIOLANUS   No, I don't work for your master.
THIRD SERVANT   What d'you mean? What's your connection with
    my master?
CORIOLANUS   It's more like honest work than a connection with
    your mistress. You talk nothing but nonsense. Go and serve the
    dishes. Get off!

> *Beats him away. Exit third servant.*
> *Enter Aufidius with the second servant.*

AUFIDIUS   Where is this fellow?
SECOND SERVANT   Here, sir. I'd have beaten him like a dog but was
    afraid I'd disturb the lords in there.
AUFIDIUS   Where do you come from? What do you want? Your
    name? Why don't you answer? Speak, man! What's your name?
CORIOLANUS If, Tullus, you don't recognise me yet,
             And do not take me for the man I am,
             Then I must name myself.
AUFIDIUS   What is your name?
CORIOLANUS A name unmusical to Volscian ears
             And harsh in sound to yours.
AUFIDIUS   Say, what's your name?
             You have a rough appearance, yet your face
             Bespeaks authority. Your rigging's torn,
             But sturdy is the vessel. What's your name?
CORIOLANUS Prepare a furrowed brow ... You know me yet?
AUFIDIUS   I do not know you. What's your name?
CORIOLANUS My name is Caius Martius, who has done
             To you particularly and all Volscians
             Great harm and mischief; witness my surname,
             Coriolanus. Service to my country,
             The fearful dangers, and the drops of blood

Shed for my thankless Rome have been repaid
Just with a surname, which may well remind you
Of all the malice and ill-feeling you
Should surely bear toward me. Only the name
Remains. The envious cruelty of the people,
Permitted by our wicked nobles, who
Have all forsaken me, devoured the rest
And seen to it that by the votes of slaves
They drove me out of Rome. Now this extremity
Has brought me to your door; not out of hope –
Don't get me wrong – of holding on to life;
If I feared death, of all men in the world
I would have avoided you. No, out of spite;
I stand before you here to free myself
From those who banished me. So if you have
A heart in you that cares, and if you seek
To be avenged for all the private wrongs
You've suffered and the shame laid on your country,
Then take immediate advantage of
My misery. Direct it so that all
My longing for revenge will serve your cause.
For I will fight against my cankered country
With all the bitterness of hell. But if
You dare not take this up, and if you're tired
Of taking chances, then, I will admit
I'm weary of this life, and would present
My throat to you and to your former malice,
Which not to cut would make you seem a fool
Since I have always followed you with hate,
Drawn pools of blood out of your country's breast,
And would disgrace you if I lived, unless
It were to serve you somehow.

AUFIDIUS   O Martius, Martius!
Each word you said uprooted from my heart
Some trace of ancient hatred. If Jupiter
Himself appeared above in godlike form
And said "It's true!", I'd no more take his word
Than yours, my noble Martius. Let me put
My arms around that body whose great strength
Has split at least a hundred of my spears
And scattered splinters to the moon. I hold
This anvil where my sword so often struck,

And claim with all the fervour that I can
A love equal to yours, as I once did
Contend with all my ambitious strength
Against your valour. Let me first assure you,
I loved the maid I married; no man ever
Displayed a truer heart. But seeing you,
You noble soul, excites my passion more
Than when I saw my wedded bride set foot
Across my threshold. You, great son of Mars,
I'll tell you that we have an army ready.
I'd planned to rip your buckler from your arm
Or lose my own in trying. You have won
In several dozen fights, and I have dreamt
Each night of our encounters, sometimes seeing
Us both down on the ground in desperate combat,
Unbuckling helmets, punching in the throat –
And then I wake half dead. My worthy Martius,
If we had no dispute with Rome except
Your banishment, we'd still conscript all men
From twelve to seventy years of age
And stuff the fight into the bowels of Rome,
Ungrateful city, swarming like a flood.
Come in with me and shake the friendly hands
Of senators who are about to leave.
Our target was the outlying territories,
Not Rome itself.

CORIOLANUS   The gods above have blessed me!
AUFIDIUS   And so, my excellent friend, if you desire
To have your own revenge, take half the troops
Assigned to me and draw up such a plan
As your experience and knowledge of
The strengths and weaknesses of Rome suggests.
Advise us whether to attack the gates
Or hound them in remoter parts, to scare them
Before the final blow. But come in, first,
Let me present you to the worthy men
Who have the final say. A thousand welcomes!
And more a friend than you were ever foe!
And, Martius, that was much. Your hand. Most welcome!

Exeunt.

FIRST SERVANT What a strange turn of events!

SECOND SERVANT I tell you, I was ready to hit him with a cudgel, yet I had a feeling his clothes gave the wrong idea of who he was.

FIRST SERVANT What an arm he has! He spun me over with his finger and thumb as if I were a top.

SECOND SERVANT No, I knew from his face there was something about him. He had the kind of face, I thought, that ... I don't know how to put it.

FIRST SERVANT He did. He looked as if ... Hang me, but I thought there was more to him than I thought.

SECOND SERVANT So did I, I swear. He's simply the most unusual man in the world.

FIRST SERVANT I think so too. But a finer soldier than him, you know one.

SECOND SERVANT Who, my master?

FIRST SERVANT No, that's not what I mean.

SECOND SERVANT Worth six of him.

FIRST SERVANT No, no way. But I take him to be the finer soldier.

SECOND SERVANT Really, I don't know. You can't tell how to say that. For defending our town, our general is excellent.

FIRST SERVANT And in attack too.

Enter third servant.

THIRD SERVANT Hey, slaves, I've got news. News, you clowns!

FIRST and SECOND SERVANTS What, what's that? Tell us!

THIRD SERVANT I wouldn't be a Roman for anything. I'd rather be a condemned prisoner.

FIRST and SECOND SERVANTS Why?

THIRD SERVANT The guy who used to thwack our general's here, Caius Martius.

FIRST SERVANT Why do you say "thwack our general"?

THIRD SERVANT I don't say "thwack our general", but he was always a fair match for him.

SECOND SERVANT Come on, we're friends, we work together. He was always too much for him. I've heard him say so himself.

FIRST SERVANT He was too much for him face to face. To tell the truth, before Corioli he scotched him and notched him like a piece of grilled fish.

SECOND SERVANT If he'd been a cannibal, he'd have broiled and eaten him too.

FIRST SERVANT What other news is there?

THIRD SERVANT   They made so much of him in there as if he were
son and heir to Mars; put at the top end of the table; no questions
asked by any of the senators without baring their heads to him;
our general behaves like a mistress to him, touches his hand as
if it were holy and looks at him admiringly in conversation. But
the main news is, our general is cut right down to half of what he
was yesterday. The other man has half, at the desire and with the
approval of the whole table. He'll go, he says, and drag the porter
at the gates of Rome by the ears. He'll mow them all down in front
of him and leave ruins in his path.

SECOND SERVANT   And he's the one to do it more than anyone I can
think of.

THIRD SERVANT   Do it? He'll do it all right, I tell you, he's got as
many friends as enemies, and these friends, don't you know, dare
not – mark my word – show themselves to be, let's say, his friends
while he's in directitude.

FIRST SERVANT   Directitude? What's that?

THIRD SERVANT   But when they see him all juiced up and in a hot
temper, they'll scamper out of their burrow like rabbits after rain,
and all join the party.

FIRST SERVANT   When does this begin?

THIRD SERVANT   Tomorrow, today, now. You'll hear the drumrolls
this afternoon. It's like a part of their feast, to be performed before
they wipe their lips.

SECOND SERVANT   Then we'll have the world in upheaval again.
This peace is just to let iron rust, for tailors to do well and ballad-
singers to breed.

FIRST SERVANT   Let's have war, say I. It's better than peace the way
day's better than night. It's lively, noisy, and smells strong. Peace
is nothing but apoplexy, lethargy; dull, deaf, sleepy, insensible; it
produces more bastard children than men destroyed by war.

SECOND SERVANT   True. If wars can be said in a way to be a ravisher,
it cannot be denied that peace is a great maker of cuckolds.

FIRST SERVANT   Ay, and it makes men hate one another.

THIRD SERVANT   Reason: because then they need one another less.
It's war, for my money. I hope to see Romans as cheap as Volscians.
They're getting up, they're getting up.

FIRST and THIRD SERVANTS   In we go! In!

Exeunt.

Act IV Scene 6

Enter the two Tribunes, Sicinius and Brutus.

SICINIUS We have no news of him, we need not fear him.
The state is cured of him; we have now peace
And quiet among the people, who before
Were in a tumult. Here we make his friends
Blush that the world goes well, for though they suffered
And were disturbed by it, they'd rather see
Rebellious crowds in busy streets than watch
Our tradesmen singing in their shops and going
About their business quietly.

Enter Menenius.

BRUTUS We did it in good time. Is this Menenius?
SICINIUS It is, it is. He has become most kind of late.
Hail, sir!
MENENIUS Hail to you both.
SICINIUS Your Coriolanus is not much missed
But by his friends. The commonwealth's secure,
And would be even if he were still here.
MENENIUS All's well, but could have been much better if
He'd compromised.
SICINIUS   Where is he, do you know?
MENENIUS No, I've heard nothing.
His mother and his wife have no news from him.

Enter three or four citizens.

ALL CITIZENS The gods preserve you both!
SICINIUS   Good evening, neighbours.
BRUTUS Good evening to you all, good evening, neighbours.
FIRST CITIZEN Our wives, our children, we ourselves, resolve
To pray for both of you.
SICINIUS   May you live and thrive.
BRUTUS Goodbye, kind neighbours.
We wish Coriolanus loved you as we did.
ALL CITIZENS The gods keep you!
BOTH TRIBUNES Farewell, goodbye.

Exeunt Citizens.

SICINIUS This is a happier and more seemly time
Than when these fellows ran along the streets
Causing confusion.
BRUTUS   Caius Martius was

A meritorious officer in the war,
But insolent, and full of pride, ambitious,
Too egoistical for words.

SICINIUS   Desiring
The throne all for himself.

MENENIUS   I disagree.

SICINIUS   If he had ruled as consul, we would all
By now be in a state of lamentation.

BRUTUS   The gods did well to intervene, and Rome
Is safe and peaceable without him.

Enter an Aedile.

AEDILE   Tribunes,
There is a slave we're holding behind bars
Who says the Volscians are on the march
In two divisions, both in Roman territory.
They press the war with brutal devastation,
Destroying all they find.

MENENIUS   It is Aufidius
Who, hearing about Martius's banishment,
Emerges bravely and thrusts out his horns
Which stayed within his shell when Martius stood
For Rome, and did not dare peep out.

SICINIUS   Come, what news is there of Martius?

BRUTUS   Have that informer whipped. The Volscians
Would surely never dare to break with us.

MENENIUS   What, never? We know well they might.
I'll give you three examples that have happened
In my lifetime. But reason with this fellow
Before you punish him: where did he hear it?
Be careful, he's the source of information;
Don't beat the messenger who brings a warning
Of what we dread the most.

SICINIUS   Don't tell me.
I know this cannot be.

BRUTUS   Not possible.

Enter a Messenger.

MESSENGER   The nobles are all heading for the senate house
In great alarm. Some news has come that fills
Them with anxiety.

SICINIUS   It is this slave.
Go, have him whipped in public, rumour-monger

That he is.

MESSENGER But, sir, the slave's report
Has been confirmed, and further information,
Worse still, has been delivered.

SICINIUS What? Worse still?

MESSENGER It's being said by many people, though
How probable it is I cannot say,
That Martius and Aufidius together
Are leading a great army against Rome.
They're bent on vengeance on a scale
As wide as that between the youngest
And the oldest thing.

SICINIUS This is most likely!

BRUTUS Just put about because the weaker sort
May wish good Martius home again.

SICINIUS The sheer deceit of it!

MENENIUS This is unlikely.
He and Aufidius can no more meet
In reconciliation than the most
Extreme contrarities.

Enter a second messenger.

SECOND MESSENGER You are to go attend the senate.
A fearful army, led by Caius Martius,
In coalition with Aufidius,
Is loose within our territories, and
Has burnt and battled its way forward
Leaving devastation.

Enter Cominius.

COMINIUS Oh, you have done good work!

MENENIUS What news? What news?

COMINIUS You've caused your daughters to be ravished, and
The city's roofs to fall as molten lead.
Before your very eyes your wives dishonoured ...

MENENIUS What's the news? What's the news?

COMINIUS Your temples burned down to the ground,
The voting rights for which you fought and argued
Reduced to nothing.

MENENIUS Please tell the news!
[*To the Tribunes*]
I fear your work is all too thorough. Please!
The news! If Martius joins the Volscians ...

COMINIUS   If?
                    He is their god. He leads them like a thing
                    Made by some other deity than Nature,
                    That shapes man better, and they follow him
                    Against us brats with no less confidence
                    Than boys pursuing butterflies in summer
                    Or butchers killing flies.
MENENIUS   Your work is all too good.
                    You and your tradesmen, you that placed so much
                    Importance on the voice of labour and
                    The breath of garlic-eaters!
COMINIUS   He'll shake your Rome about your ears!
MENENIUS   Like Hercules with apples from a tree.
                    Your work is all too thorough.
BRUTUS   But is this true, sir?
COMINIUS   Yes, and you'll be old
                    Before you find I'm wrong. All the regions
                    Are eagerly rebelling. Those who don't
                    Are mocked for knowing nothing and then die,
                    Persistent fools. And who can blame him?
                    Your enemies and his find something in him.
MENENIUS   We're done for, all of us, unless that man
                    Is merciful.
COMINIUS   And who will ask for mercy?
                    The tribunes cannot, out of shame; the people
                    Deserve such pity of him as the wolf
                    Does of the shepherd. For his best friends, if they
                    Should say "Be good to Rome", they would be just
                    Like those that had deserved his hate, and thus
                    Appear no different from his enemies.
MENENIUS   It's true.
                    If he were near my house bearing a torch
                    With which to burn it, I would not have face
                    To say "Please, don't!" Your work was all too thorough.
                    You and your crafts, you've crafted well!
COMINIUS   You've brought
                    A terror to the city such as never
                    Left everyone so helpless.
BOTH TRIBUNES   Don't say we
                    Have brought it on.
MENENIUS   So was it us? How so?
                    We loved him, but like animals and cowards

> We gave in to your gangs that shooed him
> Out of the city.

COMINIUS   But I fear they'll shout
> For mercy when he comes. Tullus Aufidius,
> Alone of men second in fame to him,
> Obeys his orders just as if he were
> His officer. The only policy
> That we can offer in defence of Rome
> Is desperation.

Enter a troop of citizens.

MENENIUS   Here come the gangs.
> And is Aufidius with him? It was you
> Who made the air unwholesome when you threw
> Your stinking greasy caps rejoicing in
> Coriolanus's exile. Now he's coming,
> And there's no hair on any soldier's head
> That won't become a whip. For every head
> On every fool that threw his cap up then
> Will tumble down in payment for your votes.
> If he could burn us to a cindery mass,
> We have deserved it.

ALL CITIZENS   It's dreadful news we hear.

FIRST CITIZEN   For my own part,
> When I said banish him, I had my doubts.

SECOND CITIZEN   And so did I.

THIRD CITIZEN   And so did I, and to tell the truth, so did very many
of us. What we did, we did for the best, and though we willingly
agreed to his banishment, it was against our will.

COMINIUS   You're a fine bunch, you voters.

MENENIUS   You've done good work, you and your pack of hounds.
To the Capitol?

COMINIUS   Yes, what else?

Exeunt Menenius and Cominius.

SICINIUS   Go, friends, and go back home. Don't be dismayed.
> These people are a faction that would be glad
> If what they seem to fear proves true. Go home
> And show no sign of fear.

FIRST CITIZEN   The gods be good to us! Come, fellows, let's go home.
I always said we were in the wrong when we banished him.

SECOND CITIZEN   So did we all. But come on now, let's go home.

Exeunt citizens.

BRUTUS   I do not like this news.
SICINIUS   Neither do I.
BRUTUS   Off to the Capitol. I'd give a half
              Of what I have for this to be a lie.
SICINIUS   Come, let's go.

Exeunt.

Act IV Scene 7

Enter Aufidius with his Lieutenant.

AUFIDIUS   Are they still rushing off to join the Roman?
LIEUTENANT I do not know what witchcraft's in him, but
              Your soldiers use him as the grace before
              They eat, they talk about him during meals,
              And then he's thanked after the meal ends.
              Your standing is eclipsed by all this favour,
              Your own men even show it.
AUFIDIUS   There's not much
              That I can do for that, except with measures
              That harm our present plan. He now behaves
              With greater pride than what I had expected
              When we embraced the first time, even with me.
              In this respect his nature never changes,
              I must forgive what cannot be emended.
LIEUTENANT As far as you're concerned, I wish you had
              Not shared the generalship with him, but either
              Had taken the responsibility
              Yourself, sir, or else left it all to him.
AUFIDIUS   I understand you well, and you should know
              That when the final reckoning is done,
              He has no inkling of what I might say
              Against him. For although it seems to him –
              And is apparent to the general view –
              That he is taking his fair share of everything,
              And shows concern for the whole Volscian state,
              That he fights furiously and always wins
              Whenever he takes up his sword, but still
              He has not yet acknowledged what he owes,
              And this default will either break his neck
              Or hazard mine when settling our accounts.
LIEUTENANT Sir, tell me, do you think he'll carry Rome?

AUFIDIUS   All cities yield to him before he ever
             Begins a siege, and the nobility
             Of Rome are on his side. The senators,
             Patricians too, adore him. Tribunes, they
             Aren't soldiers, and their people will repeal
             His banishment as rashly as they first
             Imposed it. He will be to Rome just like
             An osprey to a fish, devouring it
             By sovereignty of nature. First he was
             A noble servant to them, but he could not
             Accept his honours equably. Whether pride,
             Corrupting every winner, as it does,
             Or lack of judgment in his failure to
             Exploit his many opportunities;
             Or nature, which compelled him to
             Be one thing, only one, and not adapting
             From warfare to affairs of state, in peace
             The same commanding figure as in war,
             The same austere demeanour serving both –
             Whichever of these factors is correct –
             And he shows traces of them all, if not
             In overflowing measure, that I grant –
             They caused him to be feared, then hated, and
             Then banished. By his merit he can stifle
             All talk of character defect. Our virtues
             Are subject to the judgment of the time.
             And power, which of itself is praiseworthy,
             Is never so completely overthrown
             As when it celebrates itself.
             One fire drives out one fire, one nail, one nail.
             In face of strength, another strength will fail.
             Beware, Caius, your destiny's decline:
             When Rome is yours, then shortly you are mine.

                     Exeunt.

Act V Scene 1

Enter Menenius, Cominius, Sicinius, Brutus, with others.

MENENIUS   No, I'll not go. You heard Cominius speak,
            Cominius who was once his general and
            Was very close to him. He called me father,
            But what of that? Go, you who banished him;
            A mile before you reach his tent, kneel down
            And beg for mercy. No, if he disdained
            To hear Cominius, then I'll stay at home.

COMINIUS   Pretended not to know me!

MENENIUS   Did you hear?

COMINIUS   Yet once he used to call me by my name.
            I spoke of our once close acquaintance
            And of blood we'd shed together. "Coriolanus"
            He would not answer to. All names were out.
            He was a kind of nothing, and insisted
            He had no name until he forged a new one
            By burning Rome.

MENENIUS   Your work was all too thorough!
            A pair of tribunes who have ruined Rome
            And thus made charcoal cheap! A noble feat!

COMINIUS   Then I reminded him of royal pardons,
            Especially admired when not expected.
            He answered that it was a poor petition
            To put to one whom they had punished.

MENENIUS   Very well. Could he say less?

COMINIUS   I ventured to awaken his concern
            For friends of his. His answer to me was
            He had no patience to select them from
            A pile of stinking, dusty chaff. He said
            It would be folly just to leave a grain or two
            Unburnt, and still endure the smell.

MENENIUS   A grain or two! I'm one of those myself.
            His mother, wife and child, and this brave fellow,
            We're all these grains.
            [*To the Tribunes*]   You are the smelly chaff,
            You smell like hell, and we must burn for you.

SICINIUS   Come now, be patient. Turn away from helping
            When help was never so urgent, if you wish,
            But don't upbraid us for our troubles. Sure,
            If you would plead your country's cause, your tongue

	Might make our countryman relent, more than
	Such troops as we can scrape together.
MENENIUS	Not I. I won't go meddling.
SICINIUS	Go, see him!
MENENIUS	What could I do?
BRUTUS	Just see if your affection
	For Rome can stir him even a little bit.
MENENIUS	Supposing Martius turns me back, just like
	The way Cominius returned, unheard,
	What then? I'd simply be a wretched friend,
	Grief-stricken at his meanness, wouldn't I?
SICINIUS	Your good intentions would deserve the thanks
	Of Rome for making the attempt.
MENENIUS	I'll try.

I think he'll hear me. Yet I'm much disturbed
That he could bite his lip at good Cominius.
That wasn't well thought out. He hadn't dined.
When veins are left unfed, our blood runs cold,
We're out of sorts all morning, quite unable
To give or to forgive. But when we've stuffed
Those tubes and those conveyances of blood
With wine and food, our souls are more benign
Than when we're fasting like a priest. I'll watch him
Till he has eaten all he needs, and then
I'll set upon him.

BRUTUS	You know the clever route to earn his kindness
	And cannot lose your way.
MENENIUS	I'll do my best,
	Whatever comes of it. It won't be long
	Before I have success or failure to report. *Exit.*
COMINIUS	He'll never hear him.
SICINIUS	No?
COMINIUS	I tell you, he's enthroned in gold, his eye

Flame-red as if intent on burning Rome.
His grievance keeps compassion out of sight.
I knelt before him; very faintly "Rise",
He said, and silently dismissed me, thus.
What he would do and what he would not do
He wrote down for me, sealed with an oath,
And sent it after me. All hope is lost
Unless his noble mother and his wife,
Who, as I hear, mean to solicit him

               For mercy for his country. Therefore, let's go
               And haste them on their way with our support.

                              Exeunt.

                         Act V Scene 2

                 Enter Menenius to the Watch on guard.

FIRST WATCH   Stay there. Where are you from?
SECOND WATCH   Stand! Go back!
MENENIUS   You do your duty well. But by your leave
               I am an officer of state and come
               To speak with Coriolanus.
FIRST WATCH   Where from?
MENENIUS   From Rome.
FIRST WATCH   You may not pass. You must go back. Our general
               Will not hear anyone from there.
SECOND WATCH   You'll see your Rome engulfed in fire before
               You "speak with Coriolanus".
MENENIUS   My good friends,
               If you have heard your general talk of Rome
               And of his friends there, it's a certainty
               My name has reached your ears. It is Menenius.
FIRST WATCH   No doubt. Go back. The value of your name
               Is not accepted here.
MENENIUS   I tell you, fellow,
               Your general is my close friend. I have had
               The task of writing down his deeds, so men
               Can read about his unsurpassed acclaim,
               A glorified account in which I paint my friends,
               Of whom he's chief, with all the brag and bluster
               I can without departing from the truth.
               Like when in bowling on uneven ground
               The ball goes past the jack, sometimes I too
               Have overstated something in his praise
               And almost sealed a falsehood. Therefore, fellow,
               I must have leave to pass.
FIRST WATCH   Look here, if you've told as many lies on his behalf as
   the words you've uttered about yourself, you should not pass here,
   no, even if lying were as virtuous as the chaste life. So go back.
MENENIUS   Young man, please remember my name is Menenius,
   always active in support of your general.

SECOND WATCH   Despite you being his liar, as you say you are, I'm one who tells the truth in his name, and so must say you cannot pass. So go back.

MENENIUS   Has he had dinner, can you tell me? I do not wish to speak to him until after dinner.

FIRST WATCH   You're a Roman, aren't you?

MENENIUS   I'm the same as your general.

FIRST WATCH   Then you should hate Rome, as he does. When you pushed out of your gates the very man who defended them and gave your enemy your protector in violent popular ignorance, do you expect to confront his desire for revenge with the feeble groans of old women, the supplicating hands of your virginal daughters or with the decrepit pleas of such a decayed old dotard as you seem to be? Do you think you'll blow out the fire that your city's about to be consumed by with such weak breath as this? No, you're deceived. So go back to Rome and prepare for your execution. You are condemned. Our general has sworn not to include you for reprieve or pardon.

MENENIUS   Sir, if your captain knew I was here, he'd treat me with respect.

FIRST WATCH   My captain doesn't know you.

MENENIUS   I mean your general.

FIRST WATCH   My general doesn't care about you. Back, I say, go, or I'll spill half a pint of your blood. Back, that's as far as you get. Back!

MENENIUS   But ... but ...

Enter Coriolanus with Aufidius.

CORIOLANUS   What's the matter?

MENENIUS   Now, you fellow, I'll give a report for you. You'll see that I am well regarded. You'll see that no Jack Guardsman can keep me from my son Coriolanus by virtue of his office. Guess how I'll be entertained by him. If you don't reckon to be hanged or to undergo some death that keeps spectators longer and is crueller in suffering, watch now, and faint when you hear what'll happen to you. [*To Coriolanus*] May the glorious gods sit in hourly council on your personal prosperity and love you no less than your old father Menenius! O my son, my son! You are preparing fire against us. Look, here's water to quench it. I was disinclined to come to you, but once assured that no one but I could move you, I have been blown out of our gates with sighs, and beg you to pardon Rome and your imploring countrymen. May the good gods

assuage your wrath and turn the dregs of it on this wretch here,
the one who barred my access to you like a block.

CORIOLANUS Go away!

MENENIUS   What do you mean, go away?

CORIOLANUS Wife, mother, child, I do not recognise them.
My obligations are now owed to others.
Although revenge engages me alone,
A change of heart would come from Volscian breasts.
Ungrateful disregard of what I did for Rome
Has poisoned our past friendship, keeping pity
Away from thinking just how close it was.
So go. My ears resist your pleas more firmly
Than all the gates of Rome against my force.
Yet, since I loved you, take this letter, please.
I wrote it for your sake and would have sent it.
I will not hear another word, Menenius.
This man, Aufidius, was my good friend in Rome.
You see it for yourself.

AUFIDIUS   You keep your temper under firm control.

Exeunt Coriolanus and Aufidius.

FIRST WATCH   Now, sir, is your name Menenius?

SECOND WATCH   It's a powerful spell he casts, you can see. You
know your way back home.

FIRST WATCH   Did you hear how we were rebuked for holding your
highness back?

SECOND WATCH   What do you think I need to be nervous about?

MENENIUS   I care nothing for the world or for your general. For such
as you, I can't think there's anything worthwhile at all, you're so
insignificant. Whoever wants to die by himself does not fear it at
another's hand. Let your general do his worst. As for you, be what
you are, and for a long time, and may your misery increase with
your age! I say to you what was said to me. Be off!   *Exit.*

FIRST WATCH   A noble fellow, I give him that.

SECOND WATCH   The worthy fellow is our general. He's the rock; the
oak, not shaken by the wind.

Exeunt.

Act V Scene 3

Enter Coriolanus and Aufidius.

CORIOLANUS Tomorrow we'll set down our siege encampment
Before the walls of Rome. My partner in this action,
You must be sure to tell the Volscian lords
How open I have been with you.

AUFIDIUS   You have
Respected Volscian wishes, and refused
To hear the public pleas of Rome. In private
You have allowed no whisper, no, not even
With friends that thought they had your ear.

CORIOLANUS That last old man that I sent back to Rome,
His heart despondent, loved me like a father,
He even made a god of me. He was
Their last resort, and though I was unkind
To him, because our love was once so strong
I offered him the same terms as before.
These they refused and cannot now accept.
Because he thought he could do more, I made
That very slight concession. Fresh petitions
From state or private persons I will not
Now entertain. [*Shout within.*]

                              Ha? What was that, a shout?
Will I be tempted to infringe my vow
As soon as it is made? I will not.

Enter Virgilia, Volumnia, Valeria, Young Martius, with attendants.

My wife comes first, and then the honoured mould
In which this trunk of mine was shaped. She brings
Her grandchild by the hand. But no I say
To feeling, and to every bond of nature!
May it be virtuous not to yield an inch!
What can a curtsey do? Or those dove eyes
For which the gods themselves would tell a lie.
I melt, for I'm not made of stronger stuff
Than others. See, my mother bows, as if
Olympus begs a favour of a molehill.
And my young boy presents a pleading look
Which Nature urges me not to deny.
Let Volscians plough up Rome and harrow Italy,
I'll never be a goose enough to obey
What instinct says; I'll stick to my convictions

As though man were created by himself
And had no other kinsmen.

VIRGILIA   My lord and husband!

CORIOLANUS These eyes are not the same you knew in Rome.

VIRGILIA   Our altered aspect, broken down by grief,
Makes you think so.

CORIOLANUS   Like a poor actor
I face embarrassment when I forget my lines
And just go blank. My closest family,
Forgive my tyranny, but do not say
Because I ask you that, "forgive our Romans".
A kiss! As long as exile, and as sweet
As my revenge! The goddess Juno knows
I stole that kiss from you and ever since
Have prized it chastely. Heavens! I prate!
And the most noble mother in the world
I've not yet greeted. Sink, my knee, to earth!   *Kneels.*
Much more than that of ordinary sons,
My knee shows deep respect.

VOLUMNIA   Oh come, stand up!
'Tis I who kneel before you, on a cushion
No softer than a flint, and all the while
Defying proper courtesy in thinking
A child should treat his parent with respect.

CORIOLANUS What's this? You kneel? I stand corrected. See?
[*Raises her*]
Perhaps now pebbles on the beach will rise
And strike the stars; perhaps the mutinous winds
Will thrust proud cedars up against the sun,
Defying the impossible as though
What cannot be can be.

VOLUMNIA   You are my warrior.
I helped to train you. Do you know this lady?

CORIOLANUS The noble sister of Publicola,
Chaste as Diana, goddess of the moon,
As pure as icicles that form from snow
And dangle from her temple – dear Valeria!

VOLUMNIA   This boy's a briefer version of yourself,
Who will expand in time and may grow up
To be like you.

CORIOLANUS   May Mars, the god of soldiers,
With the consent of Jove, instil your mind

With noble thoughts, so you may prove to be
Untouched by shame and may stand out in war
A beacon to the world, resisting weakness
And standing up for those that seek your guidance.

VOLUMNIA Kneel now, then.

CORIOLANUS   That's my brave boy!

VOLUMNIA So he, your wife, this lady and myself
Are all here to entreat you.

CORIOLANUS   Please, enough.
Or if you plan to ask, remember this:
The things I've sworn never to grant should not
Be thought of as refusals. Do not ask
Me to dismiss my soldiers; I will not
Give in again to Roman working men.
Don't tell me my behaviour is unnatural.
Don't try to calm my anger or deflect
My vengeance with your cooler arguments.

VOLUMNIA Enough, enough!
You've said you will not grant us anything,
And we have nothing else to ask but what
You have already said you would deny us.
Yet we will ask, so if you still refuse,
Then your severity will be to blame.

CORIOLANUS Aufidius, and Volscians, listen; we'll
Not hear this in private. Your request?

VOLUMNIA If we were silent and said nothing, both
Our clothes and our appearance would betray
The life we've led since you were sent away.
Imagine how unfortunate we are,
More so than every living woman, since
The sight of you, which ought to make us weep
With joy and feel true comfort, draws out tears
Of sorrow and solicitude instead,
Making the mother, wife and child observe
The son, the husband and the father tear
His country's bowels out. And to poor us
Your enmity is fatal. You bar us
From praying to the gods, which is a comfort
That all but we enjoy. For how can we –
Alas – how can we pray to save our country,
To which we're bound, together with your victory,
To which we're also bound? We'll either lose

Our country, our dear nurse, or else yourself,
Our comfort equally. Calamity
Must either way befall, no matter who
We wish to win. For either you'll be led
In manacles along our streets, condemned
As a deserter, or you'll tread in triumph
On your country's ruins and win the palm
Of victory for having bravely shed
Your wife and children's blood. For myself, son,
I don't intend to wait for war to settle
The outcome. If I can't prevail upon you
To show nobility and grace to both
Instead of seeking the defeat of one, you will
No sooner march to overwhelm our country
Than you will tread upon your mother's womb,
That brought you to this world.

VIRGILIA   Mine too,
That gave you this young boy to keep your name
Alive for generations.

BOY   He won't tread
On me. I'll run away until I'm bigger,
And then I'll fight.

CORIOLANUS   It's better not to see
A woman or a child's face, or else
A woman's tenderness takes over. I
Have sat too long.

VOLUMNIA   You cannot leave us yet.
If our request was aimed at forcing you
To save the Romans and thereby destroy
The Volscians whom you serve, you might condemn us
As poisoning your honour. No, our suit
Is that you reconcile them, so together
The Volscians say "This mercy we have shown",
The Romans "This we have received", and each
On either side acclaim you loudly, crying
"Be blest for bringing us this peace!" Great son,
You know the aftermath of war's uncertain.
But this is certain: if you conquer Rome,
The benefit you gain therefrom will be
A name whose repetition will be dogged
With curses, and whose chronicle will be:
"The man was noble, but his final act

Was the obliteration of his country;
His name remains for evermore abhorred."
Speak to me, son! You do affect the fine
Particulars of honour, and dispense
Terror and mercy like the gods who blast
A thunderous gale with mighty winds
Yet load the lightning with a bolt that splits
Only an oak tree. Why do you not speak?
Is it a point of honour that a man
From the nobility should hold a grudge
For ever? Daughter, won't you say something?
Your weeping doesn't touch him. You speak, boy!
Perhaps your childish voice will move him more
Than argument. There's no man in the world
Who owes more to his mother, yet here he lets
Me prattle on as if they'd put me in the stocks
And wandered by unheeding. Never yet
In all your life did you show any courtesy
To your dear mother. She, poor hen, has clucked
Around you, wanting no more chicks, to fit
You for the wars from which to come home safely,
Laden with honour. Say my request's unjust
And send me back in scorn. But if it's not,
You are not honest, and the gods will plague you
Because you keep me from my duty which
Is a mother's to fulfil. He turns away.
Down, ladies, we will shame him on our knees.
The name of Coriolanus should stir pride,
Not pity, in our prayers. Down! Let's bring
This to an end. So we'll go home to Rome
And die among our neighbours. Look at us!
This boy, who cannot tell you what he needs
And kneels with hands held up in fellowship,
Presents a stronger argument for us
Than what you have to counter it. Let's go.
This fellow had a Volscian for a mother;
His wife is in Corioli, and his child
Resembles him by chance. Now send us off.
I will be silent till our city is in flames,
And then I'll speak a little.

    He holds her by the hand in silence.

CORIOLANUS O mother, mother!
What have you done? The heavens open up,
The gods look down, and this unnatural scene
Reduces them to laughter. O my mother!
You've won a happy victory for Rome,
But for your son – believe it, oh believe it –
It is most dangerous, if not fatality,
Because you have prevailed. But be it so.
Aufidius, though I cannot fight the war
I planned, I'll make a satisfactory peace.
Now, good Aufidius, were you in my place,
Would you have paid your mother less attention,
Or granted less, Aufidius?

AUFIDIUS   I was moved.

CORIOLANUS I'm certain that you were. And, sir, it is
No little thing to make me weep with pity.
What kind of peace you make, inform me. I'll
Not go to Rome, but I'll return with you.
Stand by me, please, in this! O mother! Wife!

AUFIDIUS [*Aside*] I'm glad you've made the separation clear,
When you must act from mercy, when from honour.
It offers me the chance to build my fortunes
Back to where they were before.

CORIOLANUS [*To the Ladies*]   Quite so.
But we will drink together, and you'll take
A better witness back than simple words;
We'll have the terms drawn up and counter-sealed.
Come, enter with us. Ladies, you deserve
To have a temple built for you. The swords
Of all of Italy, with all her allied arms,
Could not have made this peace.

                              Exeunt.

Act V Scene 4

Enter Menenius and Sicinius.

MENENIUS   Do you see that cornerstone on the Capitol over there?
SICINIUS   Yes. Why?
MENENIUS   If you can dislodge it with your little finger, there's some
hope that the ladies of Rome, especially his mother, may prevail

with him. But I say there's no hope; our throats are under sentence, awaiting execution.

SICINIUS   Is it possible for a man to change his consitution in so short a time?

MENENIUS   There's a difference between a grub and a butterfly, but your butterfly was a grub. This Martius has grown from man to dragon. He's got wings; he's more than a creepy-crawly.

SICINIUS   He loved his mother dearly.

MENENIUS   He loved me too, and he no more remembers his mother now than an eight-year-old horse would. The tartness of his face would make ripe grapes sour. When he walks, he moves like a battering-ram, and the ground quakes at his approach. He can pierce body armour with his eyes, he can talk like a church bell, and his ha-hum is like artillery. He sits in his chair of state like a statue of Alexander. What he instructs to be done is no sooner said than done. He has everything a god has except eternal life and a heaven to put his throne in.

SICINIUS   And mercy, if your report is true.

MENENIUS   I paint him true to life. Wait and see what mercy his mother can draw out of him. There's no more mercy in him than milk in a male tiger. As our city will soon find out. And all this is because of you.

SICINIUS   The gods be good to us!

MENENIUS   No, in such a case the gods will not be good to us. When we banished him, we did not respect them, so now that he's coming back to break our necks, they won't respect us.

Enter a Messenger.

MESSENGER   Sir, if you want to save your life, go home.
The plebs have taken in your fellow tribune;
They drag him up and down, all swearing if
The Roman ladies bring no comfort home
They'll give him death by inches.

Enter another Messenger.

SICINIUS   What's the news?

SECOND MESSENGER   Good news, good news! The ladies have prevailed.
The Volscians have retired, and Martius gone.
A happier day has never greeted Rome,
Not even the expulsion of the Tarquins.

SICINIUS   Friend, is this definite? Is it yet certain?

SECOND MESSENGER   As certain as I know the sun is fire.

Where were you lurking so as not to know?
No swollen tide was ever so colossal
As all the rescued coming through the gates.

Trumpets, hautboys, drums beat, all together.

The trumpets, sackbuts, psalteries and fifes,
Tabors and cymbals, and the shouting Romans
Make the sun dance. [*A shout within.*] Listen!

MENENIUS   This is good news.
I'll go and meet the ladies. This Volumnia
Is worth all consuls, senators, patricians
All put together. Tribunes, such as you,
A cityful at least! You have prayed well today.
This morning for ten thousand of your throats
I'd not have given a cent.

Continued shouting.

Listen to the cheers!

SICINIUS   First, god bless you for your news. Next, accept my
gratitude.

SECOND MESSENGER   Sir, we all have great cause to give great
thanks.

SICINIUS   Are they near the city?

SECOND MESSENGER   Almost at the entry.

SICINIUS   We'll meet them and join in the rejoicing.

Exeunt.

Act V Scene 5

*Enter two Senators, with Ladies,
passing over the stage, with other Lords.*

A SENATOR   Behold our patroness, the life of Rome!
Call all your tribes together, praise the gods,
And light triumphal fires. Strew flowers near them.
Outshout the noise that banished Martius;
Recall him with the welcome of his mother.
Cry "Welcome, ladies, welcome!"

ALL   Welcome, ladies, welcome!

A flourish with drums and trumpets. Exeunt.

Act V Scene 6

Enter Tullus Aufidius, with attendants.

AUFIDIUS   Go, tell the city's lords that I am here.
                    Deliver them this paper. Having read it,
                    Tell them to go to the market place, where I
                    In presence of the lords and common people
                    Will vouch the truth of it. He whom I name
                    Has entered by a city gate already
                    And means to stand before the people, hoping
                    To put his case before them. Proceed.

Enter three of four conspirators of Aufidius's faction.

                    Welcome!
FIRST CONSPIRATOR   How is it with our general?
AUFIDIUS   Not unlike
                    A man who's poisoned by his own munificence,
                    Killed by his charity.
SECOND CONSPIRATOR   Most noble sir,
                    If you still plan the same conspiracy
                    In which you wanted us to join, we'll save you
                    From your great danger.
AUFIDIUS   Sir, I cannot say.
                    We must proceed in concert with the people.
THIRD CONSPIRATOR   The people will remain uncertain while
                    There's argument between you, but the fall
                    Of either makes the one who's left the winner.
AUFIDIUS   I know, and my excuse for striking him
                    Can be interpreted as honourable.
                    I raised him, and to win his loyalty
                    I pledged my honour. Smiled upon by me,
                    He watered his new plants with flattering dew,
                    Seducing all my friends; and to this purpose
                    He bent his natural self, not known before
                    As anything but rough, unswayable and free.
THIRD CONSPIRATOR   Sir, when he stood for consul, his obtuseness
                    And his refusal to give way lost him the …
AUFIDIUS   That's what I planned to say. They banished him;
                    He came to me and offered me his throat
                    To cut. I took him in, made him a partner,
                    Gave way to him in all the main decisions,
                    And let him choose the freshest of my troops
                    For his campaigns. I personally served

His interests, and helped to build the fame
Which he accepted for himself. I even
Took pride in being so unfair, until
I seemed to be his follower, not his partner.
He paid me with a condescending smile,
As if I were a mercenary.

FIRST CONSPIRATOR   True.
The army was astonished, and soon after,
When he was on the point of taking Rome,
And we were looking forward to the spoils, ...

AUFIDIUS   That was the thing that made me want to fight him
With every sinew. Just a woman's tear or two,
As cheap as lies, caused him to sell the blood
And labour of our great campaign. For that
He has to die, and I will find renewal
In his fall.

Drums and trumpets sound, with great shouts of the people.

                         But listen!

FIRST CONSPIRATOR   You entered your own city like a messenger,
And had no welcome home, while he returns
Splitting the air with noise.

SECOND CONSPIRATOR   And patient fools
Whose children he has killed, wear out their throats
With yelling in his honour.

THIRD CONSPIRATOR   Seize the chance:
Before he makes a speech and woos the people
With words of flattery, let him feel your sword,
And we'll be there. As soon as he lies dead,
The story as you tell it will be sure
To lay his arguments to rest also.

AUFIDIUS   Enough. Here come the lords.

Enter the Lords of the city.

ALL LORDS   You are most welcome home.

AUFIDIUS   I have not deserved it.
But, worthy lords, have you perused my document
With full attention?

ALL LORDS   We have.

FIRST LORD   And we are sorry to have read it.
His failings up until the last I think
Might be more lightly punished, but
To end before he had begun, without

The benefit of having raised an army,
To answer us by making accusations,
And make a treaty with our prospects good,
All this admits no pardon.

AUFIDIUS   He's coming. You will hear him.

Enter Coriolanus marching with drum and colours,
the Commoners being with him.

CORIOLANUS Hail, lords. I have returned, your soldier,
No more infected with a love for Rome
Than when I parted hence, but still obedient
To your command. It pleases me to report
That I successfully achieved the march
Of war, with many a bloody fight, right to
The gates of Rome. The booty we brought home
Is recompense for one full third of all
The cost of the campaign. We have made peace
With no less honour to the city of Antium
Than shame to Rome. And now we have a treaty,
Which consuls and patricians all have signed,
Agreed by all, and sealed by the senate.

AUFIDIUS Don't read it, noble lords, but tell the traitor
He has disgracefully abused the power
You gave him.

CORIOLANUS   Traitor? What do you mean?

AUFIDIUS Yes, traitor, Martius.

CORIOLANUS Martius?

AUFIDIUS Yes, Martius, Caius Martius. Do you think
I'd grace you with that stolen name, that robbery,
Coriolanus, in Corioli?
You lords and leaders of the state, he has
Perfidiously betrayed your chief concerns
And given up your city Rome – I say
"Your city" – for a salty tear or two
Shed by his wife and mother. Thus he broke
His oath as if it were a skein of silk,
And disregarded all advice he had
From brother officers. His nurse's tears
Caused him to whine away your victory,
Embarrassing young boys, while sturdy men
Looked wonderingly at each other.

CORIOLANUS Do you hear that, Mars?

AUFIDIUS   Don't call the god by name, you boy of tears.
CORIOLANUS What!
AUFIDIUS   Enough.
CORIOLANUS You shameless liar, you have made my heart
                       Too great for its containment. "Boy"? O slave!
                       Pardon me, lords, it is the first time ever
                       That I've been forced to scold. Your judgments, lords,
                       Must give this cur the lie; he wears my wounds
                       Carved deep upon him and will bear my blows
                       Until the grave; his knowledge of the truth
                       Will therefore make him answer for the lie.
FIRST LORD   Quiet, both of you, and let me speak.
CORIOLANUS Cut me to pieces, Volscians. Men and lads,
                       Let all your blades be blooded. "Boy"! False hound,
                       If you have written truthful history,
                       You'll find it there set down that, like an eagle
                       Loose in a dovecote, I went into Corioli
                       And set your Volscians aflutter. All alone
                       I did it. "Boy"!
AUFIDIUS   Why, noble lords,
                       Let this unholy braggart bring to mind
                       His mere good luck, the cause of your disgrace,
                       Before your very eyes and ears?
ALL CONSPIRATORS   He should die for it!
ALL PEOPLE   Tear him to pieces! At once! He killed my son! My
    daughter! He killed my cousin Marcus! He killed my father!
SECOND LORD   Peace there! No outrage! Peace!
                       The man is noble, and his fame extends
                       Across the globe. His recent crimes against us
                       Will be set forth in court. Hold off, Aufidius,
                       And don't disturb the peace.
CORIOLANUS   If only I had him
                       And six Aufidiuses, or more, the tribe
                       Of them, to use my lawful sword against!
AUFIDIUS   Insolent villain!
ALL CONSPIRATORS   Kill, kill, kill, kill, kill him!

                The Conspirators draw and kill Martius, who falls;
                         Aufidius stands on him.

LORDS   Hold it, hold, hold, hold!
AUFIDIUS   My noble masters, let me speak.
FIRST LORD   O Tullus!

SECOND LORD   You have done a deed that will make valour weep.
THIRD LORD   Don't tread on him. Be quiet, masters all.
                Put down your swords.
AUFIDIUS   My lords, when you become aware – which now
                Is hard with all the rage that he provoked –
                Aware of all the danger which this man
                Presented while alive, you will rejoice
                That he is now no more. I trust your honours
                Will call me to the senate; I'll present
                Myself your loyal servant, or endure
                Your heaviest censure.
FIRST LORD   Bear away his body,
                And let us mourn for him. Let him be held
                The noblest corpse any procession
                Did ever follow to the tomb.
SECOND LORD   His own
                Impatience spares Aufidius a great deal
                Of blame. Let's make the best of it.
AUFIDIUS   My rage has gone. And I am deep in sorrow.
                Let three strong soldiers lift him up, I'll be
                The fourth. Let drums give out a mournful beat.
                Trail your steel pikes. Though in this city he
                Has widowed many, orphaned many too,
                Who all bewail their losses to this day,
                Yet he will leave a noble memory.
                Assist.

Exeunt bearing the body of Martius. A dead march is sounded.

The Tempest

CHARACTERS

Alonso, King of Naples
Sebastian, his brother
Prospero, the rightful Duke of Milan
Antonio, his brother, the usurping Duke of Milan
Ferdinand, son of the King of Naples
Gonzalo, an honest old counsellor
Adrian, a Lord
Francisco, a Lord
Caliban, a savage and deformed slave
Trinculo, a Jester
Stephano, a drunken Butler
Master of a ship
Boatswain
Mariners

Miranda, daughter of Prospero

Ariel, an airy spirit

Presented by spirits:
Iris
Ceres
Juno
Nymphs
Reapers

Other spirits attending Prospero

Act I Scene 1

A tempestuous noise of thunder and lightning is heard.
Enter a Shipmaster and a Boatswain.

MASTER Bo'sun!

BOATSWAIN Here, master! What's happening?

MASTER Speak to the mariners, good man. Get to it quickly or we'll
run aground. Get going, move!   *Exit.*

BOATSWAIN Hey there, my hearties! Come on, come on there!
Quickly! Take in the topsail, listen for the master's whistle! [*To the
storm*] Blow till you burst your guts, so long as we've enough
water …

Enter Alonso, Sebastian, Antonio, Ferdinand, Gonzalo and others.

ALONSO Good bo'sun, take care. Where's the master? Act like men!

BOATSWAIN I beg you, stay below!

ANTONIO Where's the master, bo'sun?

BOATSWAIN Don't you hear him? You're hindering our work. You're
helping the storm.

GONZALO Now, good man, be patient.

BOATSWAIN When the sea is. Be off! What do these breakers care
for the name of king? Get to your cabins. Be quiet and don't
trouble us.

GONZALO All right, but remember who you have on board.

BOATSWAIN None that I love more than myself. You are a
councillor: if you can command the elements to silence and extract
peace from this turmoil, we'd not have to touch another rope. Use
your authority! If you can't, be thankful that you've lived so long,
and make yourself ready in your cabin to face imminent disaster, if
it should occur. Come on then, my hearties! Out of our way, I say.

Exeunt Boatswain with mariners,
followed by Alonso, Sebastian, Antonio and Ferdinand.

GONZALO I have great faith in this fellow. He that is born to be
hanged shall never drown, says the proverb, and his complexion
is set rather for the gallows. Stay committed, good fate, to his
hanging. Make the rope of his destiny our cable, for our own
are little help. If he's not destined to be hanged, our situation is
desperate.

Exit. Enter Boatswain.

BOATSWAIN Bring down the top of the main mast! Lower, lower,
more! Level it with the main course! Curse that shouting! They're

louder than the weather, or us at work. [*To the lords*] You here
again? What are you doing? Shall we give up and drown? Are you
determined to sink?

SEBASTIAN   Damn your cursing, you bawling, blasphemous,
uncharitable dog!

BOATSWAIN   Lend a hand then!

ANTONIO   Hold your insolent tongue, you bastard, you dog! We're
less afraid of drowning than you are.

GONZALO   I'll guarantee he won't drown, even if the ship's no
stronger than a nutshell and as leaky as an unstaunched wench.

BOATSWAIN   Lay her to wind, to wind! Set the two sails! Off to sea
again; lay her off!

Enter mariners, wet.

MARINERS   All's lost! Say your prayers! All's lost!

BOATSWAIN   Do we have to end in the drink?

GONZALO   The king and prince are saying their prayers! Let's join
them, for our situation is no better.

SEBASTIAN   I'm out of patience.

ANTONIO   We're completely cheated of our lives by drunkards. This
big-mouthed rascal – may you be hanged at low tide and washed
by ten tides!

GONZALO   He'll survive the storm to be hanged, even if every drop
of water swears the opposite and opens wide to swallow him.

Exeunt Boatswain and mariners.

OFFSTAGE SHOUTS   Help! Mercy! We're breaking up! We're breaking
up! Goodbye, my wife and children! Goodbye, brother! We're
breaking up!

ANTONIO   Let's all sink with the king!

SEBASTIAN   Let's bid him goodbye.

Exeunt Antonio and Sebastian.

GONZALO   I'd give a thousand furlongs of sea for an acre of ground
just now. Heather, brown gorse, anything. God's will be done, but
I'd rather die a dry death.   *Exit.*

Act I Scene 2

Enter Prospero and Miranda.

MIRANDA   If you, my dearest father, by your arts
             Contrived to raise this storm, let it now end.
             The sky, it seems, is pouring pitch and tar

And causing fires the sea can only quench
By surging to the sky. I suffered so
To see them struggling there. A fine vessel,
Which carried men of noble rank no doubt,
Was dashed to pieces. Oh, their dreadful cries
Pierced me to the heart. Poor souls, they perished.
If I had been some powerful god, I would
Have sunk the sea within the earth before
It swallowed up the ship like that, and all
The souls she carried in her.

PROSPERO   Calm yourself;
Don't be alarmed! Your pitying heart should know
There's no harm done.

MIRANDA   O fateful day!
PROSPERO   No harm!
I have done nothing but take care of you,
Of you, my dear one, you, my daughter, who
Know nothing about who you are, nor even
Where I came from, or that I am better
Than Prospero, master of a humble cell,
Your humble father too.

MIRANDA   The need to learn
Such things was never in my mind.

PROSPERO   It's time
I told you more. Now help me be divested
Of all these magic garments: that's the way.
My arts are there contained. Now wipe your eyes;
The shipwreck with its fearful sights and sounds
Which did arouse such fine compassion in you
Was so commanded by my magic arts
That not a single soul, no living creature,
No, nothing in that vessel, not a hair,
Was victim to the storm or lost for ever,
Even though you heard their cries and saw it sink.
Sit down, there's more to tell you.

MIRANDA   You have often
Begun to tell me who I am, but stopped
And left me with my fruitless questions,
Saying, "No. Not yet."

PROSPERO   The time's now come;
The present moment is exactly right
For you to listen well. Can you remember

A time before we came to this poor home?
I don't believe you can, since then you were
No more than three years old.

MIRANDA   But yes, I can.

PROSPERO   Remember what? Another house? A person?
If there's a living image you can still
Recall, then you should tell me.

MIRANDA   It's far off,
More like a dream, uncertain, too remote
For me to guarantee. Were there not
Four or five women who once cared for me?

PROSPERO   There were, and more, Miranda. How is it
That this lives in your mind? What else do you see
Across the dark abyss of distant time?
If something from before you came here lingers,
The way you came here might.

MIRANDA   Not that, I fear.

PROSPERO   Twelve years ago, Miranda, twelve years now,
Your father held the dukedom of Milan.
He was a prince.

MIRANDA   Sir, are you not my father?

PROSPERO   Your mother was a virtuous woman, and
She said you were my daughter; and your father
Was Duke, his only heir a princess of Milan,
Equal in birth with him.

MIRANDA   O great heavens!
What foul deed ever drove us all from there?
Or was it fortunate?

PROSPERO   Both, both, my girl.
A foul deed, as you put it, drove us thence,
But happily we came here.

MIRANDA   My heart bleeds
To think of all the grief I must have caused you,
I don't remember that. Please tell me more.

PROSPERO   My brother, that's your uncle, named Antonio
(I ask you to observe how treacherous
A brother can be), he whom next to you
In all the world I loved, to whom I passed
The governance of my state, which at that time
Became the leading city-state in Italy,
And Prospero the leading Duke, respected
Because I was devoted to the liberal arts

Without a parallel; these being all my passion,
The government I trusted to my brother
And drew away from state affairs. My mind
Was all absorbed in study. Your false uncle ...
Are you still listening?

MIRANDA   Yes! Attentively!

PROSPERO   ... Was skilled in granting citizens' requests,
And also saying no. He knew whom to promote,
And whose ambitions to rein in; he gave
My office-holders new powers, or moved them,
Or won them over; having both the key
Of officer and office, he tuned all the city's ears
To whatever theme he chose, so he became
The ivy clinging to my princely trunk
And draining it of life. You're not attending!

MIRANDA   Good sir, I am.

PROSPERO   Please listen carefully.
Neglecting worldly things and thinking only
In solitude how to improve my mind,
And too withdrawn to read the people's view,
I let the evil in his nature rule
My treacherous brother; and my trust,
Like a good parent, only bred in him
A wickedness as great in its false way
As was my trust, which had indeed no limit,
A boundless confidence. And raised in power
Not only by the money due to me
But also by what sums a Duke can raise –
Like someone who habitually bends the truth
And falsifies his memory, in the end
Believes in his own lies – he did believe
He was indeed the Duke instead of me,
Assuming all the outward marks of royalty
And all prerogatives. His next ambition ...
Did you hear?

MIRANDA   Your story would cure deafness!

PROSPERO   To have no screen between this part he played
And him whose role it was, drove him to be
Dictator of Milan. For me, poor man, my library
Was dukedom large enough. He judges me
Incapable of daily business, craves
Secure authority at home and pays

A ducal homage to the King of Naples,
An annual tribute as from coronet to crown.
The city of Milan, unbowed, is forced
To stoop in shame.

MIRANDA   O merciful heavens!

PROSPERO   These treaties, these events: take careful note.
Is this a brother's doing?

MIRANDA   No sin could I
Impute to her, my noble grandmother.
Good wombs have borne bad sons.

PROSPERO   Now here's the pact:
This King of Naples is my enemy of old.
He pays attention to my brother's plan,
Which was that in return for homage paid
Along with tribute of I know not what,
The King should drive me and my family
Out of the dukedom and confer my city,
With all the honours, on my brother. At once
A treacherous force was raised, and at midnight
One day Antonio seized the city gates,
While under cover of the night his men
Appointed for the purpose drove me out,
Me and yourself, in tears.

MIRANDA   Alas, for pity!
I don't remember how I cried that day,
So now I'll cry again. The story wrings
The tears from my eyes.

PROSPERO   Listen a bit more,
And then I'll tell you what the present business
Is all about. Without it this account
Would be irrelevant.

MIRANDA   Why didn't they
Destroy us there and then?

PROSPERO   I'm glad you asked!
My tale provokes that question. They did not dare,
Because the people loved me very dearly.
They could not leave a bloody stain behind,
So covered up their deeds as best they could.
In brief, they hurried us aboard a boat,
Sailed out to sea some leagues where they prepared
A rotten carcass of a barrel, unrigged,
No tackle, sail or mast, so grim a ship

          The rats had even shunned it. There they left us
          To howl and hear the sea howl back, to sigh
          Into the wind, whose pity sighing back
          Was loving but unkind.

MIRANDA   Alas, what trouble
          Must I have been to you.

PROSPERO   You were an angel,
          You saved me with your smile; you were kept strong
          By generous gifts of fortitude from heaven,
          While I adorned the sea with salty tears
          And groaned with hardship. Seeing your sweet smile
          My courage rose, and I regained the stomach
          To face what lay ahead.

MIRANDA   How did we get ashore?

PROSPERO   By providence.
          We had some food and some fresh water which
          A noble Neapolitan, Gonzalo,
          In kindness (having been assigned the task
          Of setting all this up) provided us
          With clothing, linen, all necessities
          Which served us in good stead. In kindness too
          He knew I loved my books and furnished me
          With volumes from my library which I prize
          Above my vanished dukedom.

MIRANDA   Would I might
          Just once set eyes on him!

PROSPERO   Now I shall rise.
          Sit still, and hear the last of our sad story.
          Here in this island we arrived, and here
          Have I, your teacher, seen you make more progress
          Than other princes can, who spend their time
          On vain pursuits, whose tutors trouble less.

MIRANDA   May Heaven thank you for it. Now I need to ask –
          For this is whirling in my mind – your reason
          For raising this sea-storm?

PROSPERO   I'll say just this:
          A strange event, dear Lady Fortune's gift,
          Has happened, bringing all my enemies
          Here to this shore; and by my prescience
          I find my zenith does depend upon
          A most auspicious star, whose influence
          I have to court, because, if not, my fortunes

Will always be against me. No more questions!
You seem to want to sleep. Let drowsiness
Consume you! I know you have no choice.

Miranda sleeps.

Come here, my servant, come. I'm ready now.
Approach, my Ariel. Come!

Enter Ariel.

ARIEL   All hail, great master, great and good, I come
To answer your command, be it to fly,
To swim, to dive into the fire, to ride
On swirling clouds. Give Ariel instructions,
His skills serve your behest.

PROSPERO   Did you, my spirit, call the tempest up
As I commanded?

ARIEL   Fully and completely.
I boarded the king's ship. From prow to stern,
Amidships, up, below, in every cabin,
My fearful flames were seen. Sometimes I'd split
And burn in many places: on the topmast,
The yards and bowsprit one by one caught fire,
Then met and fused. Jove's lightning never flashed
More speedily when warning of the thunder,
Or more deceived the eye. The fire and cracks
Of sulphurous roars made even mighty Neptune
Cower, and caused his fearless waves to tremble,
His fearful trident shake!

PROSPERO   My brave spirit!
Was anyone so firm that such confusion
Did not affect his reason?

ARIEL   Not a soul.
They all behaved like madmen, making signs
And cries of desperation. All save the sailors
Plunged straight into the sea and left the vessel
Burning with my flame. The king's son Ferdinand,
His hair on end like reeds, was first to leap;
He shouted as he dived in, "Hell is empty;
And all the devils are here!"

PROSPERO   Why, that's my spirit!
But was this near the shore?

ARIEL   It was, my master.

PROSPERO   And are they, Ariel, safe?

ARIEL   Not a hair perished;
          No mark or blemish on their clothing found,
          All fresher than before. And as you ordered,
          I've scattered them in groups around the isle.
          The king's son I have settled by himself,
          I left him there to cool the air with sighs
          In an odd corner of the isle, and sitting
          His arms folded like this.

PROSPERO   Of the king's ship
          And crew what is the present disposition?
          And all the rest of the fleet?

ARIEL   Safely in harbour
          The king's ship lies; a hidden inlet where
          You once sent me to find some magic dew
          From the storm-wracked Bermudas; there she lies.
          Her sailors all are down below asleep,
          Exhausted from their labours and benumbed
          By magic I applied. The other ships,
          Which I had scattered, now have come together;
          They're on the Mediterranean heading home
          To Naples, with a heavy heart, convinced
          They saw the king's ship founder with all hands,
          His royal self among them.

PROSPERO   You have done
          Exactly what I charged you with, my Ariel.
          But still there's more. What time is it?

ARIEL   Past noon.

PROSPERO Two hours past, at least. Before the hour of six
          We both must use the time with real purpose.

ARIEL   Is there more work? You give me all these duties,
          So I'll remind you of the promise that you made,
          But have not granted yet.

PROSPERO   So what was that?
          What do you ask of me?

ARIEL   My liberty.

PROSPERO Before your time is up? No chance.

ARIEL   I beg you,
          Remember I have served you worthily,
          I've told no lies, made no mistakes, obeyed you
          Without grudge or grumbling. And you promised me
          A full year off.

PROSPERO   Perhaps you have forgotten

	The misery I rescued you from?
ARIEL	No.
PROSPERO	You have! You think you earn my praise
	By treading ooze upon the ocean bed,
	Or running up against a cold north wind,
	Or following my orders far beneath the ground
	When it is frozen hard.
ARIEL	I do not, sir.
PROSPERO	You lie, malignant wretch! Did you forget
	The foul witch Sycorax, malformed and envious,
	Bent double with old age. Did you forget her?
ARIEL	No, sir.
PROSPERO	You did. Where was she born? Speak. Tell me!
ARIEL	Sir, in Algiers.
PROSPERO	Oh, is that so? I must
	Remind you once a month what you have done,
	Which you forget. This damned witch Sycorax
	Was banished from Algiers, as well you know,
	For endless mischief-making and some fearful
	Sorcery. For one particular reason
	Her life was spared. Is this what you believe?
ARIEL	Yes, sir.
PROSPERO	That blue-eyed hag was pregnant, so the sailors
	Conveyed her here and left her. You, my slave,
	As you admit yourself, were then her servant.
	Because you were too delicate a spirit
	To act on her abominable commands
	And disobeyed her orders, she confined you
	With help from her more powerful servants,
	And in her quite unmitigated rage
	Imprisoned you within a hollow pine.
	And there in great distress you spent at least
	A dozen years; and in that time she died
	And left you there. You groaned and whimpered
	As loudly as a mill-wheel. At that time
	This island was distinguished by no trace
	Of human shape, save for the freckled, hag-like son
	She littered here.
ARIEL	Yes, Caliban, her son.
PROSPERO	How quick you are! It is indeed that Caliban
	In service now to me. You know quite well
	What horrible distress I found you in. Your groans

Caused even wolves to howl and touched the hearts
Of ever-hungry bears. It was a torment
Fit only for the damned, which Sycorax
Could not release you from. My art it was,
When I arrived and heard you, which split wide
The pine and let you out.

ARIEL   I thank you, master.

PROSPERO   If you give me more trouble I will gouge
An oak and cram you in its knotty entrails
Until you've howled away a dozen years.

ARIEL   Forgive me, master. I'll obey commands
And be a gentle spirit.

PROSPERO   If you do,
I will allow two days then let you go.

ARIEL   That's my noble master! What comes next?
Give me your orders what I have to do.

PROSPERO   Transform yourself into a water-nymph;
Invisible to all but you and me,
Unseen by other eyes. Go, take that shape
And then come back to me. Now off you go!

Exit Ariel.

Wake up, dear heart, wake up! You have slept well.
Wake up!

MIRANDA   The strangeness of your story brought
A heavy sleep upon me.

PROSPERO   Shake it off!
Come on, we'll visit Caliban, my slave,
Whose talk is always vulgar.

MIRANDA   He's a villain, sir,
I cannot bear to see him.

PROSPERO   But as it is,
We cannot do without him. He makes fire,
He fetches wood, and helps with various duties
That assist us. Hey there! Slave! Caliban!
You clod, you! Speak!

CALIBAN   *(Within)*

         There's plenty wood in here!

PROSPERO   Come out, I tell you. There are other jobs.
Get on with it, you tortoise.

Enter Ariel like a water-nymph.

PROSPERO   A fine disguise! My quaint, outlandish Ariel,

A word in your ear.

ARIEL   My lord, it shall be done.   *Exit Ariel.*

PROSPERO   You poisonous slave, begotten by the devil,
            Son of that wicked witch, come out!

                        Enter Caliban.

CALIBAN   May dew as lethal as my mother ever brushed
            From stinking fen, with feathers from a raven,
            Drop on you both! May noisome south-west winds
            Spread blisters on your skin!

PROSPERO   For this, be sure, tonight you will get cramps
            And stitches strong enough to stop your breath!
            Throughout the long dark night a trail of hedgehogs
            Will work you over, stinging as they go
            And leaving a broad honeycomb of bites
            More sore than bee-stings.

CALIBAN   I must eat my dinner.
            This island's mine, from Sycorax my mother,
            Which you have stolen. When first you came
            You stroked me and made much of me; you'd give me
            Water with berries in it, and teach me how
            To name the stronger light that burns by day
            And that which shows at night. And then I loved you
            And showed you all the island's special spots,
            The fresh springs, salt pits, barren land and fertile –
            I curse myself for doing it. Sycorax's spells,
            Toads, beetles, bats – may all that come to haunt you!
            For I am all the subjects that you have,
            I used to be my own king! Here you keep me
            In this hard rock, and never let me venture
            To the rest of the island.

PROSPERO   You're a lying slave!
            A flogging might persuade you, never kindness!
            Filth though you are, I've treated you with care,
            And lodged you in my cell until that day
            You tried to rape my child.

CALIBAN   Oh ho! Oh ho! I wish I had!
            But you prevented me, or else this isle
            Would now be full of Calibans.

MIRANDA   You hateful slave!
            Incapable of understanding goodness,
            And full of evil plans! I pitied you,

Took pains to make you speak, and taught you hourly
One thing or another. When you didn't know
What your own savage words were saying, gabbling
A stream of nonsense, I divined their meaning
And gave you words we'd understand. But yet,
Though you learned much, your type is one
That cannot bear to foster goodness. That is why
You were confined deservedly in rock,
Deserving more than prison.

CALIBAN   You taught me more than language, and my gain
Is, I know how to curse. A raging plague upon you
For teaching me your language!

PROSPERO   Fiend, get out!
Fetch us some fuel. You'd better jump to it
And do your other tasks. Was that a shrug?
If you neglect what I command, or do it
Only grudgingly, I'll see you bent
In two with cramps, I'll fill your bones with aches
You'll howl enough to frighten wild beasts.

CALIBAN   No, please!
[*Aside*] I must obey. His arts are of such power
He could control my mother's pagan god
And make a vassal of him.

PROSPERO   So, slave, go!

Exit Caliban.
Enter Ferdinand, and Ariel invisible, playing and singing.

ARIEL   *Song*

Come unto these yellow sands,
And take hands.
Curtsied when you have, and kissed,
The wild waves whist.
Foot it featly here and there,
And sweet sprites the burden bear.

Refrain

Hark, hark
The watch-dogs bark
Bow wow, bow wow.

ARIEL   Hark, hark, I hear
The strain of strutting chanticleer
Cry cock-a-doodle-doo.

FERDINAND Where can this music be? In the air, or on earth?
It sounds no more; but surely it is meant
For gods of the island. Sitting on a bank,
My father's shipwreck leaving me in tears,
This music crept to me across the water,
Allaying both its fury and my suffering
With the sweet song. From there I followed it,
Or rather I was drawn. But now it's gone.
No, it begins again.

ARIEL   *Song*

Full fathom five thy father lies,
     Of his bones are coral made;
Those are pearls that were his eyes;
     Nothing of him that doth fade;
But doth suffer a sea-change
Into something rich and strange.
Sea-nymphs hourly ring his knell.

                              Refrain

Ding-dong.

ARIEL   Hark, now I hear them, ding-dong bell.
FERDINAND The words recall my father, who was drowned.
This is no mortal business, nor is it
An earthly sound. I hear it now above me.
PROSPERO [*To Miranda*] Lift up those frail eyelashes of yours
And tell me what you see there.
MIRANDA   What is it?
A spirit? How it stares around! Believe me, sir,
It's handsome, certainly. But still a spirit.
PROSPERO No, girl, it eats and sleeps and has the same
Senses as us. This fine young man you see
Was in the shipwreck. If he were not sick
With grief – a cancer to good looks – you'd see
The good in him. He's lost all his companions;
He's searching for them everywhere.
MIRANDA   I'd say
He was divine; in nature I have never
Seen anything so noble.
PROSPERO [*Aside*]   Things are going
The way my soul wants! Spirit, fine spirit,
I'll free you in two days for this.

FERDINAND   For sure,
              There is the goddess that the songs are sung to.
              Forgive me, may I know if you belong
              Here on this island? And would you instruct me
              In how I should behave? My main request,
              The last I ask of you, is – O you wonder! –
              Are you a real girl?
MIRANDA   A wonder, no!
              But certainly I'm real!
FERDINAND My language! Heavens!
              I am the noblest of all those who speak it,
              If only I was where it's spoken.
PROSPERO   Noblest?
              Suppose the King of Naples heard you say that!
FERDINAND Alone now as I am, I am astonished
              To hear you speak of Naples. He does hear me,
              I weep to think of it. Myself, I'm Naples!
              For with my very eyes that never dry
              I saw my father drowned.
MIRANDA   May God have mercy!
FERDINAND It's true, and all his lords were lost, Milan
              Was with them, and his brave son too.
PROSPERO [*Aside*]   Milan's
              Real Duke and his brave daughter could correct you,
              But this is not the time. Those two have fallen
              In love at first sight. My delicate Ariel,
              I'll set you free for this. A word, good sir;
              I fear you've made a serious mistake.
MIRANDA   Why is my father so uncivil to him?
              This is the third man I have ever seen; the first
              I ever fell for. May my father share
              My feelings rather more!
FERDINAND   If you're a virgin,
              And have not promised love before, I'll make you
              The Queen of Naples.
PROSPERO   Just another word, sir:
              (They're in each other's power, but this swift business
              Must not be easy for them, else the victory
              Becomes too light a prize.) Now one word more:
              Take careful note. You do usurp a name
              That is not yours. You came here with the purpose
              Of spying on this island, just to seize it

From me, its lord.

FERDINAND   No, as I am a man!
MIRANDA   No evil can exist in such a temple!
             If evil spirits find so fair a house to live in
             Good things will want to dwell there too.
PROSPERO   Come, sir.
             [*To Miranda*] Don't speak on his behalf, he is a traitor.
             [*To Ferdinand*] Come!
             I'll manacle your neck and feet together.
             Seawater you can drink; your food will be
             Freshwater mussels, withered roots and husks
             That cradled acorns. Follow me.
FERDINAND   No, no!
             I will resist such cruel treatment till
             My enemy is stronger.

             He draws his sword but is charmed from moving.

MIRANDA   O dear father,
             Don't be too hasty to condemn him, for
             He's noble, and not threatening.
PROSPERO   What's this?
             The foot ruling the head? Put up your sword,
             You traitor! Obviously you dare not strike,
             You're overcome by guilt. Give up that posture,
             Or else I will disarm you with this stick
             And make your weapon drop.
MIRANDA   Please, father, please!
PROSPERO   Get off! Don't cling like that!
MIRANDA   I pray you, please!
             I'll stand for him.
PROSPERO   Silence! One word more
             And I'll be angry with you, even hate you.
             You'd stand for an impostor? That's enough!
             You think he is the only decent creature,
             You've seen just him and Caliban. You fool,
             Compared to most men he's a Caliban;
             Compared to him, they're angels.
MIRANDA   My affections
             Are then most humble. I have no ambition
             To see a better man.
PROSPERO   [*To Ferdinand*]   Come on, obey!
             Your sinews have a childish look again,

	There's no more vigour in them.
FERDINAND	So they are.

My feelings are all tense, as in a dream.
My father's loss, the weakness which I feel,
The death of all my friends and this man's threats,
Subduing me, are little burden on me.
If I can only once a day be blest
To see this maiden through my prison bars,
Freedom may prosper elsewhere. Space enough
Have I in such a prison.

PROSPERO (It's working!) Come on!
You have done well, fine Ariel.
[*To Ferdinand*] Follow me!
[*To Ariel*] Here's what you next shall do for me.

MIRANDA   Take courage;
My father has a better nature, sir,
Than what he said just now. This is unusual,
What came from him.

PROSPERO [*To Ariel*]   I say you'll be as free
As mountain winds; but first you have to do
Exactly everything I order.

ARIEL   To the last syllable.

PROSPERO [*To Ferdinand*] Come, follow!
[*To Miranda*] Don't speak for him!

                    Exeunt.

Act II Scene 1

*Enter Alonso, Sebastian, Antonio, Gonzalo,
Adrian, Francisco and others.*

GONZALO I beg you, sir, cheer up. You have good cause,
As we all do, for joy, since our escape
By far outweighs our loss. Distress like this
Is common; every day some sailor's wife,
Or owners of a vessel, or its master,
Have just the same lament. But for the miracle,
I mean our preservation, few in millions
Could speak like us. It would be wise, I say,
To keep it in proportion.

ALONSO   Quiet, please sir.

SEBASTIAN   [*To Antonio*] He looks at sympathy as if it were cold porridge.

ANTONIO   [*To Sebastian*] His sympathiser won't give up easily.

SEBASTIAN   Look, he's winding up his wit like a watch. By and by it will strike.

GONZALO   Sir, –

SEBASTIAN   One. Count!

GONZALO   When every mishap is complained of, the complainer gets …

SEBASTIAN   A dollar.

GONZALO   He's dolorous, it's true. You spoke truer than you meant.

SEBASTIAN   You took it more seriously than I meant you to.

GONZALO   So, my lord –

ANTONIO   My, what a waster of words he is.

ALONSO   Please, that's enough.

GONZALO   Well, I've said what I had to say. But yet –

SEBASTIAN   He'll have more to say.

ANTONIO   For a bet, say whether he or Adrian is the first to crow.

SEBASTIAN   The old cock.

ANTONIO   The young cock.

SEBASTIAN   Done. The bet?

ANTONIO   The winner gets to laugh.

SEBASTIAN   Here they go.

ADRIAN   Though this island seems to be deserted –

ANTONIO   Ha, ha, ha!

SEBASTIAN   So, you've been paid.

ADRIAN   Uninhabitable, and almost inaccessible –

SEBASTIAN   Yet –

ADRIAN   Yet –

ANTONIO   He was bound to say it.

ADRIAN   It must have a refined, tender and delicate climate.

ANTONIO   Like some girls we know.

SEBASTIAN   And crafty, like his learned delivery.

ADRIAN   The air breathes upon us here most sweetly.

SEBASTIAN   As if it had lungs, and rotten ones too.

ANTONIO   Or as if it were scented by a bog.

GONZALO   Here there is everything useful for life.

ANTONIO   True, except a means to support life.

SEBASTIAN   There's little or none of that.

GONZALO   How lush and sturdy the grass looks! How green!

ANTONIO   The ground is indeed tawny brown.

SEBASTIAN   With a hint of green in it.

ANTONIO   He doesn't miss much.

SEBASTIAN   But he does get it totally wrong.

GONZALO   But the rarity of it is – which is hard to believe –

SEBASTIAN   As many acknowledged rarities are.

GONZALO   That our clothes, having been drenched in the sea, have nonetheless kept their freshness and sheen, as if they had been freshly dyed, not stained with salt water.

ANTONIO   If just one of his pockets could speak, wouldn't it say he's lying?

SEBASTIAN   Yes, or keep its thoughts to itself.

GONZALO   I believe our clothes are now as fresh as when we first put them on in Africa, at the marriage of the king's beautiful daughter Claribel to the King of Tunis.

SEBASTIAN   It was a fine marriage, and we prosper well out of it.

ADRIAN   Tunis never before had such a paragon of a queen.

GONZALO   Not since the widow Dido was queen.

ANTONIO   Widow? Nonsense! Why did he say widow? Widow Dido indeed!

SEBASTIAN   What if he had said "widower Aeneas" too? Good lord, you pick on anything.

ADRIAN   The widow Dido, you said? You make me think hard about that. She was from Carthage, not Tunis.

GONZALO   This Tunis, sir, was Carthage.

ADRIAN   Carthage?

GONZALO   I assure you. Carthage.

ANTONIO   His words are better than Amphion's miraculous harp that built the whole city of Thebes.

SEBASTIAN   He's built the walls and houses too.

ANTONIO   What impossible thing will he do next?

SEBASTIAN   I think he'll carry this island home in his pocket and give it to his son for an apple.

ANTONIO   And then sowing its seeds in the sea he'll produce more islands.

GONZALO   Ay.

ANTONIO   Well at last!

GONZALO   Sir, we were saying that our clothes seem now as fresh as when we were at Tunis for the marriage of your daughter, who is now queen.

ANTONIO   And the loveliest ever seen there.

SEBASTIAN   Not counting, let me remind you, the widow Dido.

GONZALO   Is my doublet not as fresh as the first day I wore it? I mean in a sort of ...

ANTONIO	He did well to come up with that "sort of".
GONZALO	When I wore it at your daughter's marriage.
ALONSO	You cram these words into my ears, without
	A thought how I might feel. I wish I'd never
	Married my daughter there. On our way back
	My son was lost, and she, you might say, too,
	Being so far away from Italy
	I'll not see her again. O son and heir
	Of Naples and Milan, what hideous fish
	Has made a meal of you?
FRANCISCO	Sir, he's alive
	Perhaps; I saw him beating through the waves
	And rising on each crest; he trod the water,
	Defying its assault, and faced each swell
	And surge as it came at him. His bold head
	He kept above the hostile waves, and rowed,
	With his good arms as oars, in lusty strokes
	Toward the shore whose overhanging cliff
	Stooped over to relieve him. I don't doubt
	He came ashore alive.
ALONSO	No, no, he's gone.
SEBASTIAN	You have yourself to thank for this great loss,
	Sir, since our Europe did not win the bride.
	You did prefer to lose her to an African
	Where she at least is banished from your sight,
	Enough to cause you real grief.
ALONSO	Enough!
SEBASTIAN	We all implored you, on our knees, to think
	Again about it. She, your lovely daughter,
	Herself was torn between distaste and duty,
	A balance in the scales. We've lost your son,
	I fear, for ever. Naples and Milan
	Have now more widows than can hope for comfort
	Supposing any men return alive. The fault's
	Your own.
ALONSO	So is the heaviest of the loss.
GONZALO	My lord Sebastian,
	Your words are true but not exactly generous,
	It's not the time for that; you rub the wound
	When you should bring the plaster.
SEBASTIAN	Very well.
ANTONIO	A surgeon's needed.

GONZALO   The weather's foul for all of us, good sir,
            When you are gloomy.
SEBASTIAN   Foul weather?
ANTONIO   Very foul.
GONZALO   If I were here to colonise this island ...
ANTONIO   He'd sow just nettles.
SEBASTIAN   Or more weeds, like docks.
GONZALO   If I were also king, what would I do?
SEBASTIAN   Avoid the curse of drink, for lack of wine.
GONZALO   In my community, against the custom,
            I'd take on everything myself. No commerce
            Would I allow; no magistrates assigned.
            There'd be no learning, neither rich nor poor,
            Domestic service, none. Contract, inheritance,
            The sale of property, land, vineyards – none.
            No use of metal, corn or wine or oil;
            No occupation, all men idle, all;
            And women too, all innocent and pure;
            No sovereignty –
SEBASTIAN   Yet he'd be king, himself ...
ANTONIO   His final words forget how he began.
GONZALO   All things in common would be made by nature,
            No sweat or effort needed; treason, crime,
            Sword, pike, knife, gun, or any other weapon
            I would dispense with; leaving all to nature
            To give enough of plenty and abundance
            To feed my innocent people.
SEBASTIAN   No marrying between his subjects?
ANTONIO   No, none; all idle, playing whores and knaves.
GONZALO   With such ideals would I govern, sir,
            To attain the Golden Age.
SEBASTIAN   God save His Majesty!
ANTONIO   Long live Gonzalo!
GONZALO   Are you paying attention, sir?
ALONSO   Please, no more! There's nothing in what you say.
GONZALO   I do believe your highness. I did it to provide an
            opportunity for these gentlemen whose lungs are so sensitive and
            alert that they are always ready to laugh at nothing.
ANTONIO   It was you we were laughing at.
GONZALO   Who, in this merry jesting, is nothing to you. So you may
            continue and carry on laughing at nothing.
ANTONIO   Touché!

SEBASTIAN   If the joke hadn't fallen flat.

GONZALO   You are gentlemen of brave spirit. You'd pull the moon
out of its orbit if only it would stay still for five weeks.

Enter Ariel [invisible] playing solemn music.

SEBASTIAN   We would indeed, and then go catching birds at night.

ANTONIO   My good Lord, don't be angry.

GONZALO   No, I promise I'll not risk losing my composure over so
little. Will you laugh me to sleep; I'm very weary.

ANTONIO   Go to sleep, and listen to our laughter!

ALONSO   What's this? All suddenly asleep? I wish
My eyes would also close my thoughts. I find
They often do just that.

SEBASTIAN   May I suggest
You don't neglect the chance of sleep that's offered?
It seldom comes to people in distress,
But when it does, it's welcome.

ANTONIO   We will both
Stand guard for you if sleep is what you need;
We'll watch your safety.

ALONSO   Thankyou. Terribly weary …

[Exit Ariel.]

SEBASTIAN   What a strange drowsiness has come over them!

ANTONIO   I blame it on the climate.

SEBASTIAN   Why
Then does it not affect us too? I find
I'm not disposed to sleep at all.

ANTONIO   Nor I. My mind is quite alert.
They dropped asleep together, as if planned,
As if the thunder felled them. Just suppose,
Worthy Sebastian, just suppose … No, no.
And yet … I think I see a hint of what
You might become. An opportunity!
My strong imagination sees a crown
Descending on your head.

SEBASTIAN   Are you awake?

ANTONIO   Did you not hear me speak?

SEBASTIAN   I did, and surely
It was a sleepy language that you spoke,
As if you were asleep. What are you saying?
This a strange repose, to be asleep
With eyes wide open; standing, speaking, moving,

	And yet quite fast asleep.
ANTONIO	Noble Sebastian,
	Your destiny's asleep. Or dead! You close
	Your eyes when you're awake.
SEBASTIAN	You snore quite clearly;
	There's meaning in your snores.
ANTONIO	I am more serious than usual. You
	Must be so too, and if you heed my words,
	You will be three times greater.
SEBASTIAN	I could flow
	Forward or backward.
ANTONIO	Let me teach you how.
SEBASTIAN	Hereditary sloth is my instructor.
ANTONIO	Oh!
	If only you could see how mocking my
	Proposal shows you like it! How by stripping it
	You really clothe it! Those whose tides are out
	Most often run so near the lowest point
	From their own fear or sloth.
SEBASTIAN	Continue, please;
	Your look and your expression seem to say
	You have important things to share. The birth
	Of these ideas is causing you much pain.
ANTONIO	Although this lord, whose memory is weak – and he
	Himself won't be remembered when he's gone –
	Although he almost had the king believe –
	And it's his job as courtier to persuade him –
	He almost had the king believe his son
	Is still alive. But it's impossible
	He was not drowned. Or else you might believe
	That man is swimming, not asleep.
SEBASTIAN	No hope
	That he's alive remains.
ANTONIO	Oh, your "no hope"
	Could bring a greater hope! "No hope" that way is
	Another way to contemplate a hope
	Of something far beyond ambition's reach
	To be discovered yet. Do you agree
	That Ferdinand has drowned?
SEBASTIAN	He's gone.
ANTONIO	Then tell me,
	Who's the next heir of Naples?

SEBASTIAN   Claribel.

ANTONIO   The one who's Queen of Tunis. She's the one
             Who lives a lifetime far away. She gets
             No news from Naples, not unless the sun
             Can send it, being faster than the moon.
             The time it takes a new born babe to get
             A razorable chin is not enough.
             It was from her we came when shipwreck struck,
             Though some of us survived. And now our destiny
             Is to perform a deed for which what happened
             Is just the prologue. Now the future rests
             In our hands, yours and mine.

SEBASTIAN   What nonsense is this? What d'you have in mind?
             It's true my brother's daughter's Queen of Tunis,
             So she is heir of Naples, and the distance
             Between the two is vast.

ANTONIO   And every yard
             Of it appears to say: "How will that Claribel
             Get sooner back to Naples? Stay in Tunis,
             And let Sebastian wake." If this were death
             That's overcome them, they would be no worse
             Than they are now. And others could rule Naples
             As well as him that's sleeping there: some lord
             As full of prattle and unwanted talk
             As that Gonzalo. I myself could make
             A jackdaw chat like that. If only you
             Were thinking as I do! What you might gain
             From that deep slumber! Do you understand me?

SEBASTIAN   I think I do.

ANTONIO   And how does your approval
             Enhance your own good fortune?

SEBASTIAN   I remember
             You did supplant your brother Prospero.

ANTONIO   True.
             And look how well my royal garments fit me,
             More neatly than before. My brother's servants
             Were then my equals, now they are my staff.

SEBASTIAN   But what about your conscience?

ANTONIO   Indeed, sir, where is that? Supposing it
             Were chilblains, I'd be sore, but no, it's not;
             It does not rule my bosom. Twenty consciences
             That keep me from Milan are frozen hard;

They'll melt before they move me. Here lies your brother,
No better than the earth he lies on. Just
Suppose he were what now he seems – that's dead …
With this obedient steel, three inches long,
I could despatch him, while you do the same
And put this ancient morsel, this Sir Prudence,
To his eternal rest. He'll have no chance
To disapprove our action … Then the rest
Will take suggestion as a cat laps milk;
They'll even tell the time for us if that
Is what we ask.

SEBASTIAN   Your case, my friend,
Will be my precedent. You got Milan,
I'll come by Naples. Draw your sword! One stroke
Will free you from the tribute that you pay,
And I as king will love you.

ANTONIO   Draw together,
And when I raise my hand, you do the same
And let it strike Gonzalo.

SEBASTIAN   A quick word first.

Enter Ariel with music.

ARIEL   My master, through his art, foresees the danger
That you, his friend, are in, and sends me here
To keep them both alive (or else he fails).

Sings in Gonzalo's ear.

> While you here do snoring lie,
> Open-eyed conspiracy
> His time doth take.
> If of life you keep a care,
> Shake off slumber and beware.
> Awake! Awake!

ANTONIO   Then let us both act quickly.
GONZALO   Now, now! May heaven preserve the king!
ALONSO   What's this? Wake up! Why have you drawn?
What makes you so afraid?
GONZALO   What's the matter?
SEBASTIAN While we stood here protecting your repose,
We heard a sudden hollow burst of bellowing,
Like bulls, or rather lions. Did you hear it?
It hurt my ears severely.

ALONSO	I heard nothing.
ANTONIO	It was a din, enough to scare a monster off,
	Or cause an earthquake! Must have been the roar
	Of a whole pride of lions.
ALONSO	Did you hear it, Gonzalo?
GONZALO	To tell the truth, I heard a humming sound
	And very strange it was. It woke me up.
	I shook you, sir, and yelled. With open eyes
	I saw their weapons drawn. There was a noise,
	That's true. We'd better stand on guard and watch,
	Or else not stay here. Better draw our weapons.
ALONSO	Lead off from here and let's make further search
	For my poor son.
GONZALO	Heaven save him from these beasts,
	He must be on the island.
ALONSO	Go ahead.
ARIEL	Prospero my lord shall know what I have done.
	So, king, go safely on to seek your son.

Exeunt.

Act II Scene 2

Enter Caliban with a load of wood; a noise of thunder is heard.

CALIBAN	May all the infections that the sun sucks up
	From bogs, fens, swamps, on Prospero fall, and make him
	Inch by inch a disease! His spirits hear me,
	And yet I have to curse. They'll neither pinch me
	Nor frighten me with goblins, throw me in the mud,
	Nor lead me like a phosphorescent light
	Out of my way unless he tells them to.
	They'll set upon me at the slightest thing,
	Sometimes like apes that scowl and chatter at me,
	Then bite me, then appear like hedgehogs which
	Lie all across my path and raise their quills,
	Tormenting my bare feet. Sometimes I am
	Entwined by adders that with cloven tongues
	Enrage me with their hissing. Look there, look!

Enter Trinculo.

Here comes one of his spirits, to torment me
For bringing wood in slowly. I'll fall flat,
Perhaps he will not see me.

TRINCULO   There's not a bush nor shrub here to ward off any
weather at all, and another storm's brewing. I can hear it singing
in the wind. That black cloud over there, the huge one, looks like
a jug that's about to shed its liquor. If it thunders as it did before,
I don't know where to hide my head. That same cloud is bound
to come down in bucketfuls. What have we here, a man or a fish?
Dead or alive? A fish. He smells like a fish, a very ancient, fish-like
smell, a kind of – not the newest – dried hake. A strange fish! If I
were in England now, as I used to be once, and had this fish on a
shop sign, there's not a passer-by who wouldn't give me a piece of
silver. This monster would make a man's fortune there; any strange
beast there makes a man's fortune. They might not give a farthing
to relieve a lame beggar, but they'll lay out ten to see a dead
Indian. It's got legs like a man and fins like arms! It's warm, my
goodness! I do declare, I can hold it back no longer: this is no fish,
it's an islander recently struck by lightning. Oh dear, the storm's
got up again. My best plan is to creep under his cloak, there's no
other shelter round here. Misery introduces a man to strange
bedfellows! I'll climb in here till the last dregs of the storm have
passed.

Enter Stephano singing.

STEPHANO   I shall no more to sea, to sea,
Here shall I die ashore.

This is a sorry tune to sing at a man's funeral. Well, here's my
comfort. *(Drinks.)*

The master, the swabber, the boatswain and I,
The gunner and his mate,
Loved Mall, Meg and Marian, and Margey,
But none of us cared for Kate.
For she had a tongue with a tang,
Would cry to a sailor, "Go hang!"
She loved not the savour of tar nor of pitch,
Yet a tailor might scratch her where'er she did itch.
Then to sea, boys, and let her go hang!

That's a sorry tune too; but here's my comfort. *(Drinks.)*

CALIBAN   Don't torment me! Oh!

STEPHANO   What's the matter? Are there devils here? Are you playing tricks with us with savages and Indians? Ha! I didn't escape drowning just to be scared of your four legs; there's a saying, "As good a man as ever went on four legs cannot make him give ground." And it will be said again so long as Stephano breathes through his nostrils.

CALIBAN   The spirit's tormenting me! Oh!

STEPHANO   This is some monster from the island, with four legs, who's got a fever, I take it. How the devil does he know our language? I'll help him along, if only for that reason. If I can restore him and keep him tame, and get to Naples with him, he'd be a present for any emperor that ever trod on shoe-leather.

CALIBAN   Don't punish me, please! I'll bring my wood in faster!

STEPHANO   He's having a fit now and doesn't make much sense. He can have a taste from my bottle. If he's never drunk wine before, it will help cure him of his fit. If I can restore him and keep him tame, no price will be too high for him. Whoever gets him will pay for him, and plenty.

CALIBAN   You haven't hurt me much yet, but you soon will; I know it from your trembling. Prospero's working on you now.

STEPHANO   Come along now. Open your mouth. Here's something that'll give you language, you cat. Open your mouth. This will shake your shaking, I tell you, good and proper. [*Caliban drinks.*] You never know who's your friend; open your chops again. [*Caliban drinks again.*]

TRINCULO   I should know that voice. It could be … but he's drowned, and these are devils. Help!

STEPHANO   Four legs and two voices! A most delightful monster! His front voice is for speaking well of his friend; his back voice is to utter foul language and disparage. If it takes all the wine in my bottle to restore him, I'll cure his fever. Come. [*Caliban drinks.*] Amen. I'll pour some into your other mouth.

TRINCULO   Stephano!

STEPHANO   Is your other mouth calling me? Mercy, mercy! This is a devil, not a monster! I'll leave him alone. I don't have a long spoon!

TRINCULO   Stephano! If you are Stephano, touch me and speak to me. I'm Trinculo, don't be frightened, your good friend Trinculo.

STEPHANO   If you're Trinculo, come out. I'll pull you by your shorter legs. If any legs are Trinculo's, these are they. You are Trinculo indeed! How did you come to be this mooncalf's shit? Can he pass Trinculos?

TRINCULO   I took him to have been killed by lightning. But weren't you drowned, Stephano? I hope you weren't drowned. Has the storm blown over? I hid under the dead mooncalf's cape for fear of the storm. And are you alive, Stephano? O Stephano, two Neapolitans escaped!

STEPHANO   Please ... don't push me about. My stomach's not very settled.

CALIBAN   These are fine creatures if they're not spirits. That's a brave god who offers heavenly liquor. I'll kneel to him.

STEPHANO   How did you escape? How did you get here? Swear by this bottle how you got here. I escaped on a barrel of sack which the sailors heaved overboard. Swear by this bottle, which I made from the bark of a tree with my own hands after I was cast ashore.

CALIBAN   I'll swear by that bottle to be your faithful subject, for the liquor is not of this world.

STEPHANO   Here. Swear then how you escaped.

TRINCULO   Swam ashore, man, like a duck. I can swim like a duck, I guarantee.

STEPHANO   Here, kiss the book. [*Trinculo drinks.*] Though you can swim like a duck, you're made like a goose.

TRINCULO   O Stephano, have you any more of this?

STEPHANO   The whole barrel, man. My cellar is in a rock by the sea, where my wine is hidden. How are you, mooncalf? How's your fever?

CALIBAN   Did you just drop from heaven?

STEPHANO   Out of the moon, I tell you. I was the man in the moon once upon a time.

CALIBAN   I've seen you there, and I worship you! My mistress showed me, you and your dog and your bush.

STEPHANO   Come and swear to that. Kiss the book. I'll supply some new contents soon. Swear.

TRINCULO   In this good light, this is a very feeble monster. Me be afraid of him? A very weak monster. The man in the moon? A very poor, credulous monster. That was a good mouthful you took, I tell you.

CALIBAN   I'll show you every fertile inch of the island. And I'll kiss your feet. Please be my god!

TRINCULO   In this light a very treacherous and drunken monster. When god's asleep, he'll steal his bottle.

CALIBAN   I'll kiss your foot. I promise to be your subject.

STEPHANO   Come on, then. Down, and swear.

TRINCULO   I'll die of laughing at this puppy-headed monster. A really pathetic monster. I could easily find myself beating him ...

STEPHANO   Come on, kiss ...

TRINCULO   ... if the poor monster weren't drunk. An inhuman
monster!

CALIBAN   I'll show you all the island's springs; I'll pick you berries,
catch fish for you and fetch plenty of wood. A curse upon the
tyrant that I serve! I won't take any more sticks for him but follow
you, you marvellous man.

TRINCULO   A really ridiculous monster! To treat a poor drunkard as
a miracle!

CALIBAN   Please let me take you where crab-apples grow. With my
long nails I'll dig for pig-nuts for you, show you a jay's nest, and
instruct you how to snare the nimble marmoset. I'll find you
bunches of hazelnuts; sometimes I'll get you young shellfish from
the rocks. Will you come with me?

STEPHANO   Please just lead the way without any more talk. Trinculo,
the King, and the rest of our company having drowned, we will
inherit here. Here, take my bottle. Friend Trinculo, we'll fill it
again by and by.

CALIBAN   *(Sings drunkenly.)* Farewell, master; farewell, farewell!

TRINCULO   What a howling, drunken monster!

CALIBAN   No more dams I'll make for fish,
                            Nor fetch in firing at requiring
                            Nor scrape trenchering, nor wash dish.
                            Ban, ban, Ca-caliban,
                            Has a new master, get a new man.
                            Freedom, high-day; high-day freedom;
                            Freedom, high-day, freedom.

STEPHANO   Come on, brave monster, lead the way.

Exeunt.

Act III Scene 1

Enter Ferdinand, carrying a log.

FERDINAND Some work can be laborious, but delight
                In doing it makes up. Some kinds of labour
                Are nobly undertaken; most poor matters
                Engender rich results. This task I do
                Would be as burdensome as odious,
                Were it not lightened by the mistress that I serve.
                This makes my labour pleasant. Oh, she is
                Ten times more gentle than her surly father:

He's nothing but severity. I must
Collect and stack some thousands of these logs,
His strict command. My lovely mistress
Weeps when she sees me working; such a toil,
She says, was never done so well. I muse ...
But these sweet thoughts always revive me
Most strongly when I'm working.

Enter Miranda and Prospero.

MIRANDA   Please, I beg you,
Don't work so hard. I wish the lightning had
Burnt up those logs you have to fetch and stack.
Just put that down and rest. When these logs burn
They'll weep for having wearied you. My father
Is hard at study; so now take a rest,
He's there the next three hours.

FERDINAND   O dearest mistress,
The sun will set before I shall be done
With all I have to do.

MIRANDA   If you sit down,
I'll move your logs a while. Just give me that;
I'll carry it to the pile.

FERDINAND   No, precious creature!
I'd rather sprain my muscles, break my back,
Than see you suffer such humiliation
While I sit idly by.

MIRANDA   It's no more shame
To me than it's to you, and I would do it
With much more ease, because my heart is in it,
And yours is not.

PROSPERO   [*Aside*]   Poor worm, you are affected!
This conversation shows it.

MIRANDA   You look weary.

FERDINAND No, noble mistress, I feel fresh as morning,
While you're more nearly night. I do beseech you –
Just so that I may say it in my prayers –
What is your name?

MIRANDA   Miranda. O dear father,
You told me not to say so ...

FERDINAND   Admired Miranda!
Indeed the top of admiration, worth
The dearest in the world! More than one lady

Have I looked keenly at, and many a time
The music of their speech has captured me
And my attentive ears. For several virtues
Have I liked several women; but never any
With a soul so full that some defect did not
Conflict with all the best in her and turn
Those qualities against herself. But you,
So perfect and so peerless, are created
Of all that's best in all of them.

MIRANDA   I know
No other of my sex; no woman's face remember
Except my own, seen in a mirror. Nor
Have I set eyes on any men but you,
Good friend, and my dear father. I don't know
What's to be seen elsewhere, but my modesty
(The jewel I possess) I would not give
To any companion in the world but you,
Nor can my imagination form a shape
That I could like, except yourself. I prattle
A bit too loosely! And my father's orders
I easily forget.

FERDINAND   I am by rank and birth
A prince, Miranda; thinking like a king
(I wish it were not so!), I no more bear
The slavery of logs than if I had
A plague of flies upon me. Hear my soul speak:
The very instant that I saw you first
My heart told me to serve you, and insists
That I become your slave. So for your sake
Am I this patient log-man.

MIRANDA   Do you love me?

FERDINAND O heaven, O earth, bear witness to my words
And bring the happy outcome that I long for
If I speak true; if I do not, then see to it
That no good fortune come my way. For I,
Beyond all limits that the world can know,
Do love, prize, honour you.

MIRANDA   I am a fool
To weep at what I'm glad of.

PROSPERO   [*Aside*]   What a happy
Convergence of such rare emotions! Heaven
Pour blessings on their union!

FERDINAND   Why the tears?

MIRANDA   At my unworthiness, not having courage
Enough to offer what I long to give, much less
To take what I would die for lack of. Still,
It's true: the more I try to hide my feelings
The more they are exposed. Be coy no more,
I tell myself! Let holy innocence declare:
I am your wife, if you will marry me!
If not, I'll die your servant. Your companion
You may not let me be, but I will serve you
Whether you will or no.

FERDINAND   Beloved, dear,
Yours humbly I remain.

MIRANDA   My husband, then?

FERDINAND   Yes, with a heart as longing
As bondage is for freedom. Here's my hand.

MIRANDA   And mine, with my heart in it. Now farewell,
Till half an hour from now.

FERDINAND   A thousand thousand!

Exeunt.

PROSPERO   I cannot be as glad at this as they;
I am amazed by it, but nothing else
Could make me so content. I have to work,
Before it's suppertime, to see to much
Related business.

Exit.

Act III Scene 2

Enter Caliban, Stephano and Trinculo.

STEPHANO   Don't tell me! When the barrel's empty we'll drink water,
not a drop before; so bear up and go at 'em! Servant monster, drink
to me!

TRINCULO   Servant monster? The island freak! They say there are
just five on the island, and we're three of them. If the other two
have brains as addled as ours, the state's in a bad way.

STEPHANO   Drink up, servant monster, when I tell you to. Your eyes
are almost set in your head.

TRINCULO   Where else would they be set? He'd be some monster if
they were set in his tail.

STEPHANO   My man-monster has drowned his tongue in drink. For
my part, the sea cannot drown me – I swam around a hundred
miles to get to shore. I tell you, monster, you can be my lieutenant,
or my standard-bearer.

TRINCULO   Your lieutenant, if you like. He's no standard-bearer.

STEPHANO   We won't flee from battle, Monsieur Monster.

TRINCULO   Nor walk either. You'll lie, like dogs, and yet say nothing.

STEPHANO   Moon-calf, speak for once in your life, if you're a good
moon-calf.

CALIBAN   How is your honour? Let me lick your shoes. I won't serve
him. He's not brave.

TRINCULO   You're lying, you ignorant monster! I'm ready to jostle
a constable! Why, you drunken fish, has anyone who'd drunk as
much sack as I have today ever been a coward? Are you telling a
monstrous lie because you're half a fish and half a monster?

CALIBAN   Listen to him making fun of me! Will you let him do that,
my lord?

TRINCULO   "Lord" he calls you! What an idiot a monster can be!

CALIBAN   Listen again! Bite him to death, please!

STEPHANO   Trinculo, keep a civil tongue in your head! If you behave
like a mutineer, you'll hang on the nearest tree. The poor monster's
my subject, and he'll not suffer any indignity.

CALIBAN   Thankyou, my noble lord. Would you be prepared to listen
once again to the petition I made to you?

STEPHANO   Of course I will. Kneel and repeat it. I will stand, and so
will Trinculo.

Enter Ariel invisible.

CALIBAN   As I told you before, I am enslaved by a tyrant, a sorcerer
that cheated me out of the island by his magic.

ARIEL   You are lying.

CALIBAN   You're lying, you jesting monkey, you! I wish my brave
master would destroy you! I do not lie.

STEPHANO   Trinculo, if you trouble him any more when he's
speaking, I'll knock your teeth out.

TRINCULO   Why, I said nothing.

STEPHANO   Be quiet, then, and say no more. Continue.

CALIBAN   I say: by sorcery he got this island.
From me he took it. Please, your majesty,
Reclaim it for me, for I know you dare to,
While this thing doesn't.

STEPHANO   That's very certain.

CALIBAN	You will be lord of it and I will serve you.
STEPHANO	How's this to be achieved? I need to see
	The person you refer to.
CALIBAN	Yes, yes, my lord. I'll find him for you sleeping,
	So you can knock a nail into his head.
ARIEL	You're lying. You can't.
CALIBAN	Who is this jesting fool? You miserable clown!
	If only you would knock him down, your highness!
	And take his bottle from him. When that's gone,
	He'll have to drink the sea, for I'll not show him
	Where the fresh springs are.
STEPHANO	Trinculo, don't run into any more danger. Interrupt the monster one more time and I'll abandon all sense of mercy and beat you like a dead fish.
TRINCULO	Why? What did I do? I did nothing! I'll move away a bit.
STEPHANO	Didn't you say he lied?
ARIEL	You're lying.
STEPHANO	Am I? Take that! If you enjoy it, call me a liar again!
TRINCULO	I didn't call you a liar. Your mind's adrift, and your hearing too. To hell with that bottle! This is what wine and drink can do. A plague on your monster, and damn your fingers!
CALIBAN	Ha, ha ha!
STEPHANO	Carry on with your tale. [*To Trinculo*] Please stand further away.
CALIBAN	Keep beating him; after a little while I'll beat him too.
STEPHANO	Further away! [*To Caliban*] Come on, continue.
CALIBAN	Well, as I told you, it's his usual custom
	To sleep in the afternoon. Then you can brain him,
	Having first seized his books, or with a log
	Batter his skull, or stab him with a stake,
	Or cut his wind-pipe with your knife. Remember,
	First take away his books, for without them
	He's just a fool, as I am, and has lost
	His power to command. His spirits hate him
	As bitterly as I do. Just the books
	Should burn; utensils, as he calls them,
	Will serve to decorate his house some time.
	Remember always the important thing:
	The beauty of his daughter; he himself
	Calls her his non-pareil. I'd never seen
	A woman, only Sycorax, my mother;
	But she as far surpasses Sycorax

As greatest is to least.

STEPHANO   Is she that fine?

CALIBAN   She is, and worthy of your bed, I promise;
              She'll bear you quite a brood.

STEPHANO   Monster, I will kill this man. His daughter and I will be
    king and queen – save our graces – and Trinculo and you will be
    viceroys. Do you like the plot, Trinculo?

TRINCULO   Excellent.

STEPHANO   Give me your hand. I'm sorry I hit you. But while you're
    alive, keep a civil tongue in your head!

CALIBAN   Within the next half hour he'll be asleep. Will you attack
    him then?

STEPHANO   I will, on my honour.

ARIEL   This I will tell my master.

CALIBAN   You cheer me up. I'm full of happy spirits.
   So let's be merry. Will you sing the round
   You taught me recently?

STEPHANO   At your request, monster, I'll do anything reasonable.
   Come on, Trinculo, let's sing.

> Flout 'em and scout 'em
> And scout 'em and flout 'em
> Thought is free.

CALIBAN   That's not the tune.

Ariel plays the tune on a tabor and pipe.

STEPHANO   What's that one?

TRINCULO   That's the tune of our song, played by a disembodied
    voice.

STEPHANO   If you're a real man, show yourself as one. If you're a devil,
    do whatever you like.

TRINCULO   O forgive me my sins!

STEPHANO   A dead man pays all his debts! I defy you! Mercy on us!

CALIBAN   Are you afraid?

STEPHANO   No, monster, I'm not.

CALIBAN   Don't be afraid! The island's full of noises
            And sounds that please and do no harm to anyone.
            Sometimes a thousand twanging instruments
            Will jangle in my ears, and sometimes voices
            Which, if I'd just then woken up from sleep,
            Send me to sleep again; and then I dream
            Of clouds that open up and shower me

With untold riches, so that when I wake
I long to dream again.

STEPHANO   That will be a fine kingdom where I can get my music for
nothing.

CALIBAN   When Prospero is destroyed.

STEPHANO   That'll be soon. I remember the story.

Exit Ariel, playing music.

TRINCULO   The sound's going away; let's follow it, and afterwards do
our work.

STEPHANO   You lead, monster, we'll follow. I wish I could see that
drummer, he's going at it!

TRINCULO   Are you coming? I'll follow Stephano.

Exeunt.

Act III Scene 3

*Enter Alonso, Sebastian, Antonio, Gonzalo,
Adrian, Francisco and others.*

GONZALO   O Holy Mary, I can go no further.
My old bones ache. This is a real maze
With straight and winding paths. Bear with me, please!
I have to rest.

ALONSO   Old lord, I cannot blame you,
Being myself worn out with weariness
And dull in spirit too. Sit down and rest.
It's time to give up hope; let's not deceive
Ourselves in this. We search around in vain,
But he is drowned. By searching here on land
The sea just mocks us. Well, let him go.

ANTONIO   I'm glad to hear that he's abandoned hope.
So don't let one rebuff deter you from the goal
You set your mind to reach.

SEBASTIAN   The next advantage
We'll seize for certain.

ANTONIO   Let it be tonight;
For now they're quite exhausted from the strain
Of travel, and are not as vigilant
As when they're fresh.

SEBASTIAN   I say tonight. That's it.

Solemn and strange music, and Prospero on the top, invisible.

ALONSO	What music do I hear? My good friends, hark!
GONZALO	Marvellous, lovely music.

Enter several strange shapes, bringing in a banquet,
and dance around it with gentle gestures of salutation.
Inviting the King and the others to eat, they depart.

ALONSO	Angels protect us! Heavens! Who were they?
SEBASTIAN	A living puppet show! Now I'll believe
	That there are unicorns, that in Arabia
	There is one tree in which one phoenix
	Sits reigning there.

ANTONIO   I'll believe both;
And what else tests belief, just come to me
And I will swear it's true. For travellers don't lie,
Though fools at home condemn them.

GONZALO   If in Naples
I should report this now, would they believe me?
If I should say I saw such islanders –
For certain these are people from the island –
Who, though they are of monstrous shape, behave
Politely and more kindly than any
Our human race can offer, or perhaps
I should say *almost*.

PROSPERO   Honest lord,
You are quite right, for some of you there present
Are worse than devils.

ALONSO   I cannot have too much
Delight from shapes and gestures such as these.
The sound, although they use no tongue, is like
An excellent dumb discourse.

PROSPERO   Save praise for later.

FRANCISCO They've vanished! Strange!

SEBASTIAN   No matter, since they
Have left their food behind; we still have appetites.
Do you wish to try what's offered here?

ALONSO   Not I.

GONZALO But sir, you need not worry. When we were boys,
Who would believe that there were mountain people
With sagging bands of skin and swollen throats
With flesh beneath? Or that there were such men
Whose heads grow from their breast? These curious tales
May be confirmed by anyone who travels

And then comes safely back.

ALONSO   I'll have the meal,
Even if it is my last; that doesn't matter,
The best in life is past. Brother, my lord the Duke,
Sit down and join us.

Thunder and lightning. Enter Ariel, like a harpy, who claps his wings
on the table, and with a quaint device the banquet vanishes.

ARIEL   You are three sinful men, whom destiny –
That uses as its instrument this world of ours
And all that's in it – caused the greedy sea
To belch you up and plant you on this island,
Where no man lives. Since you of all people
Are least deserving, I have made you mad.
With madness comes the courage such men feel
To hang or drown themselves.

Alonso, Sebastian, Antonio draw their swords.

                                    You fools! For we
Are ministers of fate. The elements
Of which your swords are fashioned might as well
Destroy the wind, or kill the surging water
With useless stabs, as lunge at me and slice
A single feather from these plumes. My servants
Are both invulnerable too. Moreover
Your swords are now too heavy for your strength,
Too heavy even to lift. But remember
(This is my message to you) that you three
Did force good Prospero to leave Milan,
And put him out to sea (which saved him),
Him and his innocent child; this dreadful crime
Is not forgotten by the heavenly powers,
Who have incensed the seas and shores against you,
And every creature too. Your son, Alonso,
They've taken. Through my voice they now
Pronounce a sentence of eternal ruin,
Worse than instant death. This punishment
Will step by step apply. Your only hope,
To save you from the fate that will befall you
Here in this wretched island, is repentance
And a blameless life.

He vanishes in thunder; then, to soft music, enter the shapes again,
and dance, grinning and grimacing, and carry out the table.

PROSPERO   You have performed the role of harpy well,
            My Ariel, disposing of that meal
            With grace. You left out none of my instructions
            In what you had to say. My lesser spirits
            Have equally performed their various duties
            With energy and skill. My magic works,
            And these, my enemies, are all tied up
            In their confusion. They are in my power,
            And in that state I'll leave them while I visit
            Young Ferdinand (who they suppose is drowned)
            And his, and my, beloved.

                            Exit Prospero.

GONZALO   In the name of all things holy, sir, why do you
            Stare like that so strangely?

ALONSO   Oh, it is monstrous, monstrous!
            I thought the waves were speaking to me,
            The winds were singing also, and the thunder –
            That deep and dreadful organ pipe – pronounced
            The name of Prospero. Its low bass voice
            Accused me. So my son is buried in the mud
            Of the ocean, deeper than the lead can sound.
            I'll join him there myself.

SEBASTIAN   However many fiends there are, I'll fight
            One at a time.

ANTONIO   I'll be your second.

                Exeunt Sebastian and Antonio.

GONZALO   All three of them are desperate. Their great guilt,
            Like poison that can kill a long while later,
            Begins to eat their conscience. I do beg you,
            You who have suppler joints than I, to follow
            Them quickly, and forestall whatever harm
            Their madness might provoke.

ADRIAN   Then follow me!

                    Exeunt omnes.

Act IV Scene 1

Enter Prospero, Ferdinand and Miranda

PROSPERO   If I have too austerely punished you,
Then your reward will make amends, for I
Have given you here a part of my own life,
What most of all I live for. Once again
I offer you her hand. All your vexations
Were just trials of your love, and you
Have fully passed the test. Heaven be my witness,
I here confirm this precious gift. O Ferdinand,
Don't laugh at me because I boast about her!
You'll find she far outpaces all my praise
And leaves it far behind.

FERDINAND I do believe it, and I give my word.

PROSPERO   Then as my gift, and as your acquisition
Worthily purchased, take my daughter. But
If you should plunder her virginity
Before the sacred ceremony and
The full and holy rites be done,
The heavens will deny the sprinkled water
That guarantees the contract. Bitter hatred,
Mistrust and scorn will strew the marriage bed
With loathsome weeds, not flowers, and both
Of you will come to hate it. So take heed,
Obey the laws of Hymen.

FERDINAND   As I hope
For quiet days, fair children and long life
With love as we have now, no murky cave,
No shady corner where temptation might
Assail my baser instinct, ever will
Let lust betray my honour and deprive
Our great day's celebration of its joy,
When I shall think the sun will never sink
And night will never fall.

PROSPERO   Fine sentiments!
Sit then, and talk with her, she is your own.
Hey, Ariel! My industrious servant, Ariel!

Enter Ariel.

ARIEL   You need me, mighty master? Here I am.

PROSPERO You and your crew did excellently serve me
In that recent business. Now I have to use you

	For something else. Go fetch that rowdy rabble

          For something else. Go fetch that rowdy rabble
And bring them here. They're at your orders.
Make sure they spring to action, for I need
To offer this young couple something new,
Some trifling trick of magic. This I've promised,
And they expect it from me.

ARIEL   Immediately?

PROSPERO   Yes, in a flash.

ARIEL   Before you can say "come" and "go",
                And breathe twice and cry "so, so",
                Each one tripping on his toe,
                Will be here with mop and mow,
                Do you love me, master? No?

PROSPERO   Dearly, my delicate Ariel. Do not return
Until you hear me call.

ARIEL   I understand.

Exit Ariel.

PROSPERO   Be true to your word. Do not let dalliance
Get out of hand. The strongest vows can lose
Against fire in the blood. Restrain yourself
Or else goodbye to your vow.

FERDINAND   I promise, sir,
The ice-cold snow that rules my heart
Abates the ardour of my lust.

PROSPERO   Very well.
Come here, my Ariel. Bring an extra spirit,
Rather than manage without. Appear! Quickly!

Soft music.

No words! All eyes! Silence!

Enter Iris.

IRIS   Most bounteous goddess of the earth, Ceres!
Your wheat, rye, barley, vetches, oats and peas;
Your turfy mountains where live nibbling sheep;
And flat fields thick with grasses, them to keep;
Your banks with trenched and reeded brims,
Which spongy April at your bidding trims,
To make cold nymphs chaste crowns; and your green groves
Whose shadow the rejected suitor loves,
Having no girl; your well pruned vineyard,
And your sea-shore, sterile and rocky-hard,

Where you do walk, Juno, queen of the sky,
Whose rainbow and whose messenger am I,
Bids you leave these, and with her sovereign grace,
Here on this grass plot, in this very place,
To come and sport. Her peacocks fly amain.
Approach, rich Ceres, her to entertain.

Enter Ceres.

CERES Hail, many-coloured messenger, that ne'er
Would disobey the wife of Jupiter.
Who, with your saffron wings, upon my flowers
Diffuse sweet honey drops, refreshing showers,
And with each end of your blue bow do crown
My leafy acres, and my shrubless down,
Rich scarf to my proud earth. Why has your queen
Summoned me here, to this grass-covered green?

IRIS A contract of true love to celebrate,
And some donation freely to estate
On the blest lovers.

CERES Tell me, heavenly bow,
If Venus or her son, as you will know,
Do now attend the queen? Since they did plot
The means dark Pluto once my daughter got,
Her and blind Cupid's shameful company
I have forsworn.

IRIS Of her society
Be not afraid. I met her deity
Cutting the clouds towards Paphos, and her son
Dove-drawn with her. Here thought they to have done
Some wanton charm upon this man and maid,
Whose vows are, that no bed-right be paid
Till Hymen's torch be lighted – but in vain.
Mars's hot minion is returned again;
Her waspish-headed son has broke his arrows;
Swears he will shoot no more, but play with sparrows,
And be a boy right out.

Juno descends.

Highest queen of state,
Great Juno comes, I know her by her gait.

JUNO How does my bounteous sister? Go with me
To bless these two, that they may prosperous be,
And honoured in their issue.

They sing.

JUNO   Honour, riches, marriage-blessing,
                 Long continuance, and increasing,
                 Hourly joys be still upon you,
                 Juno sings her blessing on you.

CERES   Earth's increase, and foison plenty,
                 Barns and garners never empty,
                 Vines, with clust'ring bunches growing,
                 Plants, with goodly burden bowing;

                 Spring come to you at the farthest,
                 In the very end of harvest.
                 Scarcity and want shall shun you,
                 Ceres's blessing so is on you.

FERDINAND This is a most impressive vision, and
                 Delightful to the ear. Would I be bold
                 In thinking these are spirits?
PROSPERO   Yes, they are,
                 Called up by me to play whatever part
                 My fancy has for them.
FERDINAND   Oh let me stay here!
                 So rare and generous a father and a wife
                 Make this place paradise!

Juno and Ceres whisper, and send Iris on employment.

PROSPERO   Be silent, now.
                 Juno and Ceres are whispering together.
                 There's something else to do. Hush, and be quiet,
                 Or else our spell is marred.
IRIS   You nymphs, called naiads of the winding brooks,
                 With your sedges crowns, and ever-harmless looks,
                 Leave your crisp channels, and on this green land
                 Answer your summons, Juno does command.
                 Come, temperate nymphs, and help to celebrate
                 A contract of true love. Be not too late.

Enter certain nymphs.

                 You sunburned sicklemen of August weary,
                 Come hither from the furrow, and be merry,
                 Make holiday; your rye-straw hats put on,
                 And these fresh nymphs encounter every one
                 In country dancing.

Enter certain reapers, properly clothed.
They join with the nymphs, in a graceful dance, towards
the end of which Prospero starts up suddenly and speaks.

PROSPERO   I had forgotten the conspiracy
                  Of that beast Caliban and his confederates
                  Against my life. The action of their plot
                  Is almost due. [*To the spirits*] Well done! Be off! That's all.

To a strange, hollow and confused noise the spirits heavily vanish.

FERDINAND This is strange. Your father's in a passion
                  That affects hims strongly.
MIRANDA   Never till today
                  Have I seen him so angry and distraught.
PROSPERO   You look, my son, as if you were dismayed
                  By something. That's not good. Be cheerful!
                  Our revels now are over; all these actors
                  Were spirits, as I told you, they have melted,
                  Quite vanished into air, into thin air.
                  And like the flimsy fabric of this vision,
                  The cloud-capped towers, the gorgeous palaces,
                  The solemn temples, the great globe itself,
                  Those who inherit it, will all dissolve,
                  And like this insubstantial pageant fade
                  And leave not a trace behind. We are the stuff
                  That dreams are made of, and our little life
                  Begins and ends in sleep. Sir, I am vexed.
                  Bear with my weakness, my old brain is troubled.
                  Don't be disturbed at my infirmity.
                  Be good enough to go back to my cell
                  And rest awhile. I'll take a gentle walk
                  To calm my restless mind.
FERDINAND, MIRANDA   We wish you peace.

Exeunt Ferdinand and Miranda.

PROSPERO   Come, Ariel, please, at my command, yes come.

Enter Ariel.

ARIEL   Your words command me. What's your pleasure?
PROSPERO   Spirit, we must prepare to deal with Caliban.
ARIEL   Yes, gladly sir. When I presented Ceres,
                  I thought I should remind you, but I feared
                  That it would make you angry.
PROSPERO   So tell me where you last saw all those rogues.

ARIEL   I told you, sir, they'd had too much to drink.
             So full of valour they attacked the air
             For breathing in their faces! Beat the ground
             Because it kissed their feet! Yet still they kept
             On with their wicked aims. I beat my drum,
             At which they pricked up their ears like skittish colts,
             Opened their eyes and turned their noses up
             As if to smell the music. I bewitched their ears
             By mooing, which they followed like young calves,
             Through briars, thorns and bushes, prickly gorse,
             That scratched at their frail shins. At last I left them
             In that scum-covered pool quite near your cell,
             Up to their chins in mud, whose stink was worse
             Than even that of their feet.

PROSPERO   Well done, my bird.
             Remain invisible for some while yet.
             The worthless stuff in my house, go bring it here,
             A bait to catch these thieves.

ARIEL   I go, I go.   *Exit.*

PROSPERO   A devil, a born devil, on whose nature
             Nurture can never stick; I took great pains
             On his behalf. Now lost, all lost, quite lost!
             His body's ever uglier with age,
             His mind too festers. I'll torment them all
             And yell if need be. Hang them on this line.

             Enter Ariel, laden with glittering apparel, etc.
             Enter Caliban, Stephano and Trinculo, all wet.

CALIBAN   Tread softly, don't let the blind moles hear our footsteps.
       We're now near his cell.

STEPHANO   Monster, your fairy, which you call a harmless fairy, has
       done little better than play a trick on us.

TRINCULO   Monster, I smell of horse piss, which offends my nose no
       end.

STEPHANO   Mine too. Do you hear that, monster? If I should get
       annoyed with you, look out!

TRINCULO   You'd be finished, monster.

CALIBAN   My good sir, bear with me still. Be patient, for the prize I
       bring you will make up for these troubles. So speak softly. It's as
       quiet as midnight.

TRINCULO   Yes, but to lose our bottles in the pool …

STEPHANO   There's not only disgrace and dishonour in that, monster, but a considerable loss.

TRINCULO   To me it's worse than our wetting. Yet this is your harmless fairy, monster.

STEPHANO   I'll go and fetch my bottle, even if I have to go up to my ears to get it.

CALIBAN   Please, be quiet, my king. Do you see here? This is the mouth of the cell. No noise, and go in. Do that nice piece of mischief which will make this island yours for ever, and I, your Caliban, will lick your boots for ever.

STEPHANO   Give me your hand. I'm beginning to have murderous thoughts.

TRINCULO   O King Stephano! O worthy Stephano! Look at the wardrobe set out here for you!

CALIBAN   Leave it alone, you fool, it's just trash.

TRINCULO   Oh ho, monster, we know what rubbishy old clothes are. O King Stephano!

STEPHANO   Take that gown off, Trinculo. Believe me, that gown's for me.

TRINCULO   Your Grace shall have it.

CALIBAN   May dropsy drown the fool! What do you mean,
Getting excited by such trash? Leave it alone.
And do the murder first. If he wakes up,
He'll pinch each bit of skin from head to toe
And turn us into something strange.

STEPHANO   Be quiet, monster! Madame line, this jacket's for me, isn't it? Now the jacket's under the line. So, jacket, you're below the equator and so you'll be shaved by sailors and become a bald jacket!

TRINCULO   Yes, yes! We steal by plumb-line and level, if it please your grace.

STEPHANO   Thanks for the joke. Here's a garment in payment. Wit will not go unrewarded while I am king of this country. "Steal by plumb-line and level" is an excellent sally of wit. Here's another garment for it.

TRINCULO   Monster, put some sticky lime on your fingers, and get on with it.

CALIBAN   I will not put it on. A waste of time!
We'll all become like stupid geese, or apes
With sunken foreheads.

STEPHANO   Monster, put it on your fingers. Help carry this away to

where my hogshead of wine is, or I'll turn you out of my kingdom.
Go on, carry these.

TRINCULO   And this.

STEPHANO   And this too.

*A noise of hunters is heard. Enter diverse spirits in the shape of dogs
and hounds, hunting them about, Prospero and Ariel setting them on.*

PROSPERO   Hey, Mountain, hey!

ARIEL   Silver! There he goes, Silver.

PROSPERO   Fury, Fury! There, Tyrant, there! Listen!

Exeunt Caliban, Stephano and Trinculo pursued by spirits.

Go, tell my demons they must grind their joints
With sharp convulsions, tighten up their sinews
With cramps that old folks get, and bruise them
With spots more like a leopard.

ARIEL   Hark, they're roaring!

PROSPERO   Make sure the hunt succeeds. At this hour
My enemies will all be at my mercy.
My labours soon will all be done, and you
Will be as free as air. A further service
I still need, so follow me.

Exeunt.

Act V   Scene 1

Enter Prospero in his magic robes, and Ariel.

PROSPERO   My plans are now all coming to the boil.
My magic does not fail, my spirits obey,
And time is moving on. What hour is it?

ARIEL   It's six o'clock, my lord, the time at which
You said our work should cease.

PROSPERO   I did say so,
When I first raised the tempest. Tell me, spirit,
How is the King, and all his followers?

ARIEL   Confined
Exactly as you gave instruction, all together
Just as you left them, all prisoners, sir,
In the lime-grove that stands close by your cell.
They cannot budge until you say. The King,
His brother, and yours, all three losing their wits,
And the remainder mourning over them,

               Brim full of sorrow and dismay; but chiefly
               Him that you called, sir, the good old lord Gonzalo.
               His tears run down his beard like winter's rain
               From eaves of thatch. Your magic so affects them
               That if you saw them now, I know your feelings
               Would turn to tenderness.

PROSPERO   Do you think so, spirit?
ARIEL   Mine would, sir, were I human.
PROSPERO   And mine will.
               You, who are only air, have such a sense
               Of their afflictions, so can I not therefore,
               (A human being too, who feels as sharply
               As they do) be as moved to tenderness as you?
               Though I am deeply pained by their great wrongs,
               Yet with my nobler reason, I can argue
               Against my rage. A finer deed is done
               In virtue than in vengeance. They, being penitent,
               The sole aim of my actions needs to go
               Not an inch further. Go release them, Ariel.
               I'll break my spells; their senses I'll restore.
               And they will be themselves.

ARIEL   I'll fetch them, sir.   *Exit.*
PROSPERO   O elves from hills, brooks, standing lakes and groves,
               And you that chase the ebbing tide across
               The sand, no footstep in your wake, and run
               Up when it rises; and you half-sized puppets
               Who make by night green fairy-rings
               That sheep will never eat; and you whose game
               Is making midnight mushrooms, after hearing
               The curfew bell; weak masters though you are,
               You helped me when I dimmed the midday sun;
               You raised unmanageable winds for me
               And caused a roaring war between the sky
               And the green sea. I've sent down lightning
               To top the rattling thunder, I have split
               The oak tree with Jove's bolt. I've caused the earth
               Itself to tremble, and I've torn great pines and cedars
               Up by the roots. At my command graves woke
               Their sleeping guests, then by my secret art
               Let them go free. But now I will abjure
               This cruel magic. And when I have requested
               Some heavenly music – which even now I do –

To work its charm on anyone at whom
These haunting sounds are aimed, I'll break my staff,
And bury it deep, deep beneath the ground;
In deeper water than the lead can sound
I'll drown my book.

Solemn music. Here enters Ariel before: then Alonso with
a frantic gesture, attended by Gonzalo; Sebastian and
Antonio in like manner attended by Adrian and Francisco.
They all enter the circle which Prospero has made, and
there stand charmed; which Prospero observing, speaks:

A solemn melody, often prescribed
To treat disturbed imaginations, cures
Your brains (now useless) boiled within your skull.
Stand there, for you are governed by a spell.
Holy Gonzalo, honourable man,
My eyes respond to what they see in yours
And shed a brother's tears. My spells begin
To weaken, and as dawn dissolves the night,
Melting the darkness, so their wakening senses
Begin to chase the ignorant fumes that cloud
Their clearer reason. You, O good Gonzalo –
My true protector, and a loyal gentleman
And subject – I will pay for all your virtues,
Both said and done, in full. But you, Alonso,
Did treat me and my daughter cruelly.
Your brother was a party to the deed –
You suffer for it now, Sebastian. Flesh and blood,
My brother, you were driven by ambition,
Rejecting natural feelings. With Sebastian
(Whose conscience therefore is the most severe)
You would have killed your king here. I forgive you,
Inhuman though you are. Their understanding
Begins to grow, and the approaching tide
Will shortly seem to fill the shore of reason
That now lies foul and muddy. Not one of them
Has looked me in the eye or recognised me. Ariel,
Fetch me the hat and rapier in my cell;
I'll change into the costume that I wore
When I was in Milan. Go quickly, spirit,
You'll soon be free.

ARIEL *(Sings and helps to attire him.)*
>   Where the bee sucks, there suck I,
>   In a cowslip's bell I lie;
>   There I couch when owls do cry.
>   On the bat's back I do fly
>   After summer merrily.
>   Merrily, merrily, shall I live now,
>   Under the blossom that hangs on the bough.

PROSPERO Why, that's my dainty Ariel. I will miss you,
But still you'll have your freedom. So, so, so.
Go to the king's ship, still invisible;
You'll find on board the sailors all asleep
Under the hatches. The master and the boatswain,
Being awake, make sure they come straight here,
And quickly too.

ARIEL I'll drink up the air as I fly, and return
Before your pulse has beaten twice.   *Exit.*

GONZALO Here torment, trouble, wonder and amazement
Are all around us. May heaven guide us somehow
Out of this fearful country!

PROSPERO   You see, sir king,
Milan's displaced and rightful Duke, Prospero.
In order to convince you that a living prince
Is speaking to you, I embrace your body,
And to you and your company, I bid
A hearty welcome.

ALONSO   Whether you're him or not,
Or something false intended to deceive me,
As I was recently, I cannot say.
Your pulse beats as of flesh and blood. My mind,
Afflicted once with madness, now recovers
Since seeing you. This surely must deserve,
If it be truly so, the strangest explanation.
Your dukedom I resign, and here seek pardon
For all my wrongs. But how can Prospero
Be living, and why here?

PROSPERO   First, noble friend,
I pay respects to your great age, deserving
Unbounded honour.

GONZALO   Whether this be so
Or not, I cannot say.

PROSPERO   You're still in thrall
To all the island's mystery which prevents you
Believing what you see. Welcome, my friends.
But you, my pair of lords, were I so minded,
I could bring down his highness's rebuke
And prove that you are traitors. But for now
I'll tell no tales.
                                    The devil speaks in him!
SEBASTIAN   No.
PROSPERO   For you, the worst of all, whom to call brother
Would just pollute my mouth, I do forgive
Your worst offences, all of them, and take
My dukedom back, which of necessity
You must restore.
ALONSO   If you are Prospero,
Explain to us how you are still alive,
How we got here, when on this shore our ship
Was wrecked three hours ago. I lost my son,
My dear son, Ferdinand. How sharp the stab
Of pain when I recall it.
PROSPERO   I grieve too.
ALONSO   Irreparable is the loss, and there's no cure
For suffering like this.
PROSPERO   I rather think
You have not sought the help of Patience.
I've called upon her aid for my own loss
And feel the better for it.
ALONSO   Your own loss?
PROSPERO   Severe and recent, too. And furthermore
I have far fewer comforts for my loss
Than you may call on. You should know that I
Have lost my daughter.
ALONSO   A daughter?
O heavens, I wish they were both living in Naples,
As king and queen there! If that were to be,
I wish I too was buried in that muddy bed
Where my son lies. When did you lose your daughter?
PROSPERO   In this last tempest. Do you see those lords?
They're so befuddled with astonishment
They've clearly lost their reason, and refuse
To recognise the truth of what they see.
They're lost for words! Whatever caused your reason

                     To desert you, let me tell you plainly
                     That I am Prospero, the very duke
                     Driven from Milan, who ended up most strangely
                     Upon this shore, where you were wrecked, and now
                     Is lord of it. No more of this just now,
                     It is a chronicle too long to tell,
                     Not something to be finished over breakfast,
                     Nor fitting for this meeting. Welcome sir,
                     This cell's my court. I have here few attendants,
                     Nor any subjects elsewhere. Take a look!
                     Since you have given me back my rightful dukedom,
                     I will requite you with something as good,
                     And offer you a miracle to please you
                     As much as my own dukedom pleases me.

Here Prospero discovers Ferdinand and Miranda, playing chess.

MIRANDA   My lord, you're cheating!
FERDINAND   No, my dearest love, I would not for the world.
MIRANDA   But for a score of kingdoms you would wrangle!
                     And I'd call it fair play.
ALONSO   If this turns out
                     To be another of the island's tricks,
                     I'll lose a dear son twice.
SEBASTIAN   An amazing miracle!
FERDINAND   Although the sea is threatening, it can
                     Be merciful. I've cursed it without cause.
ALONSO   May all the blessings
                     Of a glad father fall upon your head.
                     Stand up, and say how you came here.
MIRANDA   O wonder!
                     How many handsome creatures there are here!
                     How beautiful mankind is! O brave new world
                     That has such people in it.
PROSPERO   It's new to you.
ALONSO   Who is this maiden you were sitting with?
                     You can have known her only for three hours.
                     Is she the goddess that divided us
                     And brought us then together?
FERDINAND   Sir, she is mortal;
                     But by immortal providence she is mine.
                     I chose her when I could not ask my father
                     For his advice; I thought I didn't have one.

> She's daughter of this famous Duke of whose
> Renown I've often heard. She's from Milan.
> I'd not seen her before, but she has given me
> A second life; this lady also brings me
> In him a second father.

ALONSO   Which I'll be.
> But, oh, how oddly will it sound, that I
> Must ask my child's forgiveness!

PROSPERO   There, sir, stop!
> Let us not spoil our memories with sad
> Events now past.

GONZALO   Within me I was weeping,
> Or else I would have said before: you gods!
> Present this couple with a sacred crown,
> For it is you who have marked out the way
> That brought us here.

ALONSO   I say amen, Gonzalo.

GONZALO Was Prospero ejected from Milan
> So that his son be king of Naples too?
> Rejoice with special fervour! Set it down
> In gold on solid pillars: the same voyage
> To Tunis for the marriage of Queen Claribel
> Brought Ferdinand, her brother, to his wife
> Though he himself was lost. For Prospero
> It brought an island dukedom; and the rest
> Of us were changed.

ALONSO   Give us your hands;
> Let grief and sorrow be the lot of those
> Who do not wish you joy.

GONZALO   So be it, amen.

Enter Ariel with the Master and Boatswain following in amazement.

> Oh look, sir, look, sir, here are more of us!
> I claimed that if there were a gallows here
> This fellow could not drown. Blasphemer, you,
> Who swore on board, d'you have an oath on shore?
> Can you not speak on land? What is the news?

BOATSWAIN   The best news is that we have safely found
> Our king and company. The next, our ship,
> Which not three hours ago we took for lost,
> Is watertight and ready, fully rigged
> As when we first put out.

ARIEL   Sir, all this service
            Is my work, done just now.
PROSPERO   My clever spirit!
ALONSO   These are not natural events, they seem
            More strange each one. Say, how did you get here?
BOATSWAIN   If I was sure, sir, I was well awake,
            I'd try to tell you. We were fast asleep
            And somehow pinioned tight beneath the hatches
            When suddenly some fearful noises woke us,
            Strange roaring, shrieking, howling, jangling chains
            And every kind of sound, all horrible.
            We found ourselves released and free,
            And saw our royal, good and gallant ship
            All trim and ready for a voyage. Our master
            Was dancing with delight. Then suddenly,
            As in a dream, the crew and we were parted,
            With us brought oddly here.
ARIEL   Did I do well?
PROSPERO   Quite fine, my clever one. You will be free.
ALONSO   This is as strange a maze as ever was,
            For it needs more explaining than just nature
            Could be responsible for. Some oracle
            Must fill in what we need to know.
PROSPERO   My lord,
            Do not disturb your mind insisting on
            The strangeness of this business. There'll be time,
            Quite soon, for me to speak with you alone;
            I will explain, in terms you can believe,
            These unforeseen events. Till when,
            Be cheerful and at ease. Come hither, spirit,
            Set Caliban and his companions free;
            Undo the spell. How are you, gracious sir?
            There are still missing from your company
            Some extra lads you seem to have forgotten.

            Enter Ariel, driving in Caliban, Stephano
            and Trinculo in their stolen apparel.

STEPHANO   Every man look to all the others and let no one take
    care of himself, for it's all up to chance. Coraggio, bully monster,
    coraggio!
TRINCULO   If these are true observers I wear in my head, this is a
    splendid sight.

CALIBAN   My god, these are fine specimens indeed!
            How splendid is my master! I'm afraid
            He'll punish me.

SEBASTIAN   Ha, ha!
            What are these things, my lord Antonio?
            Will money buy them?

ANTONIO   I dare say. D'you see,
            That one there is a fish, and no doubt marketable.

PROSPERO   Just notice these men's liveries, my lords,
            And see if they're correct. This misshapen knave,
            His mother was a witch, with strength enough
            To influence the moon, controlling tides,
            Usurping its authority to excess.
            These three have robbed me, and this half-devil
            (For he's a bastard one) had plotted with them
            To take my life. Two of these fellows you
            Must know and own; this monstrous object I
            Acknowledge mine.

CALIBAN   I will be pinched to death ...

ALONSO   Is this not Stephano, my drunken butler?

SEBASTIAN   He's drunk. Where did he find the wine?

ALONSO   And Trinculo is reeling. Where could they
            Have found liquor enough to turn them red?
            How did you get so pickled?

TRINCULO   I've been in such a pickle since I last saw you that I fear
            my bones will never be rid of it. I'll be so pickled no blow-flies will
            come near me.

SEBASTIAN   So what's it all about, Stephano?

STEPHANO   Don't touch me! I'm not Stephano, I've been turned into
            a cramp.

PROSPERO   You wanted to be king of the isle, you wretch?

STEPHANO   I'd have been a sorry one.

ALONSO   This is as strange a thing as I have ever set eyes on.

PROSPERO   He is as ill-proportioned in his manners
            As in his shape. Go, monster, to my cell.
            Take your companions with you. If you hope
            To get my pardon, be sure to make it perfect.

CALIBAN   I will, for sure. And I'll be wise in future,
            And hope for grace. What a sixfold ass I was
            To take that drunkard for a god
            And worship this dumb fool.

PROSPERO   Go on, away!

ALONSO   Away! And leave those garments where you found them.
SEBASTIAN   Or stole them, rather.
PROSPERO   Sir, I invite your highness and your friends
            To my poor cell, where you shall take your rest
            For this one night, which, part of it, I'll fill
            With tales and talk that I am sure will make it
            Pass quickly. There's the story of my life,
            And all the interesting things that happened
            Since I came to this island. In the morning
            I'll take you to your ship, and so to Naples,
            Where I shall hope to see the happy marriage
            Of this beloved couple solemnised,
            And after that retire to my Milan,
            Where each third thought will be my grave.
ALONSO   I long
            To hear the story of your life, which must
            Affect the ear most deeply.
PROSPERO   I'll tell all,
            And promise you calm seas, auspicious gales,
            And winds so expeditious you will catch
            Your royal fleet ahead. My Ariel, chick,
            That is your task. Then to the elements
            Be free, and fare you well! The rest, withdraw.

                        Exeunt omnes.

                        Epilogue

PROSPERO   Now my magic's overthrown,
            And what strength I have's my own,
            Which is most faint. Now it's true,
            I must be here confined by you
            Or sent to Naples. Let me not,
            Since I have my dukedom got
            And pardoned the usurper, dwell
            On this bare island, by your spell;
            But release me from my bands
            With the help of your good hands.
            Gentle breath of yours my sails
            Must fill, or else my project fails,
            Which was to please. No more do I
            Have spirits to command or magic by,

And my ending is despair,
Unless I be relieved by prayer
Which pierces so, that it assaults
Mercy itself, and frees all faults.
As you from crimes would pardoned be,
Let your indulgence set me free.

Exit.

Designed and typeset in Adobe Warnock Pro by
David Roberts, Pershore, Worcestershire

◈